WITHDRAWN

Modern and Contemporary Poetry and Poetics

Modern and Contemporary Poetry and Poetics promotes and pursues topics in the burgeoning field of twentieth- and twenty-first-century poetics. Critical and scholarly work on poetry and poetics of interest to the series includes social location in its relationships to subjectivity, to the construction of authorship, to oeuvres, and to careers; poetic reception and dissemination (groups, movements, formations, institutions); the intersection of poetry and theory; questions about language, poetic authority, and the goals of writing; claims in poetics, impacts of social life, and the dynamics of the poetic career as these are staged and debated by poets and inside poems. Topics that are bibliographic, pedagogic, that concern the social field of poetry, and reflect on the history of poetry studies are valued as well. This series focuses both on individual poets and texts and on larger movements, poetic institutions, and questions about poetic authority, social identifications, and aesthetics.

Language and the Renewal of Society in Walt Whitman,
Laura (Riding) Jackson, and Charles Olson
The American Cratylus
Carla Billitteri

Modernism and Poetic Inspiration
The Shadow Mouth
Jed Rasula

The Social Life of Poetry
Appalachia, Race, and Radical Modernism
Chris Green

Procedural Form in Postmodern American Poetry
Berrigan, Antin, Silliman, and Hejinian
David W. Huntsperger

Modernist Writings and Religio-scientific Discourse
H.D., Loy, and Toomer
Lara Vetter

Male Subjectivity and Poetic Form in "New American" Poetry
Andrew Mossin

The Poetry of Susan Howe
History, Theology, Authority
Will Montgomery

Ronald Johnson's Modernist Collage Poetry
Ross Hair

Pastoral, Pragmatism, and Twentieth-Century American Poetry
Ann Marie Mikkelsen

(Re:)Working the Ground
Essays on the Late Writings of Robert Duncan
Edited by James Maynard

Women's Poetry and Popular Culture
Marsha Bryant

Previous Publications

Auden and Documentary in the 1930s. 1997.

Photo-Textualities: Reading Photographs and Literature. 1996.

Women's Poetry and Popular Culture

Marsha Bryant

palgrave
macmillan

First published in 2011 by
PALGRAVE MACMILLAN®
in the United States—a division of St. Martin's Press LLC,
175 Fifth Avenue, New York, NY 10010.

Where this book is distributed in the UK, Europe and the rest of the world,
this is by Palgrave Macmillan, a division of Macmillan Publishers Limited,
registered in England, company number 785998, of Houndmills,
Basingstoke, Hampshire RG21 6XS.

Palgrave Macmillan is the global academic imprint of the above companies
and has companies and representatives throughout the world.

Palgrave® and Macmillan® are registered trademarks in the United States,
the United Kingdom, Europe and other countries.

ISBN: 978–0–230–60941–9

Library of Congress Cataloging-in-Publication Data

Bryant, Marsha, 1960–
      Women's poetry and popular culture / Marsha Bryant.
         p. cm.—(Modern and contemporary poetry and poetics)
      ISBN 978–0–230–60941–9 (hardback)
         1. English poetry—Women authors—History and criticism.
      2. American poetry—Women authors—History and criticism. 3. Popular
      culture in literature. 4. Popular culture and literature—Great Britain—
      History. 5. Popular culture and literature—United States—History.
      I. Title.

PR116.B79 2011
821'.9099287—dc22   2011013947

A catalogue record of the book is available from the British Library.

Design by Newgen Imaging Systems (P) Ltd., Chennai, India.

First edition: October 2011

10 9 8 7 6 5 4 3 2 1

Transferred to Digital Printing in 2012

For Cassandra, Gail, and Michael

Contents

List of Figures — ix

Permissions — xi

Acknowledgments — xiii

Introduction: Key Signatures, Signature Styles — 1

Chapter 1 CinemaScope Poetics: H.D., Helen, and Historical Epic Film — 21

Chapter 2 The Poetry Picture Book: Stevie Smith and Children's Culture — 51

Chapter 3 Uneasy Alliances: Gwendolyn Brooks, *Ebony*, and Whiteness — 83

Chapter 4 Everyday Ariel: Sylvia Plath and the Dream Kitchen — 121

Chapter 5 Killer Lyrics: Ai, Carol Ann Duffy, and the Media Monologue — 149

Key Notes: Manifesto for Women's Poetry Studies — 175

Notes — 189

Works Cited — 201

Index — 223

Figures

1.1 Helen entering Troy, *Helena* (Bavaria Film, 1924)   26

1.2 Helen meets Paris, *Helen of Troy* (Warner Brothers, 1956)   34

2.1 Stevie Smith's drawing for "Papa Love Baby"   58

2.2 Stevie Smith's drawing for "The Photograph"   61

2.3 Page from Edward Ardizzone's *Tim All Alone* (1957)   67

2.4 The page of Stevie Smith's "Bog-Face"   69

2.5 Stevie Smith's drawing for "Nourish Me on an Egg"   75

4.1 Bon Ami© advertisement from *Ladies' Home Journal* (1957)   145

6.1 Front cover to *Making for Planet Alice* (1997)   178

Permissions

Excerpts from H.D.'s "Helen," "Leda," and *Helen in Egypt.* Reprinted by permission of New Directions Publishing Corporation.

Excerpts and drawings from "Papa Loves Baby" and "The Photograph" by Stevie Smith, from *Collected Poems of Stevie Smith,* copyright ©1972 by Stevie Smith. Reprinted by permission of New Directions Publishing Corporation.

Excerpts from "Infant" and "Nourish Me on an Egg" (and drawing for the latter) by Stevie Smith, from *Collected Poems of Stevie Smith,* copyright ©1937 by Stevie Smith. Reprinted by permission of New Directions Publishing Corporation.

Excerpts and drawings from "Bog-Face" by Stevie Smith, from *Collected Poems of Stevie Smith,* copyright ©1942 by Stevie Smith. Reprinted by permission of New Directions Publishing Corporation.

Excerpts from "The Last Turn of the Screw" by Stevie Smith, from *Collected Poems of Stevie Smith,* copyright ©1966 by Stevie Smith. Reprinted by permission of New Directions Publishing Corporation.

Stevie Smith's poems and drawings reproduced by permission of Estate of James MacGibbon.

Page from *Tim All Alone* by Edward Ardizzone (1957) reproduced by permission of Frances Lincoln Ltd., copyright © 2006.

All excerpts from Gwendolyn Brooks's poems reprinted By Consent of Brooks Permissions.

Bon Ami© advertisement reproduced by permission of Faultless Starch/Bon Ami Company.

Excerpts from "Human Interest" and "Education for Leisure" are taken from *Standing Female Nude* by Carol Ann Duffy, published by Anvil Press Poetry in 1985.

Excerpts from "Psychopath" are taken from *Selling Manhattan* by Carol Ann Duffy, published by Anvil Press Poetry in 1987.

Front cover to *Making for Planet Alice* (1997) reproduced by permission of Bloodaxe Books.

An earlier version of chapter 3 was originally published as "Gwendolyn Brooks, *Ebony,* and Postwar Race Relations," in *American Literature*, vol. 79, issue 1, pp 113–41. Copyright 2007. Reprinted by permission of the publisher, Duke University Press.

Early work on a part of chapter 5 appeared in *College Literature* as "Plath, Domesticity, and the Art of Advertising" (2002), and is expanded here with the journal's permission.

Acknowledgments

This book generated from the synergy of two poetry networks, an interdisciplinary collaboration, and the classroom. I am grateful to the H.D. International Society, founded by Donna Hollenberg and Eileen Gregory, for enabling connections among scholars working with women's poetry. The inspiration and support I drew from this network were crucial to the project. I thank the society's co-presidents Annette Debo and Lara Vetter for their expertise and encouragement. The H.D. listserv has provided an indispensable resource for research questions.

The Modernist Studies Association (MSA) is the other generative network for this book, which is dedicated to its founders Cassandra Laity, Gail McDonald, and Michael Coyle. MSA provided the opportunity to meet other scholars working with poetry and visual culture. In particular, Elizabeth Bergmann Loizeaux and Susan Rosenbaum have offered models for such work, and have been supportive readers of my unorthodox mixtures of materials. Anita Helle widened my understanding of Plath's relationship to visual culture, while Lesley Wheeler offered insight to my analysis of Stevie Smith's drawings. Through MSA I met other scholars who helped me renew my thinking about poetry, innovation, and pedagogy: Juliana Chang, Suzanne Churchill, Alan Golding, Susannah Young-ah Gottlieb, Linda Kinnahan, Douglas Mao, Adalaide Morris, Catherine Paul, Gyllian Phillips, and Helen Sword. I am grateful to the late Lorenzo Thomas for his generous critique of my presentation on Gwendolyn Brooks and *Ebony*. These intellectual encounters have made the conference a vital space where poetry studies and cultural studies can meet. I cannot imagine the book happening without it.

My collaboration and long-standing friendship with Mary Ann Eaverly, a classical archaeologist, have played a crucial role in transitioning to this midcareer project on women's poetry. Our collaboration began with work on poems by our colleague Debora Greger, then ventured into H.D., Egyptology, and pedagogy. Writing with someone in a different field challenged me to think more broadly as a humanities scholar.

Reconnecting with Karen Jackson Ford, whom I met in graduate school at Illinois, provided inspiration and encouragement as we pursued our work on Brooks.

Like all academic workers, I am indebted to the generosity of institutions for supporting my work on this book. A fellowship from the National Endowment for the Humanities funded my writing of several chapters, as did summer support from Humanities Scholarship Enhancement Grants at the University of Florida. The opportunity to present a Shannon-Clark lecture at Washington and Lee University helped me to revise my chapter on Smith.

The Department of English at my home institution also fostered a stimulating and supportive environment in which to think and write. I am grateful to chairs John Leavey and Pamela Gilbert for their leadership, and to Kenneth Kidd and Leah Rosenberg for their thoughtful responses to individual chapters. Barbara Mennel and Mary Ann Eaverly were generous with their time in watching Manfred Noa's sprawling *Helena* with me, translating respectively its German subtitles and pan-Mediterranean iconography. The conference "Black Cultural Interventions into Gender and Sexuality Studies," organized by colleagues Amy Ongiri and LaMonda Horton-Stallings, provided a generative space to think about Ai. The department's annual conferences on American studies helped me refine my reading of CinemaScope and historical epic, as did Malini

Johar Schueller's work and Phillip Wegner's expertise in Fredric Jameson. I also thank Don Ault, Roger Beebe, Terry Harpold, Susan Hegeman, Michael Hofmann, Judith Page, Jodi Schorb, Stephanie Smith, Chris Snodgrass, Anastasia Ulanowicz, and Ed White for various synergies in the workplace.

I am especially grateful to Palgrave and its series editor, Rachel Blau DuPlessis, for the acuity of feedback they provided and for their accommodations. The reader's report gave me a clearer sense of the project's larger issues, and the editorial comments helped me to refine my methodology.

Several people gave me access to key material for the book. Rita J. Smith, curator of The Baldwin Collection of Historical Literature, University of Florida, helped me locate many of the children's books that Smith reviewed, as well as Edward Ardizzone's work. I thank Gina Minks, Special Collections Librarian at the University of Tulsa's McFarlin Library, for assisting me with press cuttings of Smith's reviews. Cary Nelson and Rachel Blau DuPlessis allowed me to cite from her contribution to the forthcoming *Oxford Handbook of Modern and Contemporary American Poetry*. I am indebted to former student Dan Hardcastle for bringing the Tawana Brawley case to my attention during a discussion of Ai's "Evidence: From a Reporter's Notebook."

The students in my women's poetry classes prompted me to think beyond counter-discursive models, inspiring me with their enthusiastic responses and discerning questions. My former and current graduate students have also been vital in prompting me to think about gender, poetry, and culture in new ways: Glenn Freeman, Cortney Grubbs, Megan Leroy, Emily McCann, James McDougall, Kirsten Bartholomew Ortega, Jill Pruett, and John Smith.

Musicians John T. Lowe, Jr., and Will Winter helped me think about key signatures and counterintuitive innovation. Exchanging ideas across disciplines with Alexandra Lucas, a biomedical researcher, also fostered my conceptualization of the book.

My research on the Bon Ami brand prompted me to switch to their earth-friendly household cleaner.

In preparing the final manuscript, Wayne Losano was an expert technical editor, requesting a donation to a dog rescue nonprofit instead of a fee. My husband Camden Pierce, another technical editor, gave generously of his time in formatting the chapters and bibliography, as well as preparing some of the illustrations. Jane Dominguez, Senior Art and Publications Production Specialist in UF's College of Liberal Arts and Sciences, did outstanding work designing the cover art. I am also grateful to Sheila M. Ryan for her expert work with the index.

For living with this project and its physical intrusions into our living space, I thank my family, Camden and Nicholas Pierce. My debt to them is immeasurable.

Introduction: Key Signatures, Signature Styles

An opening or disclosure, a *key* is also a pitch, tone, or style. I begin with the figure of the *key signature* to reconfigure our sense of how popular culture shapes modern and contemporary women's poetry. In music, a key signature is not the music itself but the point of reference for sounding its notes. Marking the home key with its pattern of sharps or flats, the key signature orients the hand and voice along each line before the music happens. Yet it also ushers in the unexpected, the accidental notes that embellish the lines and detour the music from its initial default settings. This break from expectation need not be experimental, but can come from repertoire. At such moments we often detect key elements of an artist's signature style.

This book proposes that popular culture functions as a key signature for locating women poets' signature styles. Indeed, some of the very materials that would seem to push the poets toward the margins can serve as counterintuitive means of innovation. Historical epic film inflects some of H.D.'s most compelling reinventions of Helen, and tabloid journalism underwrites some of Carol Ann Duffy's dexterous diction. Popular culture does not necessarily place women poets in a position from which they must answer back—even when it engages conventionally feminine subjects such as romance and domesticity. The screen siren does not always become a straw woman, children's books do not always demand counter-narratives, women's magazines do not always require rejection. Contrary to popular belief, women poets who incorporate popular culture do not always compose parodies or critiques—although they may choose to do these things. Women poets may choose to do a little of both while tapping popular forms to invent, to mimic, to add depth and scope. Such effects enable them to write from the cultural center as *insiders.* Rather than transgressing a dominant or patriarchal culture, these popular registers transgress our usual sense of women's poetry as an oppositional aesthetic, a counter-discourse.

Key Signatures 1

Since women's poetry emerged as an academic field in the 1970s, the counterintuitive use of popular culture has been a key signature hidden in plain sight. It was lost when second-wave feminism and women's studies brought popular culture into the academy for a necessary and ongoing critique, identifying sexist representations of women. In parallel fashion, the vital project of feminist literary criticism located ways that even established women writers such as H.D. and Edna St. Vincent Millay were systematically marginalized in literary history, countering this serial neglect with a women's canon. Addressing the poets' status as canonical *outsiders,* foundational scholars of women's poetry stressed its subversive aspects to challenge institutional practices that systematically excluded women. Louise Bernikow distills this imperative for transgression in her anthology *The World Split Open* (1974): "A woman poet, authentic and in rebellion, is subversive of standard economic, political, social, artistic, and psychic orders" (9). In the 1990s, feminist-psychoanalytic critics transposed the outsider model to the unconscious and female subjectivity, identifying unique rhythms and tonalities in women's writing that departed from the symbolic (and patriarchal) order of language—and even from the signifying system itself. This approach drew from Julia

Kristeva's theory of semiotic language (the preoedipal infant's repressed, maternal rhythms that precede the symbolic order).[1] In women's poetry studies, Kristevan and other French feminist interpretations proved especially useful in revaluing the syntactic and sonic excesses of Gertrude Stein and Edith Sitwell, the matriarchal avant-garde of modernism. Yet the blind spot in feminist-psychoanalytic criticism was a tendency to impose a universal model of women's writing that wrenched it from demographic and other cultural contexts. This transposition of the woman poet-as-outsider also continued the field's emphasis on transgression.

Ironically, the key signature of popular culture and counterintuitive innovation was misplaced when cultural studies began to reconfigure literary analysis in the 1990s. Poetry was deemed antithetical to this new methodology because of its traditional "universalizing, taming, humanizing claims," Rachel Blau DuPlessis explains, and it consequently suffered a loss of cultural capital: "Poetry, most particularly the lyric, has generally been construed (in its university and critical reception) as opposite to society and its discourses" ("Social Texts"; *Genders* 8). Given the sheer amount of feminist inquiries on women writers' relationships to literary and popular culture, it is surprising that women's poetry has received so little attention from cultural critics. As early as 1975, anthology editor Cora Kaplan insisted that "women are at the front of a continuing effort to alter the elite relationship of art to the culture that produces it" (24); in other words, women's poetry is ideally suited for a cultural approach. The impetus for my study began in the late 1990s, when I offered my first women's poetry courses. Although the field's dominant key signatures of confession, critique, and subversion proved indispensable for charting thematic links across the syllabus, they sometimes proved less successful when discussing individual poems with Gen-Xers and Millennials. In particular, my students kept resisting the idea that women poets always countered popular culture—and backlash could not account for all of their objections.

And so this book takes up the issue of how best to approach modern and contemporary women's poetry in the twenty-first century, offering flexible strategies that acknowledge gender difference without restricting women poets as cultural outsiders. Proposing a model of women's poetry studies, my approach situates the poems through their intersections with nonliterary discourses, as well as within scholarship on and anthologies of women's poetry. By *women's poetry studies* I mean several things. First and foremost, the term invokes two interdisciplinary fields—*women's studies* and *cultural studies*—to signal an expansion of primary materials beyond literature and lives. Print and visual media, crucial to both fields, prove especially important in recovering the discursive networks inflecting the poets' signature styles. My analysis reverses the long-standing assumption that the poems must criticize mass media to be taken seriously as women's poetry. While I depart from most feminist approaches by not privileging gender subversion over other cultural meanings, I do not ignore ways in which the poems can transgress the mainstream even as they invoke it. I concur with Susan Stanford Friedman that "moving *beyond* gender does not mean forgetting it" (*Mappings* 18), just as moving beyond the usual parameters of poetry criticism does not mean forgetting form and close reading. But my analysis reads the poems horizontally across other cultural practices. Like Patrick Brantlinger, I understand literature as "a leaky category because it is an ensemble . . . of representations of the world at large, including all other forms of discourse that are supposedly nonliterary" (15). Offering a wide-angle view of the poetry and the field, I consider popular cinema, children's books, magazines, and journalism to revitalize our understanding of women's poetry and its cultural contexts.

Strictly speaking, *women's poetry* refers to any and all poems written by women. Yet gender adheres to this literary and marketing category in ways it does not to poems written by men. Ascribed meanings can skew readers' perceptions; for example, some expect women's poetry to be strictly *about* women or *for* them, limiting its scope to stereotypical subjects (motherhood and romance) and its social domain to gender issues (women's identities under patriarchy). My methodology dislodges such lingering assumptions in two key ways: by departing from psycho-biographical frameworks for the poetry and by examining cultural constructions of the *women's poetry* label. Although most of the poems I assess share with lyric utterance an identifiable speaker (individual or collective), I focus on poetic modes that resist confessional readings: epic, ekphrasis, social commentary, dramatic monologues.[2] Building on the rich body of work I inherit from feminist critics and anthology editors, my study considers each poet's signature style in light of a central issue in the field and a contemporaneous popular discourse. I also take into account each poet's reception in women's poetry anthologies, revealing surprising inconsistencies that open new possibilities for interpretation. Ultimately, my approach reverses the trend of assuming that women poets set out to subvert the mainstream, the media, and the marketplace.

Field Notes

The academic wing of women's poetry studies spans from Suzanne Juhasz's American-centered *Naked and Fiery Forms* (1976), which declared "a new tradition" (1), through Jo Gill's cross-Atlantic *Women's Poetry* (2007), which offers a critical guide to a well-established and increasingly diverse field. Juhasz's title anticipates the emphasis on confession, protest, and lyric in subsequent criticism.[3] Including British poets, Sandra Gilbert and Susan Gubar published their foundational essay collection, *Shakespeare's Sisters* (1979).[4] Yet their introduction also reflects an American tendency to declare literary independence, celebrating three centuries of women's poetry as "our grand, lost heritage of poetic presumption" (xxvi). By the mid-1980s, the field had emerged as a site of connections and contentions, but the figure of the outsider manifested on both sides of the Atlantic. While most critics in the United States embraced the idea of a separate canon grounded in women's experience, their counterparts in the United Kingdom remained more invested in literary tradition. Recounting dissonant tones that inflected the field's emergence sets the stage for self-reflection and new methodologies.

Anglo-American fault lines manifested with the publication of Alicia Suskin Ostriker's *Stealing the Language* (1986) and Jan Montefiore's first edition of *Feminism and Poetry* (1987). For Ostriker, American women poets are social outsiders who break free from imprisonment in patriarchal language and embark on "a quest for autonomous self-definition" (11, 10).[5] Her focus on adversarial and "explicitly female" poems yields a "powerful collective voice" that sounds in harmony with the American women's movement (7–8). For Montefiore, who is more wary of a separate tradition, women poets are linguistic outsiders even before they enter the social sphere because their psychological entry into language—"a system of signifiers constituted purely by difference"—differs from men's (2004; 102). Rather than women's experience, then, Montefiore bases her analysis on the linguistically constituted subject theorized by Jacques Lacan.[6] But her major theoretical framework derives from his feminist inheritors, especially Luce Irigaray. If Ostriker's construction of a women's tradition reflects an American sense of self-reliance, Montefiore's model of women's poetry relies on an English sense of poetic tradition.[7] Yet despite these major rifts, their positions also overlapped. Ostriker's central model of subversion (revisionist mythmaking) hinges on literary tradition, while Montefiore's preferred conception of form (*l'écriture feminine*) hinges on the female body. Indeed, the interplay of these early studies established trends that would shape the next two decades of criticism, which emphasized American poets and French feminism. As recently as 2005, Jane Dowson and Alice Entwistle noted that twentieth-century British women writers have been "overshadowed by their American contemporaries in critical discourse" (4). That same year British poets would finally become majority stakeholders in an Anglo-American anthology, Deryn Rees-Jones's *Modern Women Poets*.

Space does not allow me to engage every study of women's poetry published since these four books opened the field. I will interact more fully with some critics in the individual chapters where they most influenced my thinking. But by pairing selected books from the last two decades, I can highlight key modulations as women's poetry studies became a wider and more nuanced field of inquiry. Liz Yorke's *Impertinent Voices* (1991) and Betsy Erkkila's *The Wicked Sisters* (1992) take different approaches to the idea of a "woman's voice" and its subversive default setting, focusing respectively on Anglo-American and American poets. Drawing on the work of Hélène Cixous to stress "insurgent gynocentric meanings," Yorke proposes a "re-visionary . . . poetic of disruption" that unites the diversity of poets through the female body and subjectivity (31, 2). If Yorke's study composes "a song out of silence" through which women affirm sisterhood and counter patriarchy, Erkkila's sounds a discordant note by examining "conflicts among women poets" themselves—including "the exclusion, silencing, or demonization of other women" across boundaries of sexuality, class, and race. Taking issue with the growing influence of French feminism, her analysis questions its tendencies "to romanticize, maternalize, essentialize, and eternalize" women writers and their affiliations (Yorke 9; Erkkila 4, 14–15, 3). But Erkkila continues the feminist project of examining how women poets defy patriarchy and form communities. My analysis focuses on discursive rather than personal networks.

Cynthia Hogue's *Scheming Women* (1995) and Cheryl Walker's *Masks Outrageous and Austere* (1991) adopt more nuanced psycho-biographical approaches, taking into account their respective American poets' social and cultural positions. Building on previous work shaped by French feminism, Hogue brings Kristeva to the forefront of her analysis. Her study locates a "gendered but provisional subjectivity" that anchors a poetics of "equivocation"— one tied to the poets' race and class privilege even as it "divests" itself of conventional privileges of poethood (xx–xxi). Walker also considers the poets' "psychosocial development," exploring "the intersection of culture, psyche, and persona" to expand critical parameters beyond uniqueness and the individual (3). While "the psychobiographical strand" remains central to her project, as Walker freely admits, she also widens her scope to the "psyche of an era"—assessing poets' "horizontal relations within a particular time period" and thus moving closer to more recent cultural approaches (1, 9). My own methodology emphasizes neither female experience nor subjectivity, but what Paula Bernat Bennett terms "the intersubjective framework of the public sphere" (5).

Karen Jackson Ford's *Gender and the Poetics of Excess* (1997) and Lesley Wheeler's *The Poetics of Enclosure* (2002) offer contrapuntal perspectives on women poets' relationship to literary conventions. Mixing lyric poets with the sonic ruptures of Stein and the Black Arts Movement, Ford locates their emergence through strategic breaks from decorum. When women poets are rebuked because "they write too much, reveal too much, and push their poetics too far," she argues, critics are drawing on cultural prescriptions that segregate "unladylike" writers while privileging other women for their stylistic transgressions (10, 14). One thinks of Marianne Moore, who found favor with her era's critical establishment and avoided the *extreme* label. If Ford shows how women poets rebel against decorum, Wheeler traces how they strategically embrace the "felicitous restrictions" of reserve—another gendered construction of poetic propriety (1). For Wheeler the reticence of "feminine discretion" armors women poets so they can "compete with or critique the received canon," as well as undo "confessionalism's poetic of presence" (8, 11). That is, what seems most traditional about the poetry offers a protective space from which to experiment. Both critics focus on American poets. My Anglo-American study considers popular culture as another means of unsettling our sense of what "properly" belongs in the domain of women's poetry.

Continuing debates over literary tradition, lyric, and innovation underscore larger questions about form, which is, of course, crucial to interpreting any poem—an act that requires close reading, or "'close-cultural' reading," as Romana Huk puts it (9). My analysis of signature style and its constitutive discourses will engage the poems' components, including not only imagery, rhythm, and sound but also rhetorical devices and page layout. Noting the tendency to "elide or erase the specificity of linguistic texture" in culturally oriented approaches, DuPlessis insists that "one wants any study of poetry to engage with poetry as such—its conventions and textual mechanisms, its surfaces and layers—and not simply to regard the poetic text as an odd delivery system for ideas and themes" (*Genders* 7). Given the trend toward topical arrangement in books on and anthologies of women's poetry, the field is always vulnerable to subsuming form within "women's themes" and identity politics. Ostriker charts key themes in her study (the divided self, identity quest, mythic revision, "body language"), while Linda Hall subdivides *An Anthology of Poetry by Women* (1994) by categories such as "Love and Passion," "Motherhood," and "Relations Between the Sexes" (Ostriker vii; Hall v–vi). Anthologies also filter women's poetry through racial, sexual, and national identities.[8] Important as these rubrics are for mapping continuities and differences in women's poetry, they can limit our understanding of form. Recently, Elisabeth Frost and Linda Kinnahan have pointed out the double exclusion of feminist experimental poetry because critics of the avant-garde usually neglect feminist practice, while "studies of American women poets have tended to focus on a poetics of personal experience" (Frost xii).[9] The interest in Carol Ann Duffy that I share with Kinnahan reflects a common emphasis on the constituent social discourses of women's poetry. Because the mainstream is so crucial to my analysis of counterintuitive innovation, linguistically experimental poetry falls outside the scope of this book. The poems I consider here remain syntactically accessible even in their ambiguities—a crucial part of the cultural work they perform.

In my wide-angle approach, I consider poetry's cross-currents with popular discourses such as Hollywood's Americanization of classical mythology, *Ebony*'s rhetoric of postwar race relations, and tabloid media's sensationalism of violence. My analysis builds on DuPlessis's feminist model of "social philology," which examines "ideologies, discourses, debates" and other "social materials" that are "activated and situated within the deepest texture of, the sharpest specificities of, the poetic text" (*Genders* 12). When Plath incorporates levitating housewives and triple repetition into the signature style of *Ariel,* she activates Madison Avenue's dream kitchen and the hard sell. When H.D. gives her epic Helen a sheer scarf to enhance her cinematic allure, she activates the Orientalist glamour of historical epic films. Adalaide Morris's comments on H.D.'s work shape my understanding of all the poems I consider here: they are "forms of cultural meditation and mediation" that operate as "agent[s] of thought, perception, and meaning in the ongoing life of a culture" (2, 1). Such horizontal perspectives call into question the cultural outsider model—including the question of whether such a position is even possible.

My thinking is also rooted in critical conversations fostered by the Modernist Studies Association (MSA), *PMLA,* and the Lifting Belly High conference on women's poetry since 1900.[10] Since the inception of MSA, women's poetry has been featured at its annual conferences. Many have furthered the field's engagement with media (photography, film, radio, magazines). If scholarship on women's poetry thrives at MSA, it can seem to fall beneath *PMLA*'s radar. Curiously, a 2005 forum claimed that poststructuralism and psychoanalysis were surprisingly absent in poetry criticism—despite their prominence in decades of work on women's poetry. In a 2008 forum on new lyric studies, which warily acknowledged poetry's proximity to media and interdisciplinarity, poems by women barely contributed to the discussion. Redressing this imbalance, the 2008 Lifting Belly High conference aimed to remap the field, revisit feminist poetics, and chart new directions. Indeed, women's poetry scholarship is an often unacknowledged site of critical innovation.

The WP Label

Women's poetry and our ways of thinking about it are constantly renewed through the publishing industry, where the poems reach a crossover market of general readers, students, and academics. While feminist literary scholars tend to recover neglected poets, contemporary anthology publishers often capitalize on the *women's poetry* label by introducing emergent ones. In her introduction to *New Women Poets* (1990), Carol Rumens notes pointedly that "new is one of the things that women poets in Britain are sanctioned to be" (13). Introducing *101 Poems by 101 Women* (2001), Germaine Greer quips that "packaging of female artists was not invented for the Spice Girls" (xi). Yet the elision of women's poetry with newness means more than a novelty act, especially in a culture where it hovers somewhere between Sappho and "chick lit." Indeed, the WP label taps a wide scope of meanings. As David Wheatley points out, anthologies often "strike a note of breakthrough and departure in their titles" (24), a trend we see in Rumens's earlier *Making for the Open* (1985), Louise Bernikow's *The World Split Open* (1974), and Maura Dooley's *Making for Planet Alice* (1997). Bernikow's title, taken from a poem by Muriel Rukeyser,[11] foregoes the elsewhere of departure by evoking social transformation—a major motif in women's poetry anthologies since Joan Murray Simpson dedicated *Without Adam* (1968) "to the young people of our time" (17). *Making for the Open* reinvents the idea of staking new territory, marking its newness as the "post-feminist" brand of women's poetry. Transporting women's poetry to an otherworldly dimension, the destination of "Planet Alice" replays the cultural outsider figure through an imagined elsewhere.[12] Eva Salzman grounds her co-edited *Women's Work* (2008) closer to home, outflanking the outsider position by laying claim to "the so-called 'special interest' group comprising over half of this planet's population" (8). Because many anthology editors work primarily as poets, they have a more vexed proximity to the women's poetry label. In turn they adopt tones of celebration, defensiveness, even denial, as they redefine a prime market through which their own work will appear.

With the exception of *Without Adam*, published in London by Femina Press, the women's poetry anthology as we have come to know it first flourished in the United States. When mainstream publishers in the United Kingdom entered this market, poet-editors mirrored some of the cross-Atlantic differences I noted in the critical survey. But they have more often pitted technical skill and feminist perspectives against one another—surely a result of England's more masculinist poetry tradition. A brief survey of the past four decades reveals key contentions over the canon of women's poetry, the issue of formal "quality," and the necessity for women's collections. As we move closer to our own cultural moment, poet-editors express increasing discomfort with the WP label even as they operate within it.

Generally speaking, Simpson and her successors in the 1970s grappled over how to represent the growing body of women poets and their work. Some anthology editors adopted gatekeeping postures that counter the wide embrace of inclusiveness that many expect from women's anthologies. "There are no *poetesses* represented in this volume," sniffs Simpson (18). Canon assembly could even take on the tone of "Daddy's girl" debates in which already established poets joined the discredited poetess in the editorial dustbin. In the American anthology *Psyche: The Feminine Poetic Consciousness* (1973), Barbara Segnitz and Carol Rainey reject "the Lady Poet"; surprisingly, H.D., Edna St. Vincent Millay, and even Anne Bradstreet occupy a "mist of chiffon" for finding favor with male publishers (15–16). Acquiring literary respectability prior to the women's movement renders poets suspect for these editors. Florence Howe's introduction to the better-known anthology *No More Masks!* (1973) centers on American poets who "write as women, and speak to women," adding emergent figures who write in tandem with the women's movement (10). At the same time, she and co-editor Ellen Bass construct a somewhat more heterogeneous canon that includes Moore and Stein, Millay and Adrienne Rich, Amy Lowell and Nikki Giovanni. African American writers find more space in this anthology and in Bernikow's *The World Split Open,* which also admits working-class women. *Salt and Bitter and Good* (1975), another Anglo-American collection that spans several centuries, gathers poems "that do not appeal to male anthologists"

(11). Edited by Cora Kaplan, this anthology of twenty-four poets enshrines the American figures that *Psyche* maligned. Kaplan dedicates her anthology to our most notorious confessional poet, Anne Sexton, while Howe claims Rukeyser as her collection's rebellious matriarch.

In the 1980s American anthologies continued to diversify, and their British counterparts gained critical mass. Erlene Stetson's important collection *Black Sister* (1981) intersects with key themes from its predecessors (such as subversion and identity quest). But Stetson notes pointedly that the trope of unmasking cannot apply to all women poets: "For black women, masks are not something they can choose to wear" (xxiii). Calling into question the idea of an inherently confessional and universal women's poetry, *Black Sister* anticipated later work in the field that acknowledged African American and black British traditions. Stetson also emphasizes the stylistic variety of the poems she selects, putting the blues in dialogue with Georgia Douglas Johnson's traditional forms and Giovanni's revolutionary poetics. Form became a vexed issue for many British poet-editors, who feared that the growing popularity of women's anthologies lowered the product's overall quality. Examining this phenomenon of editor's remorse, Vicki Bertram detects "the anxiety of the well-respected women poets commissioned to undertake the publishing of what they regarded as a flood of inferior poetry" (5). In her introduction to *Making for the Open,* for example, Rumens faults women's anthologies for emphasizing "specifically female experiences" and feminist themes at the cost of form and technique, claiming they are "swamped by the noisy amateurs proclaiming that women, too, have a voice" (xvii, xv). Likewise, Fleur Adcock insists that this rising tide of women poets will not lift all boats. In *The Faber Book of 20th Century Women's Poetry* (1987), she conveys her distaste for "slabs of raw experience" masquerading as poetry, excoriating Sexton and preferring the "perfectionist" tendencies she finds in Moore, Plath, and Elizabeth Bishop (13, 5). Conversely, Jeni Couzyn imports Plath into her British collection, *The Bloodaxe Book of Contemporary Women Poets* (1985), to foreground voice, experience, and "female consciousness" (16). Form does not figure largely in her biographically driven introduction.

Along with her predecessor Diana Scott, editor of *Bread and Roses* (1982), Couzyn offers one of the few British-focused collections published before the 1990s. Both editors share an affinity with American feminist perspectives that shaped the previous decade of anthologies. For example, Scott points out that nineteenth-century poets who gained literary respectability had to adopt "a safe literary style"—although she concurs with Adcock that all "serious poets" rely on literary tradition (12–13). In her American anthology *Early Ripening* (1987), Marge Piercy saw contemporary women's poetry making a clean break with its male counterpart and, more fundamentally, with the dominant culture: "vis-à-vis almost any institution or holiday or habit or idea, there is a confrontational aspect, a remaking, a renewing, a renaming, a re-experiencing and then recasting" (1). Piercy's invocation of the subversive outsider hearkens back to Bernikow's, as does her dedication of the anthology to Rukeyser.

Since the 1990s American editors have begun to join their British counterparts in expressing ambivalence about the WP label, sometimes casting doubt on the whole enterprise even as they acknowledge the differential treatment that women poets receive in criticism and collections. In her forward to *The Extraordinary Tide* (2001), for example, Eleanor Wilner acknowledges the "uneasiness that necessarily accompanies a women-only anthology" (xxiii). Some British poet-editors go so far as to violate editorial protocol by voicing their reluctance to assume the task. Dooley states the matter most plainly (and plaintively) in *Making for Planet Alice*, confessing her horrified reaction to being asked: "One of my first thoughts was 'another anthology of women poets? Not again, not now, surely not?'" She worries that the popularity of women's anthologies has created "a separate culture" or "cultural sideshow," underscoring the outsider theme (12). While Simpson and Scott addressed their earlier collections to general readers of poetry with no apparent discomfort, Linda France takes pains to note that

Sixty Women Poets (Bloodaxe, 1993) is not intended "to exclude or alienate the male reader"—a common concern among contemporary editors (14).

Backlash alone cannot account for such rhetorical maneuvers to hold the very idea of *women's poetry*—and even *woman*—at arm's length. Many British and American poet-editors try to extricate their anthologies from the *f*-words *feminine* or *feminist*,[13] often with the rhetorical sneering that inflected their predecessors' attacks on women's experience and amateurism. In *Making for the Open*, Rumens had marshaled women poets to resist the expectation to be ladylike "purveyors of a versified 'Body Shop' ethic," declaring that "niceness has very little to do with poetry" (14). The elision of women's poetry with upscale consumption and "feel good" aesthetics seems rather curious in the year of Duffy's edgy debut, *Standing Female Nude* (1985). If Rumens felt that more schooling would remove the taint of femininity, Susan Aizenberg and Erin Belieu propose less cheerleading. In their millennial anthology *The Extraordinary Tide,* these editors declare that "it is not possible to celebrate poetry written by women without such poetry being relegated to the perfumed category known as 'women's poetry'"—a far cry from their predecessors' ready embrace of woman-centeredness in collections that were hardly dainty. Aizenberg and Belieu make a point of choosing poems that "leav[e] the visible and invisible walls of women's identity ghettoes behind" (xxviii), intersecting with Salzman and Amy Wack's desire to dispel the assumption that "gender-segregated anthologies . . . take gender politics as their main subject" (Salzman 17). By contrast, Greer's millennial collection features poems "written from the point of view of a woman" and mostly "about being female." Her frank acknowledgment of the "intensity of anger in them" ventures as close to the second *f*-word as most recent editors dare to tread (xii).[14] In justifying selections for her cross-Atlantic *Modern Women Poets* (2005), Deryn Rees-Jones foregrounds the problem of "how to negotiate and value women's experience in relation to poetry" without limiting the WP label. "to important but not exclusively female or feminist concerns" (23).

Dowson's assessment of contemporary women poets' discomfort with female affiliation points out "the continuing difficulty in formulating a satisfactory critical terminology for reading women's poetry" ("'Older Sisters'" 7). Perhaps the problem lies not in women's poetry, but in our ways of talking about it.

Key Signatures 2

The field and market of women's poetry are now sufficiently established to require self-reflection and new methodologies. Thus I invoke *key signatures* in a second sense: the poets I consider here are known in the women's poetry canon. I have chosen these figures from the repertoire for several reasons. First, established poets allow for a reorientation of the field that continues its generative issues, from women's mythmaking to media relations. Second, the poets I discuss circulate in a wide variety of anthologies, making their work accessible to current and emergent critics and teachers. Third—and most important to my argument—the poets I assess prove difficult to position as cultural outsiders. Carol Ann Duffy is the current poet laureate of Britain, where she is known as the people's laureate. The American Academy of Arts and Letters honored H.D. at the culmination of her career, and Stevie Smith received the Queen's Gold Medal for Poetry at the culmination of hers. Gwendolyn Brooks won the Pulitzer Prize for her second volume, while Ai won the National Book Award for her volume of selected poems, *Vice* (1999). Although Sylvia Plath's renown came posthumously, *Time* magazine named her among its one hundred artists of the twentieth century. My point here is not the (sometimes belated) recognition of women poets, but the mainstream institutions that have conferred these distinctions. This should prompt us to revisit the poets' signature styles and see how they lay claim to the cultural center—even as we acknowledge the fact that women are positioned differently in culture than men. The poems I discuss have multiple proximities to the mainstream, which I chart by situating each signature style alongside a popular discourse. In addition, I pair each poet with a key inquiry in the field to show how her work unsettles traditional *and* revisionist conceptions of women's poetry.

I begin with two modern matriarchs who would influence contemporary poets in the United States and United Kingdom, respectively. Recovered as a major modernist by feminist critics, H.D. remains central to our understanding of women's mythmaking. Chapter 1 restores her most ambitious epic, *Helen in Egypt,* to its cultural moment—the resurgence of historical epic films about the ancient Mediterranean world. The poem's formal excesses, expansive framing, and grand romance transform H.D.'s late signature style into CinemaScope poetics. Completed the same year that Warner Brothers released *Helen of Troy* (1956), H.D.'s long poem intersects with its cinematic counterpart in fashioning a woman-centered epic that hinges on timeless love. Both emphasize emotions over action as they call into question the martial masculinity of Homeric epic. In addition to recirculating the Helen myth in the 1950s, epic filmmakers returned to ancient Egypt—most notably in Cecil B. DeMille's second *Ten Commandments.* As with *Helen in Egypt,* the staggering scope of these productions spread across the ancient Mediterranean as the United States exerted more control over the modern Middle East. Dispelling myths of the poem's historical belatedness, I show that the overwrought style of H.D.'s feminized epic reflects the ruptures of popular film and postwar geopolitics.

Chapter 2 reconsiders the illustrated poems of Smith, reclaimed as a foundational figure in contemporary British women's anthologies. Known for her representations of childhood and performances in children's trappings, Smith produced a poetry picture book that ultimately resists the kind of outsider readings it would seem to invite. I situate her work within the Century of the Child, departing from the psycho-biographical approaches that dominate discussions of Smith's child speakers. Instead of grounding my analysis in Smith's own childhood, I show how her poems affiliate themselves with Child Study and other aspects of children's culture. My analysis also recovers the poet's work as a reviewer of children's literature for popular magazines, an activity that kept her attuned to new possibilities for altering character relations and page design within the mainstream. The innovative work of author-illustrator Edward Ardizzone offers an especially productive analogue for reorienting our sense of how her pictures operate on the page. Drawing on such intersections with children's culture, I show how Smith's work departs from the Romantic constructions of the child that she saw in her modernist peers. Smith's picture book also invites us to acknowledge the limiting ways that Romanticism's vulnerable/rebellious child inflects formulations of women's poetry.

My next three chapters examine intersections between poetry and the media—a key inquiry in studies of women's poetry, as well as of contemporary poetry more generally. Reassessing Brooks's postwar career in chapter 3, I show how she reinvents the protest poem by tapping the mainstream discourse of race relations featured in *Ebony*. Her first volume and America's first black picture magazine entered culture from the same Chicago neighborhood in 1945, sharing stylistic proximities that others have overlooked. While Brooks would counter *Ebony*'s portrayal of black beauty, signature pieces such as "The Sundays of Satin-Legs Smith," "Beverly Hills, Chicago," and "The *Chicago Defender* Sends a Man to Little Rock" were part of a national conversation the magazine fostered through its "photo-editorials" and letters to the editor. The poet's and magazine's depictions of whiteness and liberals made them central interpreters of race relations for their cross-racial audiences. Each wielded whiteness with a rhetorical flourish that marked the uneasiness of cross-racial coalitions in an era that culminated with Emmett Till and the Little Rock Nine. I also address these poems' problematic reception in the women's poetry canon.

In chapter 4 I revise standard readings of Plath and domesticity, departing from myths about her life to explore mythologies of everyday life and the postwar dream kitchen. Hardly a diary of a mad housewife, Plath's signature poems tap Madison

Avenue's extraordinary realm of kitchen magic and mechanized marriage—a popular discourse Plath knew well from her years of reading *Ladies' Home Journal.* Her turn toward domesticity intersects with the everyday theories of Henri Lefebvre's second volume of *Critique of Everyday Life* (1961) and Roland Barthes's *Mythologies* (1957), which also drew on women's magazines to reveal the inherent ambiguities and strangeness of automatic appliances, volatile cleaners, and ornamental cookery. While Plath's first volume took hesitant steps toward making domesticity the stuff of poetry, *Ariel* completes her project of finding transcendence within it. The animated machines, household apparitions, and levitating housewives that mark her signature style find their popular counterparts in magazine advertising. Breaking down the domestic/poetic dualism that can stymie our understanding of women's poetry, I show how Plath's everyday Ariel anticipates the dynamic domesticities of Pamela Gemin's recent collection *Sweeping Beauty: Contemporary Women Poets Do Housework* (2005).

My final chapter examines Ai and Duffy, who create disturbing *media monologues* from tabloid journalism, talk shows, and popular songs. By taking on the personae of male killers, each poet violates deep-seated expectations of women's poetry with graphic depictions of violence. Duffy shocked critics with "Psychopath," a poem that evokes the Yorkshire Ripper, while Ai's cast of characters seems to intersect with America's Most Wanted. Confronting these poems reveals the gendered double standard of dramatic monologue, which assigns perpetrators to male poets and victims to women. Ai and Duffy refuse these rules and perform commodified masculinities that go over the edge, composing *killer lyrics* that embrace toughness. The poets' counterintuitive innovations construct a mainstream extreme, blurring boundaries between poetic language and media discourse in ways that do not limit themselves to irony and critique. This unexpected degree of media affinity also plays a role in each poet's uneasy relationship to women's poetry criticism and anthologies, a bias that has led to the suppression of Duffy's killer lyrics—and of Ai's canon. Both monologists turn

women's poetry inside-out with the front-page tactics of their signature styles.

As the field of women's poetry studies nears the half-century
mark, we need to reassess its central premise that women poets operate primarily as cultural outsiders—invaluable as this model has
been for forming alternative canons and histories. The wide scope
of women's poetry does not conform to the contours of a loyal
opposition. Even the signature styles of our key figures are more
vested in the mainstream than we think. Resounding the poems'
proximities to popular culture provides a means of recovering this
fundamental relationship. As we move from the cinematic stage
to the lyrics of popular songs in the following chapters, we can
reorient standard accounts of women's poetry by reclaiming the
cultural center.

CHAPTER 1

CinemaScope Poetics: H.D., Helen, and Historical Epic Film

From the Hellenism of her early Imagist poems to her late epic *Helen in Egypt*, H.D. displayed a career-long passion for ancient Mediterranean cultures. She also consumed the modern medium through which their myths and artifacts circulate most widely: historical epic film. Filling the screen with grandiose sets, sprawling combat, and star-crossed lovers, popular images of what George MacDonald Fraser dubs the "Egypto-Biblo-Classic era" emerged and resurged alongside H.D.'s portrayals of mythic figures (7). Indeed, the romantic sensibility and pan-Mediterranean scope of epic film inflect H.D.'s most ambitious rendering of Helen. Along with *Trilogy*, her long poem *Helen in Egypt* prompted a feminist reappraisal that made H.D. a matriarch of modern and contemporary poetry. And yet curiously, her Hellenism proved divisive even as her mythmaking poems shaped criticism on and anthologies of women's poetry.

Foundational studies of H.D. by Susan Stanford Friedman and Rachel Blau DuPlessis value the Helen poems for contesting gender stereotypes and subverting literary tradition. In Alicia Suskin Ostriker's analysis of American women's poetry, *Helen in Egypt* serves as an exemplar of such "revisionist mythmaking"

(212). But Jan Montefiore's cross-Atlantic assessment claims that readers do not "feel the strong pressure of feminist intention" in H.D.'s work (5). For editors of pioneering women's poetry anthologies, her classical leanings were detrimental traits that could become grounds for her exclusion. Florence Howe assigns H.D. token status in *No More Masks!* (1973), while the editors of *Psyche: The Feminine Poetic Consciousness* (1973) shun her as a "Lady Poet" who used Hellenism to court male editors (Segnitz and Rainey 16). Given such surprising dissonance in feminist responses to H.D.'s mythmaking, we must reexamine its cultural meanings in her Helen epic. Do H.D.'s borrowings from popular film and romance prevent, augment, or reinvent the kind of revisionism we expect from women poets? Is *Helen in Egypt* mostly innovative or traditional, subversive or conformist? What significance lies in the text's emergence at a time when most producers of epic were filmmakers rather than poets?

The grand sweep of *Helen in Egypt* (1961) transformed H.D., Imagiste, into a poet of the wide screen during the era of CinemaScope and VistaVision. This monumental poem was the last volume that H.D. saw to print, the culmination of her work in the long form, and the fullest manifestation of her late signature style. Like other modernist long poems, its stylistic excesses resemble the "hyperformalism" that Vivian Sobchack locates in historical epic film (282). Indeed, Friedman's distillation of *Helen in Egypt* as "all-time, all-war, all-love" could double as a promotional blurb for Hollywood's postwar epic blockbusters ("Hilda Doolittle" 139). In 1954, the year that H.D. finished her epic's verse sections, Hedy Lamarr brought Helen to the big screen in the Italian-produced *Loves of Three Queens*.[1] Twentieth-Century Fox stretched the staggering range of CinemaScope photography in *The Egyptian* (1954).[2] This postwar innovation also freed directors from relying on tight close-ups to reveal the nuances of actors' facial expressions, allowing ample room in the shot for panoramic views or grandiose sets.[3] H.D. completed the prose parts of *Helen in Egypt* in 1956, a year of lavish epics about the ancient Mediterranean world: Warner Brothers' *Helen of Troy,* MGM's *Alexander the Great,* and Paramount's *The Ten Commandments* (Cecil B. DeMille's second version). Widening her epic's scope, H.D. went beyond her usual poetic proportions by enlarging its dimensions, inflating images, and escalating emotions. At its most grandiose, the epic style of *Helen in Egypt* bridges high modernism and high camp.

Although H.D.'s wide-ranging cineliteracy included the popular genres of "comedy, melodramas, and epic spectacle," as Rachel Ann Connor points out (28), the critical conversation about H.D. and film gravitates toward nonnarrative, avantgarde productions from Europe. Notable exceptions include Charlotte Mandel's early work on the poet's responses to Greta Garbo, as well as Jean Gallagher's and Katherine Hopewell's more recent analyses of H.D.'s acting and fiction, respectively, in the context of melodrama.[4] By situating *Helen in Egypt* within the postwar resurgence of historical epic film, my horizontal reading reconsiders H.D.'s late signature style as a "formproblem" that does not fall squarely within standard frameworks of revisionist mythmaking.[5] I borrow Fredric Jameson's use of the term to signal a wide-angle approach that considers genre and geopolitics—while keeping gender issues fully in view. The diverse materials I examine reflect "the dialectical opposition and profound structural interrelatedness of modernism and contemporary mass culture" that Jameson identifies (*Signatures* 16). As we shall see, the poem's proximity to popular film demands that we locate H.D.'s ultimate epic closer to the mainstream than we are accustomed, acknowledging that it does not prove as revisionary as we thought. In particular, I show how this poem's epic-romance form yields a production as stylistically and emotionally overwrought as its cinematic counterparts. Indeed, H.D. parallels Helen's ruminations over relationships with Theseus's pursuit of the Golden Fleece. Viewing *Helen in Egypt* through the analogue of CinemaScope, I extend Adalaide Morris's desire to move away from psychobiographical approaches to H.D. and "toward a wider discussion of the relationship between poetic forms and cultural meanings" (13). Finally, my return to H.D.'s epic mythmaking challenges myths of the poem's belatedness by arguing for its timeliness in a period of American expansionism.

Modernist Long Poems, Historical Epic Film, and Hellenism

Ambitious, stylized, and meticulously researched, poetic and cinematic epics often gravitate toward the ancient Mediterranean cultures enshrined in classical, biblical, and Egyptian traditions. Both employ a spectacular breadth of space, time, and characters held together by myths and symbols. Sobchack argues that "it is by means of iconographic expansiveness and formal excessiveness that the Hollywood historical epic creates a field of temporality experienced as subjectively transcendent and objectively significant" (286)—a claim that holds equally true for *The Cantos, The Waste Land,* and *Helen in Egypt.* The producers of epic poems and films achieve their expansive historical sense through extended labor. To authenticate their productions Pound compiled notebooks, Eliot wrote footnotes, H.D. re-created ancient monuments, and studios employed research teams. *Intolerance: Love's Struggle Throughout the Ages* (1916), D. W. Griffith's most ambitious epic, cites information about ancient Babylon,[6] while the opening credits to DeMille's 1956 *The Ten Commandments* include scholars from the University of Chicago, the Department of Antiquities in Luxor, and the Metropolitan Museum of Art in New York. The tendency toward citation aligns these productions with Pound's and Eliot's long poems, but their archaeological grounding and popular-romance plots align them more fully with *Helen in Egypt.* Epic films often drew on best-selling novels to reshape heroic plotlines; for example, the love triangle in *The Ten Commandments* came from Dorothy Clarke Wilson's *The Prince of Egypt* (1949). Paradoxically, this softer side of the historical epic brought strong women to the cast of characters.

Janice Radway asserts that historical romances "tend to portray more independent and defiant heroines" than do other subgenres of romance fiction; moreover, the heroine does not always "figure in a larger plot simply as a hero's prize"—an especially attractive feature for rescripting Western culture's ultimate war prize (582, 589). Cinematic Helens rebuke kings and rescue princes, reversing traditional gender roles even as they provide the emotional center for their respective romance plots.[7] The woman-centeredness of historical epics about Helen, Cleopatra, and other legendary figures offered H.D. a counterintuitive form of innovation, one that reconfigures our sense of revisionist mythmaking.

Ready-made for expansive treatment, Helen and the Trojan War soon became staples of what the Germans would dub *Monumentalfilm,* a genre that parallels the chronology of the modernist long poem. Historical epic cinema began in 1908, the year before Pound began his *Cantos,* with the Italian production of *The Last Days of Pompeii.* The golden age of Italian cinema brought new magnitude to film form with *The Fall of Troy* (1911), with on-location shooting and hundreds of extras. This film's romantic rerouting of Homer saw a successful run in American theaters (Solomon 4–5). In Hollywood Griffith produced his monumental *Intolerance,* which features spectacular pageantry, extravagant costumes, and mammoth sets. Writing for the avant-garde journal *Close Up* in 1927, H.D. concedes the lure of Griffith's feast of images—even for literati who sneered at popular cinema:

> I am lost myself in a tangle of exciting detail, am myself so startled and amazed by certain swiftness, certain effects of inevitable precise mass movement (such as . . . the crowd again crossing sand in Babylonian *Intolerance*) that I lose my own clue, become sated and lost and tired. ("The Cinema and the Classics" 33–34)

The poet succumbs to the palpable effects of epic spectacle. Critics often invoke H.D.'s call for directors to "slash and cut" their excesses, casting her own epic production as an oppositional aesthetic. H.D. does fault historical epic films for their "ornate, over-crowded, over-detailed and confused" images of the classical past ("The Cinema and the Classics" 30–33). Yet she later turns such criticism on her-self in *Trilogy,* where she imagines a reader who finds "imagery / done to death" and "historical parallels . . . done to death" (44, 51)—words that might as easily apply to Griffith or DeMille.

Helena (1924), directed by Manfred Noa, was the first Helen film of truly epic proportions, sharing with *Intolerance* a duration of over three hours. Its hyperformalism features stately processions, daring chariot races, and grand romance. The heroine, played by Edy Darclea, establishes the cross-cultural dimensions of epic women through costume and other props. For example, she enters Troy in a chariot drawn by lions (alluding to Cleopatra entering Rome), donning an anachronistically sequined bodice and a wreath similar to those of Greco-Roman goddesses (see figure 1.1).

H.D.'s response to the film was mixed, finding it "excellent in particulars" if overdone in its "paste board palaces" and Helen's "hair stream[ing] in the wind" ("The Cinema and the Classics" 30). Four months after this response to *Helena,* Hollywood re-leased its first Helen epic—a freehanded version of John Erskine's farcical bestseller, *The Private Life of Helen of Troy* (1927).[8]

Figure 1.1 Helen entering Troy, *Helena* (Bavaria Film, 1924)

Directed by Alexander Korda, the film pushed feminization to high frivolity by making Greek women's lust for Trojan fashions the cause for war. This box office hit drew praise in the *New York Times* as "an ambitious affair, with great hosts of people and monster stage settings" (Hall 14). Noa also produced an unsuccessful remake of *Helena* (*La Regina de Sparta*) that appeared three years before DeMille's lavish *Cleopatra* (1934). Historical epic film waned on both sides of the Atlantic during the censorship movements of the 1930s and World War II, but it resurged in the 1950s during geopolitical struggles for control of the Middle East. During this time Pound published his *Rock-Drill* (1955) and *Thrones* (1959) installments of *Cantos*, and H.D. projected the Helen myth across a span of 303 pages.

Although H.D. had not begun writing long poems during the flowering of historical epic film in the 1920s, two early poems show the interplay of revisionist and romantic tendencies that would shape her grandiose Helen epic. The first of these, "Helen," is among her best-known works; written in 1923, it appeared in the volume *Heliodora* (1924). With its compact lines and strong visual orientation, this poem displays the chiseled precision of the Imagist aesthetic that first established H.D.'s reputation. She renders Helen as a statue, in effect stripping the poem's subject of its subjectivity:

> All Greece hates
> the still eyes in the white face,
> the lustre as of olives
> where she stands,
> and the white hands.
> (*Collected* 154)

Here the classical world's most beautiful woman is not so much an icon as a target. Friedman points out that "all Greece" ultimately bears "the entire weight of a cultural tradition" the poet calls into question (234). In other words, H.D. exposes Helen's dubious enshrinement as a character assassination that has shaped centuries of Western literature. Paradoxically, this eighteen-line poem and its static Helen better fit the conventions of revisionist mythmaking than does *Helen in Egypt,* which devotes scores of pages to the protagonist's words and thoughts. Although Helen remains silent in the earlier poem, its critique sounds clearly: Greece "could love indeed the maid, / only if she were laid, / white ash amid funereal cypresses" (*Collected* 155). That is, even virginity (maidenhood) could not redeem Helen for the Greeks—unless she was also purified through death.

The closest that "Helen" ventures toward epic intonations is H.D.'s epithet "God's daughter, born of love," an unexpected phrase that romanticizes the consensus myth of Helen's conception resulting from rape (*Collected* 155). But the discourse of romance dominates the prequel poem, "Leda," a factor that surely contributes to its virtual absence from H.D. studies. Appearing in *Hymen* (1921), "Leda" is her first poem about the Helen story—and among H.D.'s earliest about mythic women. Significantly, it reveals that popular romance was already shaping the poet's Hellenism from the outset of her career. Transforming an act of inflicted violence into one of consensual lovemaking, the poem presents softened images of Zeus that anticipate H.D.'s refashioning of Achilles as the romantic hero of her Helen epic. Her Zeus is not terrifying like the assaulting figure of W. B. Yeats's later "Leda and the Swan." Instead, H.D. emphasizes the god's "soft breast" and redness to describe an erotic encounter that mingles caresses and colors; Leda becomes a lily enriched by golden hues (*Collected* 102). Fittingly, the poem situates Zeus and Leda within a "liminal landscape . . . where sweet water overcrosses salt," to borrow Eileen Gregory's characterization of the same border terrain of Helen and Achilles's lovemaking in *Helen in Egypt* (192). H.D. also softens her mythic scene with languid pacing. The shortest line ("he floats") draws attention to Zeus's near stasis, and its assonant links with *slowly, gold,* and *old* reinforce this slow-motion effect. If "Helen" hinges on the statuesque, "Leda" suggests the aesthetics of watercolor and *tableau vivant.*

H.D.'s most surprising invocation of romance comes at the declarative turn in the final stanza. For here "Leda" counterpoises one kiss with both the Trojan War and Helen's resulting censure by "all Greece":

> Ah kingly kiss—
> no more regret
> nor old deep memories
> to mar the bliss . . .
> (*Collected* 120–21)

Helen in Egypt will repeat this fraught balancing act when the protagonist asks, "Can one weigh the thousand ships against one kiss in the night?" (39) In "Leda," the audible exhalation of breath— "Ah"—attempts to expel any trace of violence from the myth of Helen's origins and its aftermath, banishing our "deep memories" of her mother's violation. While the poem's climax allows Leda the agency of sexual pleasure, its palpable "bliss" signals the "all encompassing" state of romantic thralldom that DuPlessis detects in many of H.D.'s later literary productions ("Romantic Thralldom" 406). Moreover, the poem does not present the ready platform for critique that we found in "Helen."

"Leda" offers important clues for the ways H.D. complicates revisionist mythmaking in *Helen in Egypt*. According to Montefiore, this enterprise cannot succeed because the poet's source materials prove so "resistant to recasting" that prior cultural meanings will "return to haunt the poem that overtly discards them" (56). The same myths that give such poems their legibility and cultural authority often come ready-made with plots and characters that undermine the position of women, as Ostriker and her successors point out. While this conundrum certainly applies to "Leda," I find that H.D.'s rerouting of the myth confronts us with more vexing problems. For the poem's romantic Hellenism not only pushes its source narrative to the breaking point, but also departs from the adversarial subversion we have come to expect from revisionist mythmaking. In short, H.D.'s heavy investment in romance resists traditional *and* revisionist approaches to myth. Her ultimate epic will oscillate between the mythmaking modes of "Helen" and "Leda," fashioning a protagonist that questions her legendary status within an overarching romance plot.

Helen in Egypt *and the Cosmic Kiss*

H.D. sets her hybrid epic after the Trojan War, which Achilles, Paris, and Helen will recall through flashbacks of her iconic appearance on the rampart walls. These main characters occupy an alternative dimension that is simultaneously physical, psychological, metatextual, and cosmic. The text reconfigures these classical characters as a love triangle so Helen can embark on her "Quest of Love" and enter an unassailable "'eternal moment'" with Achilles (*Helen* 181, 269). At one level this clearly empowers the protagonist, because rather than being bartered, taken, and scripted by others, she chooses her ideal lover. Yet even as H.D.'s Helen plays a more active role than her classical counterpart, her enthrallment punctuates her agency with near-incapacitating states of emotion. Not surprisingly, feminist critics do not usually look to romance plots as vehicles for epic heroines and woman-centered writing, even though Radway reminds us that "a romance is, first and foremost, a story about a woman" (589).[9] But we must take into account the fact that Achilles also succumbs to thralldom, making the destined couple's power relations complicated and inconsistent. This Achilles gazes upward into Helen's eyes before he falls in battle, and this Helen proclaims that "Love's arrow" slew him—in effect, transforming Homer's avenging Paris into an unwilling Cupid figure. If the *Iliad* is essentially a chronicle of the great warrior, *Helen in Egypt* is, at heart, a love story. H.D.'s epic-romance does more than fuel the poem's fraught gender relations: it activates the form-problem of an emotionally and stylistically overwrought style that straddles popular and literary culture. The poem acknowledges the importance of romance to its formal innovations, declaring that "the numberless / tender kisses" and "soft caresses" have no part in traditional epic. For H.D., the Trojan War is neither a focal point nor a backdrop, but a conduit through which "two soul-mates should meet" (*Helen* 9, 289, 5).

The interplay of concise, visually oriented poems and prose head notes contributes to the formal excess of *Helen in Egypt,* remixing the earlier poems' rhetorical declarations and romantic lyricism with the ambiguities we expect in modernist long poems. While Helen utters most of its individual lyrics, Achilles, Paris, and Theseus speak substantial portions of the text. The individual head notes range from a single sentence to multiple paragraphs, varying in their function and length as well as in the proximity of their meanings to the accompanying poems. Generally speaking, these prose sections either chart events and themes (like Milton's summations in *Paradise Lost*) or Helen's insights and emotions (like third-person narration in romance novels). For example, an early head note informs us that Helen's "concern is with the past, with the anathema or curse" of her reputed role in the war, while another reveals that her newly kindled love for Achilles veers between "fear" and "defiance" (*Helen* 5, 18). At other times H.D. uses head notes to point out the significance of a mythological figure or ancient site (like the citations in epic films and modernist long poems).[10] Yet on the whole, the head notes in *Helen in Egypt* can prove more tentative than definitive. After qualifying that Helen and Achilles "are not shadows, not shades, not ghosts," for example, the prose narrator simply asks, "What are they?" We find a similar elusiveness in head notes that comment on the protagonist's movement through the epic-romance plot: "Has her knowledge made her happier? Perhaps." (*Helen* 43, 26). Whenever I teach *Helen in Egypt,* students have difficulty determining whether certain sequences depict the protagonist's memories, fantasies, or actions. Navigating the poem's three sections ("Pallinode," "Leuké," and "Eidolon"), we encounter a text with the look of a free-verse epic, the hybrid narrative of epic-romance, and the fluid geography of historical epic film. In short, the act of reading *Helen in Egypt* proves an epic task in and of itself.

Critical discussions have emphasized Helen's search for identity, but *Helen in Egypt* consistently subordinates this psychological quest to romantic pursuit. Indeed, H.D.'s working title was *Helen and Achilles*. Helen activates the plot in Egypt by using "magic greater than the trial of arms" to summon Achilles, and he ushers in its resolution by following a new command (cosmic Love) to transport her back. In the middle section Helen goes to the primary site of Achilles worship in the ancient world—the isle of Leuké. This proves a fitting place for Helen to sort through the "heart-storm" of emotions triggered by their night on the beach, a scene she recalls during her encounters with Paris and Theseus (*Helen* 5, 159). As in most romance stories, the heroine controls the point of view while her beloved controls her movement through the narrative. Besides plotting the union of her ideal lovers, H.D. fashions their meeting across gender boundaries: Achilles will soften into a male romantic lead, while Helen will acquire attributes of a woman warrior. Their interactions in the Egyptian present and Trojan past form the poem's emotional center.[11]

There are classical as well as more contemporary precedents for pairing Helen and Achilles so that the innovations of H.D.'s epic-romance rely more on augmenting and combining diverse sources than on countering a patriarchal tradition or master narrative. Given the sheer amount of time that she and fellow Imagists Pound and Richard Aldington spent in the British Museum between 1911 and 1913, H.D. would surely have seen its famed Portland Vase. According to James Davidson and other Classicists, one of its amorous scenes might portray Achilles and Helen (Silverstein 34; Davidson 331–32). Guy Hedreen notes that variant Achilles lore joins him with either Iphigenia or Helen in his afterlife on Leuké and that one ancient text refers to a temple statue of Helen and Achilles making love (320). H.D. alludes to the legend of their son, Euphorion, in the opening head note to her epic's "Leuké" section. The context of historical epic film provides another possible source. *Helena*, the Helen epic H.D. assessed in *Close Up*, anticipates the love triangle of Helen, Achilles, and Paris in *Helen in Egypt*. The romance plot begins when Achilles sees Helena at the Adonis

Games that precede Paris's arrival in Sparta. Struck by her beauty, the warrior enters the requisite chariot race to best Menelaus and presumably win Helena as well as the victor's crown. After Helena leaves the palace with Paris, it is Achilles who calls for war. In the Troy sequences we see more of Achilles's interactions with Helena than of his legendary confrontation with Hector. In Achilles's final scene, he is felled by Paris as he gazes up at Helena for the last time. This softer side of epic cinema inflected the genre from its beginnings—including films with warrior heroes such as Odysseus, Alexander, and Ben-Hur. While Helen films drew many of their spectacular effects from sprawling combat scenes, they relied heavily on the discourse of romance to swell the intensity of close-ups and dialogue—aspects that made women's emotions rather than martial masculinity the focal point of epic narration.

The protagonist and signature style of *Helen in Egypt* intersect with popular cinema's feminization of epic form, positioning H.D. as a cultural insider. The poem's interplay of cinematic and classical inflections begins by relocating Helen from the towering walls of Troy to the colossal architecture of Egypt. We first view her in Karnak's "Amen" temple, a vast space in which she appears as a series of images (and studies hieroglyphics). Like ornate movie palaces inspired by the Tutankhamun excavations, such as Grauman's Egyptian Theatre in Hollywood, the temple functions as a monumental site for projecting the past.[12] Whether moviegoers were watching an epic film about Cleopatra or the Exodus story, Antonia Lant explains, such theater designs rendered ancient Egypt as oracle of a "hieroglyphics revealed by light," a cinematic picture-language that simultaneously condenses the ancient past and transmits modernity (71). In H.D.'s epic picture palace, Egypt operates as a site where "images and pictures flow through" the protagonist, to borrow a filmic phrase from her memoir *The Gift* (134). Throughout *Helen in Egypt* Helen will project her distant and more recent past in an epic that "may like cinema, be remembered, re-pictured, re-played," as Mandel puts it ("Redirected Image" 44). In the "Pallinode," H.D. projects two structuring images that replay in the other sections: Helen's eternal moment with Achilles in Egypt and Helen's iconic appearance on the Walls of Troy. While we see the first only through Helen's eyes, we view the second from the perspective of each character in the love triangle. H.D. will gradually superimpose the first image over the more familiar one to form a new emblem of Helen-and-Achilles.

"Pallinode" presents the eternal moment through the popular romance trope of mistaken identity, launching the central conflict between Achilles's actions and Helen's emotions. Radway distills this mainstay formula as "the story of a woman who is misunderstood by the hero, mistreated and manhandled as a consequence of his misreading, and then suddenly loved, protected, and cared for by him because he recognizes that he mistook the meaning of her behavior"(75). Helen masks her identity when Achilles approaches her on the shore, fearing his anger should he recognize her. She first passes herself off as a common slave ("I am a woman of pleasure"), a remark that not only comments "ironically" on her notoriety, but also intersects uncannily with *Helen of Troy*—in which the heroine disguises herself as a palace slave and encounters a ragged Paris on Sparta's shore. Director Robert Wise makes effective use of widescreen framing, centering on Helen's puzzled response to her future lover while showing the rippling sea, massive cliffs, and Paris's ship that will take them to Troy (see figure 1.2).

Figure 1.2 Helen meets Paris, *Helen of Troy* (Warner Brothers, 1956)

H.D.'s Helen compounds her requisite scene of misrecognition by deciding to "blacken her face" and arms with a charred stick so that she resembles what the prose narrator terms "the prophetic *femme noire* of antiquity"—one of several manifestations she assumes in the poem (*Helen* 12, 15). Susan Edmunds reads this dramatic alteration as "a moment of actual racial conversion" in which "Helen becomes a black woman in becoming Isis," noting that British Egyptologist E. A. W. Budge portrayed the goddess as a black African (120). H.D. was certainly familiar with the work of Budge and other Egyptologists, as I have discussed elsewhere with Mary Ann Eaverly. While H.D.'s image of a black Helen is unusual, it is not unprecedented; Orson Welles cast Eartha Kitt as Helen in his 1950 stage production of *Faust.* In terms of popular culture, H.D.'s cross-cultural figure replays the racial ambiguity of Egyptian royal women in historical epic film. Claudette Colbert portrayed a Cleopatra with art-deco pallor, but Gene Tierney spoke of having "'to make up as a dark-skinned Queen'" for her appearance in *The Egyptian* (Lux 137). In the 1956 version of *The Ten Commandments,* Anne Baxter presents a well-tanned Princess Nefretiri. H.D.'s Egyptianized Helen projects an amalgam of the primal goddess, the Hollywood vamp, the noble queen, the classical ideal, and the modern romance heroine.

Through his forceful reaction to Helen's dissembling, Achilles displays the trappings of popular romance heroes as well as epic warriors. Mistaking her for Hecate and then for a corrupt version of Isis, Achilles launches a series of invectives that culminates in an outburst of violence.[13] When he recognizes Helen at last ("for you were the ships burnt"), Achilles grabs her throat with "his fingers' remorseless steel," an image that evokes combat. But this rage of Achilles veers suddenly into lovemaking, "a touch in the dark" that brings "Helen / to sleep in his arms." She does not reject her volatile lover, but wishes to "remember, / forever, this Star in the night" (*Helen* 17, 42, 19)—a romantic revision of Homer's avenging Achilles "blazing like a star" on the Trojan plain (*The Iliad* 542). Strange as Helen's response may seem, it is all too predictable in romance fiction. In her landmark analysis of Harlequin romances, Tania Modleski points out that "the puzzling behavior of the hero" constitutes the "basic enigma" of such novels, in which his initial "brutality comes to be seen as a manifestation not of contempt, but of love" (30, 33). If there is any doubt that H.D.'s heroine has similarly swooned, the prose narrator informs us that "this 'attack' meant more to her than the approaches of her husband, Menelaus, or the seduction of her lover, Paris." In other words, she perceives her traumatic experience as a heightened form of love. Musing over her rough treatment, Helen envisions Achilles through a montage of warrior/lover images: he is a lady-killer who "flouted his power, / while women fell, as the scythe / of his visored glance swept them over" (*Helen* 39, 33). By blurring the boundary between his martial and sexual prowess, Helen can justify Achilles's prior actions and pursue their ultimate union.

Ultimately, H.D.'s epic protagonist is neither a traditional nor revisionist questing figure because her desire for Achilles ultimately outweighs her independent goals of cosmic and self knowledge. Sometimes an individual poem's expression of romantic desire undercuts its head note's claim that Helen engages in philosophical inquiry (*Helen* 198). As she presumably contemplates the division of body and spirit, for example, she rhapsodizes over Achilles's face and hands. Initially Helen "feel[s] the lure of the invisible" in the Amen temple, but her interest in metaphysical pursuits succumbs to "the lure of his sea-eyes." Indeed, she "flings knowledge away," as the prose narrator puts it (*Helen* 21, 37, 32). Achilles also interferes with Helen's much-discussed search for identity. She would "fight for Helena" so she is not "lost," but the sound of his voice returns her mind to the scene of their lovemaking. As with typical romance heroines, heart trumps head to resolve her inner turmoil:

> the heart does not wonder?
> the heart does not ask?
> the heart accepts,

> encompasses the whole
> of the indecipherable script;
> take, take as you took
>
> Achilles' anger, as you flamed
> to his Star,
> this is the only answer . . . .
> (*Helen* 37, 86)

Here the cosmic plane telescopes into her passion, and Helen instructs herself to *take* (to withstand as well as to secure) any resulting agitations. Throughout the poem Helen's interactions with Achilles unsettle, detour, or refocus her independent aims so that her trajectory adheres to neither the classical voyage out that her gender traditionally prohibits, nor the sustained "voyage in" that feminist critics brought to light in women's writing.[14]

Achilles's enthrallment with Helen began in Troy, which he recalls in a romantic flashback of her appearance on the Walls—the poem's second structuring image. Projecting this memory in "Pallinode," Achilles displays a softer masculinity as he becomes fixated on Helen's scarf and pacing movements:

> I saw her scarf
>
> as the wind caught it,
> one winter day; I saw her hand
> through the transparent folds,
>
> and her wrist and her throat . . . .
> (*Helen* 56)

Here Helen's Orientalized appearance makes her kinswoman to the alluring, veiled women of epic films about Egypt and Babylon.[15] While the voyeuristic aspect of Achilles's gaze reinforces conventional masculinity, the passage also calls his warrior identity into question by confessing that Helen is "the Power / that swayed" him (*Helen* 56). Achilles looks to Helen for his fate in the war, measuring her footsteps with his own "heart-beats" to determine whether he should break with "the Command" of Agamemnon, Menelaus, and Odysseus (*Helen* 53). Creating a close-up view of Helen despite their great physical distance, the scene simulates CinemaScope photography's merging of panoramic perspective and emotive expression. Achilles anticipates the reader's dubious response to his cinematic feat:

> you say, I could not see her eyes
> across the field of battle,
> I could not see their light
>
> shimmering as light on the changeable sea?
> (Helen 54)

Here Helen looks back, no longer the object of a voyeuristic gaze but the subject of a desiring(and knowing) one. Like his counterpart in *Helena*, Achilles dies as her eyes meet his, searing into his memory this immortal emblem of their love.[16]

H.D.'s romantic refashioning of Achilles also anchors a critique of martial masculinity that better fits our expectations of women's revisionist mythmaking. Not surprisingly, then, this oppositional aspect of *Helen in Egypt* has garnered the most critical attention—despite its relatively small proportion of the whole. In "Pallinode" Helen declares, "I do not want to hear of Agamemnon / and the Trojan Walls" because the Greek warriors "fought, forgetting women, / hero to hero, sworn brother and lover, / and cursing Helen through eternity." She disputes their legendary heroic status as vigorously as she contests the false image they impose on her: "I am not nor mean to be / the Daemon they made of me" (*Helen* 18, 4, 109).[17] Under the tyranny of Agamemnon and her husband Menelaus—immortalized with grandiose battle scenes in the *Iliad*—Greece is not a source of civilization but "a place / where desolation ruled." Helen characterizes her brother-in-law as a "war-Lord" who "blighted" the peaceful "Harmony and Grace" of Clytemnestra and Iphigenia. The prose narrator expands this critique by linking Agamemnon to a "death-cult" that sacrifices women (*Helen* 90, 74, 99). H.D. gives postwar resonance to this patriarchal band through anachronistic descriptions. As Friedman points out, Achilles's Myrmidons are "fair-haired" like the Nazi ideal, and their leader is an "indisputable dictator" who is promised "Helen and world-leadership" if he continues with Agamemnon and Menelaus (*Helen* 9, 51; Friedman, "Creating" 382–83). This hypermasculine Achilles will switch loyalty to the new command of divine love in "Eidolon," where his thralldom takes on epic proportions.

H.D.'s negative projection of martial masculinity presents foils to Helen's ideal mate, intersecting with popular cinema's depiction of Homer's legendary kings. Classicist Jon Solomon faults Helen epics for supplanting "the heroic qualities of men like Achilles, Agamemnon, and Hector" with "the amorous qualities of heroine Helen" (103), thus feminizing their Homeric sources. In *Loves of Three Queens,* Menelaus is a war monger longing to invade Troy before Paris's arrival in Sparta. In *Helen of Troy* Menelaus is the villain who jeopardizes an ideal love and Paris the dashing hero who rescues Helen from a despotic husband. Brutish and menacing, Sparta's king grabs Helen's throat in her iron-barred chamber—a stark domestic space that reflects her imprisonment, as Martin Winkler points out (*Cinema* 225, 227). Just as Menelaus has no finest hour in *Helen of Troy,* bellicose Agamemnon has no day of glory. He pushes for "a war of defensive aggression" before Paris enters his brother's palace, eager for a united Greece that controls Mediterranean trade. When Agamemnon assembles the Greeks to rouse them for war, the scene floods with red light to highlight the men's frenzied movements and battle lust. In contrast, the film's pastel-clad Paris is a suave, diplomatic figure who aims to "spread civilization" to the Spartans.[18] Like H.D.'s Achilles, he also displays for Helen the requisite prowess that will secure her love. Both characters perform a hard/soft masculinity like their counterparts in romance fiction, yet these hybrid heroes are contained within their relationships. It would be a stretch to claim that they ultimately threaten the status quo in their respective texts.

H.D.'s Paris is the false lover that Helen must reject because he would dissuade her from Achilles and restore her to iconic status. When Paris finds Helen on Leuké, he mistakenly believes that Aphrodite has given his beloved to him for a second time. To win back her affections, he plays on her sympathies by recounting the series of losses he has endured since Troy. Against his will, Paris's avenging arrow became "Love's arrow" that joined Helen with her new lover. He now replays for Helen his memories of their last days in Troy, projecting a reverse-angle of Achilles's sequence to reveal bitterness over losing her love before she fled the palace. For him the alluring scarf marked the transfer of Helen's love to Achilles, "a visible sign, / to enchant him, / to draw him nearer" (*Helen* 139). Because Paris sees her most vividly in his memories, he lacks the cosmic capacity that Helen requires to achieve a love beyond her legend. So she must reject his offer of a shared afterlife on Leuké. By walking out on him, the narrator informs us, Helen renounces "all claim to the world and her past affiliations with it" (*Helen* 145). Even so, her ensuing distress undercuts her bold action so that she conforms to romance heroines. "Troubled by the old questions," as Linda Wagner puts it, Helen wonders: "how is it she is here? why is this happening? why does she deserve this 'heart-storm?'" (Wagner 513; *Helen* 162) To emerge from this turbulent state, Helen finds her first lover.

Like Paris, Theseus mistakes Helen's arrival at his door as a sign that she loves him. Both characters try to nullify her attraction to Achilles—and her new affinity for Egypt—by pulling her farther back into the past.[19] Attempting to undo Helen's desire for Achilles, Theseus relays to her the warrior's abandonment of his wife and his desire for Paris's sister Polyxena, as well as his ghost's demand for her sacrifice. However, the prose narrator intervenes to maintain our investment in the hero, brushing aside this potentially damning information as "unrelated to our Achilles concept." As if on cue, Theseus transforms into an enabling character that can get Helen "half-way to that Lover"; he will even make an off-stage alliance with Achilles to transport Helen back to Egypt. His domestication makes this former "Master of the Argo" a fitting confidant as he nurtures her with a fire and woolen shawl. Displaying a more feminized version of hard/soft masculinity than Achilles, Theseus's hybridity of "power and tenderness" allows Helen to ponder the mysterious nature of romance (*Helen* 172, 165, 206–07).

Although Achilles does not appear physically in "Leuké," Helen gives him palpable presence through her passionate accounts of him—the poem's only form of Achilles-worship on his legendary island. "Do you know his hands?" she asks Theseus, asserting that "they are powerful but thin; / too fine for strength"—a description that counterpoises her repeated image of Achilles's "remorseless steel" fingers about her throat. She compares this violent embrace to the talons of "a gerfalcon / fall[ing] on his prey," the unrivaled "touch" the "Absolute." Indeed, the narrator's introduction to this poem states that "Helen seems to ask, how can I compromise? My soul or my spirit was snatched from its body, or even more miraculously, *with* its body, by this 'gerfalcon.'" Carnal and cosmic at once, Achilles's predatory lovemaking in Egypt yields the ecstasy of "an ever widening flight" into the eternal moment in timeless-time. Equally expansive is Helen's rhapsodic account of her lover's eyes as the sea itself. Paradoxically, this metaphoric extension of Achilles's earlier "sea-eyes" telescopes the terrain of epic questing *and* stretches the romance to epic proportions. Proclaiming that she "would renew the Quest" for cosmic love, Helen plots her course for the Zodiac Wheel, relying on her lover for orientation (*Helen* 198–99, 205). Like the widescreen projections of CinemaScope, H.D.'s extended framing enables heightened portrayals of emotion within an enlarged and multiplaned frame.

Writing in CinemaScope: Epic Returns

In "Eidolon," the culminating section of *Helen in Egypt,* the poem becomes more emotionally and stylistically overwrought as Helen extricates herself from the love triangle—and her iconic image. She projects the poem's structuring images in a nonlinear sequence that ejects Paris from the plot and replaces her legendary child (Euphorion) with the mutual ecstasy of her eternal moment with Achilles. In the opening lyrics to this aptly named section of the poem (*eidolon* means image), a proliferation of romance and representation heightens the grandiosity of H.D.'s late signature style. Here the softening of Achilles takes on epic proportions as he pledges allegiance to "Formalhaut [sic], / the Initiator, royal, sacred / High Priest of love-rites." This inflated lover's discourse borders on unintentional self-parody, like epic cinema's over-blown love scenes. No longer the martial "'Lord of Legions'" and "'King of Myrmidons,'" the narrator informs us, H.D.'s hyperro-mantic Achilles prays before Helen "as before the high-altar," car-rying a torch literally and figuratively for his ultimate lover (*Helen* 208–10). The poet does not contain her epic's amorous outbursts by deflecting them into quotations from foreign languages or juxta-posing them with ironic voicing, departing from Eliot and Pound. Instead, the passionate lyricism of *Helen in Egypt* revels in its amo-rous excesses. Anticipating readers' confusion at the poem's sudden shift from Greek, Trojan, and Egyptian mythological figures to an indeterminate one, the narrator's explanation spreads across the Mediterranean to stretch the limits of legibility. The poem's par-allel escalation of mythic and archaeological allusions pushes its epic dimensions well into the overwrought:

> Who is Formalhaut? We gather that this is a synonym for "the Nameless-of-many-Names," Proteus, King of Egypt. It is the same Amen-temple, at all times, in all places, on all planes of existence, whether they are symbolized by Athens, the intellect, or by Eleusis, the mysteries. (*Helen* 212)

This proliferation of unwieldy references spans Persia, Greece, and Egypt, intersecting with the "wantonly expansive" quality of epic cinema's "excess of temporality" (Sobchack 280, 295). H.D. also continues a key characteristic of modern epic that Franco Moretti has traced through male writers since Goethe: the nonlinear sense of time as "a zigzag that leaps from one epoch to another without any consistency" (52). *Fomalhaut* is not, in fact, the name of a deity but a first-magnitude star in the Piscis Australis (Southern Fish) constellation.[20] One of four guardian stars for the ancient Persians, Fomalhaut was also worshipped at Demeter's temple in Eleusis. But neither the star nor the amorous meanings H.D. assigns it connect to Amen, the primal Egyptian sun-god.[21] *Helen in Egypt* pulls both Fomalhaut and its most ancient deity out of cultural alignment as Achilles's diction pushes past conventions of epic gravitas. In effect the poem has reconstructed its monumental set, Amen's temple of cosmic instruction, as "Formalhaut's" temple of love.

Before Helen can fashion a new image of herself in this rapture of representation, she must exit the confinement of a love triangle that interferes with her quest for cosmic love. Paris makes a final attempt to turn Helen from Achilles, but he cannot operate within the poem's increasingly panoramic scope. Ultimately, he would limit Helen's domain to her orthodox text so he can assume that he alone truly knows her: "I read all your thoughts." Helen has no choice but to banish Paris to the representational bind that he and poets of her legend have fashioned; they are "caught in the maze of the Walls / of a Troy that never fell." Forever imprisoned within this "Labyrinth" that Helen escapes, Paris is cut off from the domain of questing and cross-cultural transformation that Helen shares with Achilles. "What could Paris know of the sea," she asks pointedly in the poem's culminating stanzas. Freed from her love triangle and its emotional turmoil at last, she can now liberate herself from the burden of misrepresentation (*Helen* 218, 232, 304).

Helen is the last major character to project the poem's image of the Walls, which she mixes with her third projection of the eternal moment. In effect, both images combine in a cinematic dissolve so that the latter can replace the former—and Helen can create her eidolon of cosmic love. While Achilles depicted Helen pacing the ramparts and Paris showed her escape from the tower, Helen completes the poem's Troy sequence by removing herself from the city. Significantly, Helen begins her final projection at the harbor (her point of departure); this border zone merges in her memories with the Egyptian shore, further blurring the space-time continuum. As "Helena, cursed of Greece" she had disguised herself to avert Achilles's anger; here she is "an enemy in a beleaguered city" who dissembles to gain safe passage to Egypt (*Helen* 16, 234). Helen's bartering tools—bracelets and scarves—recall her cinematic allure in Achilles's and Paris's projections, while her indeterminate status ("is she a slave or a queen?") mirrors the earlier trope of mistaken identity. Like a plucky romance heroine, Helen shows her mettle in these scenes, "fight[ing] . . . through the crowd," contemplating a "leap from the Walls," eluding a palace guard, and finally commanding a boatman at the wharves: "here is silver, / let me pass." This expansion of her displays heroic qualities that complement Achilles's romantic ones (*Helen* 233–34, 265).

With nothing left to hold her in Troy after Achilles dies, Helen's seven years there distill into a composite single day—her last day in the city and her first encounter with her new lover. Such flash forwards to Egypt punctuate all of Helen's flashbacks to Troy so that her projection succumbs to the poem's inevitable pull toward the eternal moment. The text racks between competing focal points before its superimposition is complete, a technique we first see when Helen tries to recall her time with Paris:

> I can not remember . . .
>
> I only remember the shells,
> whiter than bone,
> on the ledge of a desolate beach.
> (*Helen* 235)

These lines repeat her earlier echoing of Achilles describing the same Egyptian shore, merging point of view and blurring temporal boundaries to expand the frame of narration.[22] Through his eyes Helen replays their night by the fire, feeling his despair and desire. As she continues her recollections of Troy, her projections of the eternal moment enlarge and "break through the legend" of her classical image (*Helen* 259).

The poem stretches even more as Helen shifts its focal images from the circles of her bracelets and Achilles's shield, to his hands that "ringed" her throat, and finally to the "circlet" pattern in the Zodiac Wheel. Achilles, the "Star in the night," now joins with Helen to "form a frieze, / the Zodiac hieroglyph, / on a temple wall" and in the heavens (*Helen* 268, 262, 271). They are unmoored not only from Troy but also from the space-time continuum itself. Instead of Hector and Achilles circling one another before their single combat, we now have Helen and Achilles forever circling the fire as they "stare and stare / over the smouldering embers," treading the sand like wary beasts in their "preliminary tension" before ecstasy. As the cosmic couple ascends to their "ultimate experience, *La Mort, L'Amour*," the text circles back to its origins in H.D.'s Egyptian picture palace—the only space that can accommodate the full scope of Helen's projections. It is the place where "light moves over the wall," the place where the "Amen-script" of hieroglyphics merges with the star-script of constellations, the place where "the old pictures are really there" as "a new pattern" emerges (*Helen* 269, 271, 288, 21, 264).

There is a timeliness to H.D.'s construction of timeless love. Poised to enter culture as Helen and Achilles are poised before their eternal moment, *Helen in Egypt* was completed during a resurgence of epic film production in the United States fueled by the advent of widescreen photography—and a postwar wave of Egyptomania. The discovery of Pharaoh Khufu's solar boat in 1954 renewed America's fascination with Egypt in ways that impacted the big screen, this time with more staggering depictions of its colossal architecture than those inspired by Tutankhamun (Solomon 143–44, 13–14).[23] *The Egyptian* and *The Valley of the Kings* appeared that same year, followed closely by *The Land of the Pharaohs* (1955); the first and third films were shot in CinemaScope. Ancient Egypt and historical epic film were reinvented through this new technology. With its stretched aspect ratio, CinemaScope and other widescreen formats allow for striking horizontal compositions that feature a vast expanse of space, off-center framings of focal characters with dramatic backgrounds, and crowded shots that offer competing points of interest (Bordwell and Thompson 165). For example, *The Egyptian* opens with a survey of screen-filling monuments: the Great Sphinx, the Pyramids, the temple of Hatshepsut, and several pharaonic statues. No American film-maker displayed the staggering scope of cinema's epic aspect ratio like DeMille, who in 1956 remade *The Ten Commandments* in VistaVision. His earlier version of 1923 displayed the vastness of epic space by evoking the American West, reconstructing Karnak's Avenue of the Sphinxes in California, and drawing our eye to the imposing mountain range in the background.[24] For the 1956 version he created a composite set based on monuments from different locations, incorporating an obelisk, Hatshepsut's temple at Deir el-Bahri, and the temple of Horus at Edfu into the imagined city that Moses builds for Sethi (Solomon 146, 148–49). In the film's most self-reflexive moment, Moses opens a drapery to reveal the spectacular shot, prompting an admiring "Superb!" from the pharaoh as viewers share his perspective on a scene overloaded with stately sphinxes, proliferating columns, and massive pylons. By reconstructing an ancient Egyptian temple complex, DeMille showcases the sheer magnitude of widescreen photography, the cinematic magic of matting and superimposition, and the wide scope of his own epic sensibility. Like DeMille, H.D. drew on Egyptian temples to launch her stylistic expansions. In particular, the Amun temple complex at Karnak was her *image of wide scope,* to borrow Gregory Ulmer's term. For thinkers and artists, he explains, it is "the core image guiding their creativity" (10). In H.D.'s case this image shaped what Mary Ann Eaverly and I have termed the "Egypto-modernist" turn in her late career—a crucial element in her move to the long poem. The poet had toured Egypt in 1923, visiting Karnak as well as Luxor and the Valley of the Kings. Replaying images of Karnak's colossal structures in *Trilogy* and

Helen in Egypt, H.D. creates an archaeological anchor and alternative dimension for her epic ambitions: "It is the same Amentemple, at all times, in all places, on all planes of existence" (*Helen* 212). In such passages H.D. writes in CinemaScope.

This expansionist aesthetic also reflects the widening of American influence over Egypt and the Middle East. It is here that the poem's form-problem reveals itself not only through the sustained tensions of epic-romance, but also through the ruptures of Cold War geopolitics. H.D. completed her poem during the year of the Suez Crisis; controlling the canal and an emergent Egyptian nation played key roles in shaping the Eisenhower Doctrine. As Edmunds rightly insists in her reading of *Helen in Egypt,* "we need to ask what declared political purposes, feminist or otherwise, are served by the poem's use of an ancient Egyptian setting and mythology"—especially since H.D. followed news of Egyptians' uprising against the British occupation and declaration of a republic (97). The year she finished the verse portions, 1954, began with the forced withdrawal of British troops from Egypt. While the critical conversation on H.D. tends to focus on British-Egyptian relations during this period, we must also bear in mind that American involvement in the Middle East increased as British influence waned. In 1956 Britain, France, and Israel invaded Egypt, while the United States and the Soviet Union intervened separately to halt the war, marking a major flashpoint in Cold War geopolitics. At the same time, Hollywood film companies were producing some of the most widely circulated images of Egypt as an ancient—and spectacular—Middle East. Moretti points out that "the present does not exist in epics" because their modern incarnations depict "the specific *historicity* of a universe in which fossils from distant epochs coexist with creatures from worlds to come" (88). The romance plot of *Helen in Egypt* gives H.D.'s epic a parallel dynamic because its heroine mostly looks back to the past or forward to her ecstatic union with her lover. Modern Egypt's fight for independence is displaced onto a distant

Trojan War that is overlaid with the ancient past of an eternal Egypt.

Although *Helen of Troy* was not part of Hollywood's latest wave of Egyptomania, it nonetheless forms part of the cultural nexus I have laid out. The first widescreen treatment of the Trojan War, this CinemaScope production touted its "Olympian scope and vastness" in the trailer (Winkler, *Troy* 17; Trailer). Its unprecedented global premiere in fifty-six countries greatly expanded Hollywood's domination of film distribution, participating in a larger Americanization of classical culture. *Helen of Troy* presents "a woman of self determination," as Hecuba puts it—a phrase deeply ingrained in national ideology. Winkler has discussed how the film's Americanization of Helen also absolves her of any blame, because "her marriage is enslavement" and "her love will give her liberty" (*Cinema* 228). With Greece rendered barbarous and Troy facing ruin, American values substitute as the civilizing force that sutures fractured Mediterranean relations. At the same time, Hollywood formulas substitute for Homeric themes to appropriate the *Iliad* as what the trailer terms "inspired romance." Like H.D.'s poem, the film's investments in classical, national, and other popular mythologies present a mode of revisionism that ultimately proves more feminizing than feminist—even as it calls into question the privileged masculinity of Homeric epic.

Spreading its scope across the ancient Mediterranean world as the United States exerted more power in the modern Middle East, *Helen in Egypt* manifests the "geographical extension" and "supranational dimension" that marks a "world-text" in Moretti's sense (47, 2). The poem is hardly the cultural latecomer that traditional literary histories would have us believe. Indeed, its elaborate intertwining of literary and vernacular cultures widens our understanding of modernity and monumental form. Through a hybrid structure of epic-romance, it parallels *Helen of Troy* in rearticulating earlier genres and styles in the wake of new geopolitical configurations. H.D.'s most overwrought poem manifests this form-problem through a woman-centered, love-driven plot—performing a counterintuitive means of revisionist mythmaking to expand legendary gender roles. Viewing the poem as a CinemaScope production calls for a widescreen mode of reading, a horizontal method that bridges cultural studies with formal analysis of signature styles. But more fundamentally, H.D.'s major epic compels us to acknowledge women poets' long-standing articulations of and through popular culture.

CHAPTER 2

The Poetry Picture Book: Stevie Smith and Children's Culture

Curiously, Stevie Smith circulates as matriarch of contemporary British women's poetry *and* as child-poet of modernism.[1] Beginning with her first volumes of poetry in the 1930s, Smith actively affiliated her work with childhood and children's culture—from the cartoonish drawings that accompanied her poems to the Peter Pan collars she donned for her readings. Browsing her *Collected Poems*, readers encounter philosophical inquiries and nursery rhythms, social satires and fairy tales, mythological figures and frolicking animals. This combination of gravitas and girlishness makes Smith a challenging figure for women's poetry studies. Because childhood plays such a key role in her signature style and reception history, critics tend to elide her poems' child speakers with Smith herself. By shifting our focus from Smith's childhood and personality to her sustained engagement with children's culture, we can resituate Smith's poems and pictures within the multiple meanings of childhood that they reiterate, revise, and reinvent. As we shall see, this horizontal approach not only removes Smith from the literary nursery, but also prompts us to reconsider how conceptions of childhood shape women's poetry studies.

Since Smith first gained critical attention, detractors and defenders alike have rendered her as a poet in a pinafore—a trend we often see in their titles: *Stevie Smith: Little Girl Lost,* "Stevie Smith: Girl, Interrupted." The first critical book, first biography, and first essay collection on Smith all refer to their subject as "Stevie," suggesting unintentionally that the poet never grew up.[2] So strong is this critical current that some critics even assign the child-voice to poems with adult speakers. For example, Eleanor Risteen Gordon compares their persistent questioning of authority to that of "a three-year-old," while Janice Thaddeus likens "Not Waving But Drowning," Smith's most famous poem, to "the cry of a child" (Gordon 239; Thaddeus 95). Romana Huk's more recent figuration of the poet falling prey to "cultural corruption" invokes the child more subtly (218). In another critical tactic, some of Smith's rehabilitators invoke childhood to convey artistic freedom and social rebellion. Martin Pumphrey links her use of fairy tales and nursery rhymes to the "anarchic force of children's culture (89). For Julie Sims Steward, Smith's unruly drawings function as a "Pandora's playbox" (69). Playing on Smith's gender-bending poem "Childe Rolandine," Laura Severin's studies give us "Childe Stevie"—perpetrator of "resistant antics" against the status quo.[3] While such subversive images of Smith-as-child are certainly preferable to trivializing ones, they can still reinforce the view that she operates primarily as a cultural outsider. Indeed, this kind of reading implicitly draws on Robert Louis Stevenson's "Child's Play" (1881) and Charles Baudelaire's *Intimate Journals* (1887), both of which invoke the spontaneity of childhood as a model of artistic genius.

Smith was hardly immature, eccentric, or anomalous in making childhood central to her work. The child as figure proved foundational to "making it new" for writers, psychologists, and other thinkers who ushered in the modernist turn. In *Children's Ways* (1897), the trade edition of his landmark *Studies in Childhood* (1895), psychologist James Sully popularized the view that child's play was an analogue for the creative process. As Holly Blackford explains, the cross-Atlantic Child Study Movement that emerged through Sully, G. Stanley Hall, and other psychologists offered "an inspiring mode of speculative composition" that sought access to the "elusive object" of the child's mind, constituting a "sister field" for fiction writers who began to experiment with capturing consciousness (371). While Henry James's *What Maisie Knew* (1897) centers the modern novel on a child's development, modernist *künstlerromans* such as James Joyce's *Portrait of the Artist as a Young Man* (1916) and Virginia Woolf's *To the Lighthouse* (1927) render childhood as a developmental stage in artistic sensibility. Children's drawings also figured prominently in the discourses of Child Study and modernist art. Roger Fry's influential "An Essay in Aesthetics" (1909) positioned these images as windows on "the imaginative life," asserting that they express children's "delightful freedom" rather than copying nature (80). Early responders to the paintings of Pablo Picasso and Paul Klee often compared their lack of verisimilitude to the work-as-play of children's hands. Modernism's child and children's culture were, in short, ongoing discursive constructions across a spectrum of media.

This enmeshing of modernism and children's culture offers important orientation to Smith, who also entered the discourse of children's culture to foster innovation in her work. By *children's culture* I mean material and social practices that are *about* or *for* children. This includes not only literature that foregrounds childhood (such as William Blake's poetry, Charles Dickens's novels, and Lewis Carroll's *Alice* stories), but also images of childhood in visual culture; commercial accoutrements of childhood such as toys and clothing; the children's book market; and social institutions that shape childhood such as child rearing manuals, psychology, and the educational system. Engaging with this rich nexus of artistic, intellectual, and popular material, Smith did not simply appropriate or parody childhood, but rather brought its diverse meanings to bear on her poetry's interplay of text and image.

The poet shaped children's culture most directly by reviewing scores of British and American children's books between 1941 and 1968—nearly the full span of her career. With capsule commentary on as many as fourteen books for children per column, Smith's reviews appeared in a diverse range of popular and more literary periodicals: *Britain To-day, Daily Telegraph, John O'London's Weekly, Modern Woman, The Observer,* and *The Spectator.* The fact that such columns were not restricted to women's magazines reflects the growth of the children's market, especially in the postwar years. Smith reviewed new editions of classical, biblical, and fairy tales; reissued children's classics by Lewis Carroll and Beatrix Potter; and emergent classics such as C. S. Lewis's *Chronicles of Narnia,* Mary Norton's *The Borrowers,* P. L. Travers's *Mary Poppins in the Park,* and Newbery Medal winners *Johnny Tremain* (Esther Forbes) and *Rifles for Watie* (Harold Keith).[4] Smith also reviewed the first literary study of the child, Peter Coveney's *Poor Monkey: The Child in Literature* (1957). Although Smith never wrote poems for the children's market, she was commissioned to introduce and caption *Cats in Colour* (1959), a picture book, and edit *The Batsford Book of Children's Verse* (1970). Such extensive cultural work could hardly be marginal in the "Century of the Child," so dubbed by Swedish child advocate Ellen Key in her international bestseller on education reform. Indeed, the dissemination of Friedrich Froebel's *kindergarten,* the emergence of children's sections in department stores, the new prominence of children in advertising, and the growing market for children's literature position Smith's verbal and visual images of childhood very much in the cultural mainstream (Kline 101–04).

Smith's Child and Child Study

Many of Smith's poems echo nursery rhymes, nonsense verse, and fairy tales, while others such as "Little Boy Lost," "Darling Daughters," and "The Orphan Reformed" voice or otherwise feature child characters. I will focus on dramatic and interior monologues because they show most clearly how modernist stream-of-consciousness and modern children's culture inflect Smith's signature style. My first examples, "Papa Love Baby" and "The Photograph," voice infant speakers who do not rest easily within their respective family scripts. Resisting critics' constructions of Smith-as-child, both poems situate babyhood within contemporary debates about developmental psychology. "Papa Love Baby" is many current readers' first encounter with the poet, appearing on the first page of both *New Selected Poems* (1988) and *The Norton Anthology of Literature by Women* (Gilbert and Gubar 2007). Given its title and subject matter, this poem strikes many critics as her quintessentially childlike voice, a kind of infant avatar.[5] While "Papa Love Baby" certainly bears a biographical layer (Smith, too, had an abandoning father who bolted for the sea), the poem is not exactly the elegy for lost childhood that some have claimed. Inflected heavily with Child Study, its simulation of a young child's consciousness is cultural inheritor of Charles Darwin's diary of his infant son, as well as Sigmund Freud's essay on infant sexuality.

Voiced by a child recalling her formative years, "Papa Love Baby" ponders her parents' misguided marriage and her father's premature departure from the family. Smith fashions an emergent sensibility that is governed not by instinct, but by a studied dislike of household relationships. Investigating her own psychological development, this precocious speaker claims that she saw through the flimsy basis of her parents' attachment as a mere toddler:

> My mother was a romantic girl
> So she had to marry a man with his hair in curl
> Who subsequently became my unrespected papa,
> But that was a long time ago now.
>
> (*Collected* 16)

Smith's tone maintains emotional distance to avoid the extremes of Dickensian woe or Georgian glow in English poems about childhood. The matter-of-factness of "she had to" positions the child as seasoned observer of her mother's fall into romantic determinism. When "papa" first appears as a discordant end word paired with "now," Smith deviates from the poem's pattern of couplet and quatrain rhyme to signal his role as family misfit. In what would become one of her signature moves, the poem redraws adult/child boundaries—in this case by fashioning a humorously "censorious baby," as

Jack Barbera and William McBrien put it (9). From her diminutive perch, the child pronounces her verdict on her parents' behavior with the feminine end-rhyme poets typically employ for light verse and satire: "I sat upright in my baby carriage / And wished mama hadn't made such a foolish marriage" (*Collected* 16). Although she lacked the ability to articulate her opinion at the time, the speaker tried to express her disapproval through body language—reversing parent-child relations with a silent scolding of her mother. By shifting diction from *mother* to *mama,* Smith heightens the contrast between the speaker's young age and mature sensibility.

Besides discounting her mother's youthful infatuation, this tiny girl questions her alleged father fixation in Freudian romances—even as Smith acknowledges Freud's tremendous impact on children's culture. At one level, "Papa Love Baby" reads as a challenge to imagine vexed father-daughter relations *without* the father of psychoanalysis:

> What folly it is that daughters are always supposed to be
> In love with papa. It wasn't the case with me
> I couldn't take to him at all
> But he took to me . . .
>
> (*Collected* 16)

The word *case* acquires institutional meanings as the child gives an account of her father's unrequited daughter fixation, balancing the family dysfunction of her mother's unrequited love for him. She claims that her own "sad fate" arose from the awkwardness of a fundamental dislike for papa, which she tried unsuccessfully to hide. Implying that he "ran away" over hurt feelings, the speaker suggests that she tried to handle the situation maturely while he behaved childishly. As Huk asserts about Smith's poetry more generally, the poet "portrayed adulthood itself as being continuingly juvenile, which of course complicates romanticised readings of her childlike speakers" even as critics try to impose them (42). In the final stanza of "Papa Love Baby," Smith thwarts Freudian models of maturation by inoculating her abandoned child against melancholia. The daughter asserts that she "could not grieve" over papa's departure, then deflects any diagnosis of repression with a rollicking outburst of anapests: "But I *think* I was *some*what to *blame*" (*Collected* 16, my emphasis of stresses).[6] By mixing the rhythms of children's poetry, the Romantic poets' suspension of disbelief, and modern theories of developmental psychology, Smith's poem interrogates the normative family as a cultural insider.

Readers of "Papa Love Baby" might expect its visual accompaniment to depict the seasoned toddler in her baby carriage or with her father, but the drawing shows a lone little girl unmoored from the poem's domestic enclosure (see figure 2.1).

Hidden beneath her cape, her arms might be hanging at her sides (which would indicate smallness and vulnerability) or folded across her chest (which would indicate stubbornness or defiance). The girl stands on a hilltop, dressed as if she has just left the church below—or wasn't going to church at all. Paradoxically, her distance from an institution that sanctions marriage is the closest the drawing comes to the poem's contexts. Smith's visual rendering of the girl presents an ambiguous image of childhood. Her dimpled knees convey a natural cuteness, while her ruffled skirt and fancy hat reflect manufactured constructions of girlhood. While her attire appears English, her close-cropped hair and slanted eyes seem Chinese. How might we account for this visual slippage between domestic and foreign, self and other? We could read the incongruities as a mirror for the dislocations of Smith's childhood: her father's truancy, her mother's early death, her own stints in a convalescent home. But if we shift our focus from nuclear to national family, we must acknowledge the larger *discursive* links to childhood—specifically to the imperialist inflections of developmental psychology.

Child Study drew from recapitulation theory to render the young child simultaneously as precultural and as a repository of early cultural history. For Freud, the child is a "little primitive creature" who "must pass through an immensely long stretch of human cultural development in an almost uncannily abbreviated form" (66). Viewed through an evolutionary lens as a microcosm

Figure 2.1 Stevie Smith's drawing for "Papa Love Baby"

of civilization's emergence, the Western child thus straddles racial as well as temporal boundaries. Ancient African and Asian cultures figured prominently in this imperialist discourse. Sully claimed that children's drawings resemble the drawings of modern aborigines and the art of ancient non-European civilizations. As an example, he linked young children's "schematic treatment" of the human eye to the stylization of dynastic Egyptian art (340), making modern childhood the imperial apex of primitive adult development. Put another way, Sully perceived a similar lack of cultural maturity and *development* in his unparallel points of comparison. Just as Child Study perceived the child as cultural outsider and cultural incubator, imperialist ideology constructed non-Western cultures as free from and fuel for modernity. Kenneth Kidd notes the latter trend in American children's literature of the modernist era, pointing out that Newbery Medal winner *Shen of the Sea* (1926) ushered in a trend of "depicting other cultures as exotic, primitive, and 'historical'" (176–77).[7] Shaping the modern maturation narrative with these racial meanings, the discourse of Child Study requires the act of becoming Western as a key marker of growing up. Smith's drawing reflects the vexed nature of this enterprise in its rendering of the young girl. On the one hand, her crinolines and overly adorned hat seem as exotic as her apparent Chineseness; that is, the trappings of modern femininity become strange. On the other, incongruent image/text relations yoke together the Orientalist trope of Asian inscrutability and the English speaker's self-disclosure of her formative years, casting doubt on the monologue's seeming transparency. As with so many of her poems about childhood, Smith's interplay of text and image in "Papa Love Baby" complicates our understanding of what (and how) "growing up" means.

"The Photograph," spoken by another tiny tot, situates developmental psychology within the popular practice of family photography to reveal children's underlying savagery, in effect creating a double exposure of modern childhood through text and image. Like "Papa Love Baby," this poem from Smith's second volume voices the recollection of a formative experience that yields unexpected results.

Here the tyke objects to being posed in "fashion fancy" upon a tiger rug, presumably to accentuate the preciousness of childhood:

> They photographed me young upon a tiger skin
> And now I do not care at all for kith and kin,
> For oh the tiger nature works within.
>
> (*Collected* 145)

Criticizing the performance of middle-class parenthood, the speaker claims that the photograph backfired by reversing rather than hastening her development. Coming into contact with the tiger skin rug activated an innate force that acculturation represses, so that the poem links "the association of childhood with primitivism and irrationalism or prelogicism" in Child Study (Ariès 56). Although "lately born," Smith's speaker can nonetheless "scent the savage he sits upon" and recognize a kindred spirit that the poet renders as an amalgam of Blake's Tyger, Freud's Id, and Kipling's Mowgli. The poem's meter becomes more irregular as it continues, reinforcing the child's recapitulation and pressing against the unchanging triplet rhyme scheme that simulates children's poetry. As Pumphrey argues, Smith often seeks "to exploit the contradictory possibilities in the cultural construction of the child (as innocent/depraved, conservative/anarchist, naïve/gifted-with-insight)" by using "children's expressive forms" such as nursery rhymes (89, 88). Yet here the final stanza combines off and slant rhyme in its line endings (*young, upon, human*), a dissonant echo of the *in* rhyme quoted earlier. Through this formal disorientation, Smith sounds uncertainly what should be the most reassuring words in the poem—the closing phrase "all things human." Mimicking and disrupting elements of children's poetry as it reverses Child Study, "The Photograph" casts doubt on children's fundamental nature through the speaker's startling self-assessment.

The poem's accompanying drawing has more obvious connections to the poem than the one for "Papa Love Baby," even though its opposition of refined and uncivilized elements would appear to work against it (see figure 2.2). Gendering the child explicitly, commercialized markers of girlhood (smocked dress, petticoats, bloomers, anklet socks) contrast with what Kristin Bluemel aptly terms "the vicious energy of the tiger skin" (118). Yet both figures manifest their respective resistance to being stilled—the posed girl by the vehemence of her displeasure and the ambiguously dead tiger by its tummy-up position, predatory expression, and protruding claws.

Moreover, the uneasy alignment of vulnerable girl and wild animal reminds us that "children are always the ones 'taken'" in family photography, as Judith Williamson puts it (122).[8] By depicting her fictive snapshot with a line drawing, Smith both revises

Figure 2.2 Stevie Smith's drawing for "The Photograph"

and reinscribes the belief in photographic veracity that circulated widely when this poem appeared toward the end of the documentary decade. Her hand-drawn image shows what family albums repress, functioning like Walter Benjamin's "optical unconscious" by inadvertently revealing their darling child's nature—despite the artifice of her trendy attire and background (47). Like many of Smith's poems from her first three volumes, in which children figure heavily, "The Photograph" and "Papa Love Baby" show that her work does not simply mimic or counter children's culture, but engages it in diverse and even contradictory ways.

Smith, Children's Literature, and the Mise-en-Page

Like her poems, Smith's reviews often encourage readers to look beyond formulaic plotlines and sentimental images of childhood. "Children have wonderfully fresh minds and deserve the best food for them," she asserts in a 1945 review for *Modern Woman,* reinforcing the consensus view of educators and developmental psychologists ("Children's" 81). Surprisingly, Smith's reviews of children's literature have not struck her editors, biographers, and critics as significant. Yet they reveal her attraction to its fluid sense of genre and formatting; both elements proved fundamental to her signature style. Smith found children's literature aesthetically interesting because its less restricted conventions could foster formal innovation. For example, she was struck by Gianni Rodari's "dazzling" *Telephone Tales* (1965), an avant-garde assemblage of a father's stories in which "nothing comes amiss to the author's fancy"—including a man with a market stall for comets and an encounter between real mice and their comic-strip counterpart ("Dumb Friends" 23). Smith expresses her enjoyment of children's literature most directly in a 1949 review, "World of Practical Girls":

> I like children's books; at least I liked these books. Why? Well, to begin with, I like the complicated plots and the uncomplicated people. Above all, no tinkering with the moral values.

These children are so practical, too. They know about trains, aeroplanes. They also know all about horses. Also, I like pictures, and children's books have pictures. I like historical books and a lot of them are historical. (729)

Child protagonists have more maneuverability than their counterparts in popular adult fiction, and their "uncomplicated" nature also means that girls are not emotionally preoccupied like the heroines of romance novels. Morality may be clear in children's literature, but "practical girls" and women can cross gender boundaries. Moreover, children's fiction can "complicate" plots because it ventures beyond the romance triangle—and even the nuclear family. In the "exciting and original" *An Explorer for an Aunt,* for example, a heroic woman creates an alternative family of nephews, nieces, and an abandoned girl. Smith also points out that girl-oriented stories can have "plenty of adventures" ("Books" 73; "Goodness" 750). In short, children's literature could be both mainstream and unconventional at once.

Smith's poem "My Hat" plays on the girls' adventure story by freeing the young protagonist from entering a marriage plot. Obediently following her mother's instruction to don the adornment for fetching "the right sort of chap," the young speaker reroutes the intended narrative with Smith's punning phrase, "How this hat becomes me" (*Collected* 315). To her delight, the hat flies her away to a remote island of perpetual morning and greenery—a ripe setting for the girl to pursue whatever fancies she chooses. Like her adult counterpart "Lady 'Rogue' Singleton," she prefers the freedom of the outdoors to the confines of courtship and domesticity. In Smith's accompanying drawing, the hat takes on fantastical proportions as it hovers between a diminished moon and sun, its chin strap looped about the girl's waist as she flies through the air. In the context of children's books, this particular drawing proves conventional in adhering closely to the narrative and appearing in frontispiece position. But in some of Smith's best-known work—including her poems about children—she pushes image-text relations in directions similar to the work of innovative author-illustrators such as Maurice Sendak and her contemporary Edward Ardizzone (1900–79).

The wide field of children's culture inflects not only Smith's subject matter, but also the mise-en-page of her signature style. In film studies, mise-en-scene refers to artistic control of everything that appears within the frame: sets, props, lighting, actors. Mise-en-page also signifies an active totality. As book artist and visual theorist Johanna Drucker insists, "The graphical presentation of a text" on the page (or screen) is fundamentally a "relational, dynamic, dialectically potential *espace* that constitutes it" (162). While such perspectives on expanding our sense of the page may bring to mind postmodern practices such as language poetry and new media, the concept of mise-en-page in children's literature is a long-standing one. Diana Klemin explains that "as offset printing gradually superseded the letter-press" in the late 1920s, children's book illustrators were no longer as confined by the page and thus able to "bleed" their illustrations "by drawing or painting to the extreme edges." Through this technological innovation—and illustrators' increasing responsibility for the mise-en-page—the children's book became "an entirety stamped with . . . individuality" (15). As with the extended narrative possibilities of children's literature, these visual inscriptions of authorship brought flexibility to the style and presentation of images, allowing illustrators and author-illustrators to move beyond the standard formats of frontispiece/text and image/caption. Offset printing also allowed publishers to brand a series with a particular look, such as the full-page reproductions of color photographs that distinguished the Batsford Colour Books series, in which Smith's *Cats in Colour* appeared.

In her reviews of children's literature, Smith would note when the pictures struck her as especially "lovely" or off-key. Smith admired Ardizzone's work, pronouncing "perfect" his illustrations for H. J. Kaeser's *Mimff-Robinson* ("Skating" 775). A prolific artist in both watercolor and pen-and-ink, Ardizzone collaborated on poetry collections as well as contemporary stories for children—including *A Ring of Bells: Poems of John Betjeman Selected for Young Readers*

(1962), Graham Greene's books about little vehicles, and Dylan Thomas's *A Child's Christmas in Wales* (1979). But he remains best known for his Little Tim books, which feature a whimsical boy in love with ships. Alone or with a friend, Tim typically stows away on a vessel, learning more about the sailing life and high-seas dangers in each story.[9] Sometimes he boards with an old boatman who forgets him upon departure. Tim's parents never seem to notice that he is away. The first in this signature series, *Little Tim and the Brave Sea Captain* (1936), appeared the year before Smith's first volume of poems. *Tim All Alone* (1956) was the first recipient of the Kate Greenaway Medal, which honors distinguished work in British book illustration. Comparing Smith's work with Ardizzone's offers a strategy for reorienting our sense of how her pictures operate on the page.

Smith surely found attractive not only Ardizzone's marginal positioning of children in his pictures, but also his tempering of sentiment in the matter-of-fact tone of the stories. *Mimff-Robinson* (1958) reflects his signature style by making the boys appear insignificant in the scene, often turning their heads away from the viewer. Paradoxically, the protagonist of the Little Tim stories is also diminished on the page, typically turning his head to present the "back view" that Ardizzone claimed was "the best view of a hero" (qtd. in Graham 30). In the 1955 edition of *Little Tim and the Brave Sea Captain,* Tim first appears in a distant plane, the profile of his head reflecting Ardizzone's tendency to offer "a suggestive sketch" rather than a delineated portrait of his main character, as Judith Graham notes (29). Like Smith, he typically uses minimal marks to convey facial expressions while making more expressive uses of body posture; sometimes the eyes are closed or represented by tiny dots. In the Little Tim series, Ardizzone's protagonist typically appears out of place as the lone child in the frame and becomes literally misplaced because he is usually forgotten by the adults who are his caretakers—his parents, his friend the old boatman, and various crews that find him aboard their ships. When Little Tim prepares to face his death on sinking—and sometimes burning—ships, Ardizzone resists sentimental treatment of his tiny protagonist's seemingly imminent demise. In *Little Tim and the Brave Sea Captain,* for example, the lad is quite forgotten in the rush to the boats after the ship's midnight crash: "He was so small and frightened that nobody had noticed him" (n.p.). Tim finds the steadfast captain on the deck, who commands stoically that he "stop crying and be a brave boy" because "tears won't help us now." Like Smith, who quipped in her "Practical Girls" review that "children are made of stouter stuff" than adults, Ardizzone took issue with the tendency to "shelter" them "too much from the harder facts of life." In his essay "Creation of a Picture Book" he insisted that "sorrow, failure, poverty, and possibly even death, if handled poetically, can surely all be introduced without hurt" (351). Smith apparently agreed, as she not only chose the Romantics' "fiercer poems" for her children's poetry anthology (including Blake's "The Sick Rose" and an excerpt from Shelley's *The Masque of Anarchy*), but also the macabre traditional ballad "Lord Rendall" (*Batsford* 3).

Like Smith's volumes of poetry, Ardizzone's Little Tim books sometimes yield creative tensions by venturing beyond standard formats for pairing text and image. Typical layouts in the children's books that Smith reviewed were facing-page illustration, pages with pictures above or below the related text, and pages with text sandwiched between pictures. Even when these formats are not intermixed, they make the picture book an "inescapably plural" form that belies the belief that illustrations are mere readerly "crutches," as Stuart Marriott puts it (4, 2). In addition to the formats mentioned earlier, the Little Tim books sometimes employ chiasmus by placing images in two diagonal corners and text in the other. Such layouts prove especially effective in depicting chaotic scenes at sea, especially given the understated diction and minimized facial expressions with which Ardizzone typically depicts danger. Here uneven patches of white space actively break apart the visual and verbal narration, intersecting with experimental tendencies in children's literature and in modernism. In his signature style, Ardizzone also used dialogue balloons to make mise-en-page more incongruous. For example, in this page from *Tim All Alone* the balloons *augment*, rather than simply reiterate, the text's rather perfunctory account of Tim being "signed on" as a cabin boy (see figure 2.3). Ardizzone found dialogue balloons "invaluable" for developing character ("Creation" 348), and Tim's polite "Thank you Sir" certainly fulfills this function. But the first mate's statement about him being "a bright boy" has no basis in the narration.

Although the protagonist appears toward the center of the page, his diminutive size and turned body minimize his importance. Moreover, he appears confined within the rectangular-shaped panel immediately behind him, further restricting his visual impact. Even the dialogue balloons occupy more space than he does, and his is the smallest of the three. Viewing the page from top to bottom, we see that Tim is outnumbered in the dialogue balloons, marginalized in the drawing and yet emphasized in the text. As with Smith's

he found they were short of crew and he was signed on at once as a cabin boy.

Once at sea Tim was kept so busy painting, scrubbing, running errands and helping the steward serve the officers' meals that he had little time to fret.

Figure 2.3   Page from Edward Ardizzone's *Tim All Alone* (1957)

illustrated volumes of poetry, Ardizzone's picture books foster a dynamic page in which readers shuttle across the spectrum of congruity and incongruity.

Despite the flexibility of her mise-en-page, Smith was inflexible about including the drawings in her volumes. Indeed, she threatened to break her coveted publishing contract with Chatto & Windus when they initially refused. Jack Barbera notes that she often introduced her poems at readings by describing their accompanying drawings, thus reinforcing her sense of them as "units" (224). Clearly the dynamics of mise-en-page shaped Smith's understanding of her signature style, which reminds many of my students of Shel Silverstein's. In addition to using the standard page formats mentioned earlier, Smith's books place drawings in corners and alongside poems, where they take on the appearance of visual annotations or marginalia. The layout for "Bog-Face" is perhaps her most heterogeneous and incongruent, reproduced here from *Collected Poems* (see figure 2.4). Competing for the viewer's attention, the two drawings and title offer radically different orientations to the poem, emphasizing respectively adult women and the poem's ungendered child speaker, Bog-Face.

Like Ardizzone's dialogue balloons (and the drawing for "Papa Love Baby"), these images create tensions on the page by pressuring one another as well as the poem's overt meanings. Smith's punning title (*bog* is British slang for toilet) does not adhere with the lower drawing because the child's face is not soiled and the landscape is tropical. Appearing even smaller on the page than Ardizzone's Little Tim, Bog-Face is marginalized by the larger female figures that dominate each drawing. The topmost image depicts a smiling woman with prominent breasts and hips, a trope we find in several of Smith's pictures of women unencumbered by domesticity. Well appareled in her hat, cape, and dress, she stands near a hill topped with palm trees, suggesting that she is on vacation. Her position on the page makes her look down at the bent figure of the mother in the lower image. And yet this smiling woman has no bearing on either of the poem's speakers and bears no resemblance to Smith's drawing of the mother.

Bog-Face

Dear little Bog-Face,
Why are you so cold?
And why do you lie with your eyes shut? –
You are not very old.

I am a Child of this World,
And a Child of Grace,
And Mother, I shall be glad when it is over,
I am Bog-Face.

Figure 2.4   The page of Stevie Smith's "Bog-Face"

If women's relations to domesticity form one axis of meaning in the mise-en-page, the major one reiterates and revises the Romantic child through the poem and accompanying portrait of little Bog-Face. Surprisingly, the poem begins with mother asking why her child is much colder than one such a young age should be, creating a contrast with the sunny tropical setting above this stanza. Her second question—"And why do you lie with your eyes shut?"—multiplies the meanings of coldness, ranging from emotional distance to more deathly possibilities. The child speaks in the second stanza, channeling the language of Romantic poets as he or she straddles the duality of the innocent/knowing child. Like Wordsworth's child "trailing clouds of glory," Bog-Face is both "a Child of this World, / And a Child of Grace." Yet Smith's child strikes a disturbing posture of world-weariness that rivals the children in Blake's *Songs of Experience*: "I shall be glad when it is over" (*Collected* 171). Bog-Face's anticipation of ending sounds suicidal. In the bottom drawing we see the mother and child who presumably utter this exchange. Although the poem portrays the mother's concern, the picture gives her clawlike fingers and a "menacing expression" similar to those Bluemel detects in the drawing for "The Sad Mother," another of Smith's devouring mother figures (125–26). In "Bog-Face" these characteristics make the mother's act of stooping to pick up her child appear more predatory than loving. If the mother's expression is fairly straightforward, the child's is not. The closed eyes and slightly downturned mouth might appear sad or resigned, while the upraised left arm could indicate feigning. Is the child punishing the mother who gave him or her life by preferring death, or is the mother about to punish her child for throwing a tantrum? In addition to these unresolved tensions, the picture reinforces the poem's gender ambiguity by dressing Bog-Face in a long-sleeved tunic and either a diaper or a short skirt. Taken as a whole, "Bog-Face" offers a striking example of not only the modernist effect in Smith's mise-en-page, but also the counterintuitive innovations that her immersion in children's literature brought to women's poetry.

"Angels and Horrors": Smith and the Innocent/Knowing Child

In 1957, the year of her volume *Not Waving But Drowning*, Smith assessed a landmark in children's culture and the maturation of modernism in her review of Peter Coveney's study *Poor*

Monkey: The Child in Literature. Surprisingly, this substantive response has thus far escaped critics' notice—even though it is here that Smith addresses most explicitly the cultural mythology of the Western child. Later revised as *The Image of Childhood,* Coveney's survey traced the emergence of the modern literary child from Jean-Jacques Rousseau and Blake to Joyce, Woolf, and D. H. Lawrence. In Coveney's narrative the literary child is offspring of Romanticism and thus symbolic of innocence, nature, feeling, and imagination. For Blake especially, deploying this natural child heightens the corruptions of industrial society. His innocent chimney sweeper disarms readers with a pointed poignancy lacking in his experienced counterpart:

> There's little Tom Dacre, who cried when his head,
> That curled like a lamb's back, was shaved; so I said,
> "Hush, Tom! never mind it, for, when your head's bare,
> You know that the soot cannot spoil your white hair."
>
> (*Collected* 51)

Assuming the role of guardian because society offers no other, the orphaned speaker becomes a vehicle for the poet's outrage at a "rich and fruitful land" with "babes reduced to misery," as Blake writes in "Holy Thursday" (67).[10] The quintessential Victorian child becomes a locus for moral debates, moribund rather than robust, and often confined to bed rather than romping outdoors. Accordingly, this child becomes an overly sentimental figure who wastes away under harsh schooling and labor in Dickens and expires angelically in overblown deathbed scenes such as Mrs. Henry Wood's *East Lynne.* Eschewing sentiment for analysis, Coveney contends, modernist writers depict the child as far less innocent than its Romantic predecessor, especially in its sexuality. Following in the wake of Freud's work, modernism's child becomes especially significant to writers as a window to the unconscious. Yet the modern child often stands in for the artist's alienation from an increasingly mechanized society, a refuge from modern culture; in other words, modernism often *recirculates* the Romantic child even as it assumes a more grown-up aesthetic of objectivity. According to Coveney, "major" modernists such as Joyce and Lawrence employ the child figure as a symbol of growth and fertility, while Woolf supposedly reflects her own neurosis and arrested emotional development by over-engaging with it (285).

As another woman modernist often accused of over-affiliating with childhood, Smith used the occasion of her review to air her own opinions about what constitutes apt and inept portrayals of child characters. Rather than perceiving a conceptual as well as chronological progression like Coveney, she believed that the "Romantic idea" of childhood as "Wordsworth's child of nature, Blake's bedevilled little ones and Dickens' wronged angels" permeates modern literature—and the popular imagination. Smith finds that even "good" modern writers "are not free from romanticism, in the sense of using the child, if not plainly to score off old offences against themselves, at least as in some way innocent—innocent and at bay" ("Angels" 49). In her favorable review of Carson McCullers's *The Member of the Wedding,* for example, Smith detected a Romantic strain in its "fairly scarifying tale of a precocious American twelve-year-old, brooding page long," despite the novel's innovations in depicting pubescent sexuality ("Book Notes" 40). She concurs with Coveney's assessment about "the free discussion of a child's sexual problems" in "many post-Freudian novels," but disagrees that this modern tendency "denotes objectivity" because of their one-sided portrayals of idealized, fundamentally innocent childhood: "How rarely in serious literature, how very rarely, is the child presented as a nasty little thing. Yet we are often nasty, and we are as much the child's old age as he is our youth" ("Angels" 49). In her rather wicked inversion of Wordsworth's "the Child is father of the Man,"[11] Smith eschews the idealization of children she finds in her modernist peers because, as the title of her review indicates, Smith perceives them as both "angels and horrors."

Smith's review of Coveney also provides a springboard for charting ways her child characters can press against their Romantic, Victorian, and modern models—or straddle these categories. In her volumes of poetry, she often reinvents childhood by recirculating these images while thwarting expected trajectories of child development. "Infant" depicts the youngest of Smith's child characters, playing on assumptions about children's innate disposition through an interpreter of the child who anticipates a disagreeing reader. Surprising us with its abrupt opening lines, the poem pushes Romantic suspension of disbelief to the breaking point: "It was a cynical babe / Lay in its mother's arms" (*Collected* 33). Ostensibly, the babe's premature birth and its mother's isolation twist its disposition, and yet this stated explanation leaves open the issue of whether nature or nurture is the prime mover. Blake's babes suspend our disbelief by articulating the strong emotions that drive their fundamental nature. "Joy is my name," says the two-day-old speaker of "Infant Joy" in *Songs of Innocence,* while its experienced counterpart in "Infant Sorrow" recalls a miserable entry into the world: "Bound and weary I thought best / to sulk upon my mother's breast" (*Collected* 35, 58). Troubling these fixed positions, Smith's third-person poem rejects both Rousseau's and Thomas Hobbes's respective models of innate goodness and depravity that shaped Romantic conceptions of the innocent/knowing child. When Smith echoes the Romantic child, we are less likely to ask if it is innocent or experienced than we are to wonder if it is childlike at all.

In *Collected Poems* "Infant" appears underneath "Intimation of Immortality," further emphasizing Smith's wink at Romantic sensibility even as the poet invokes it. In that poem she presents an older speaker who does not wish to be "sib to eternity," preferring to forego Wordsworth's return to the original heavenly state of his famous Ode (*Collected* 33). The drawing that accompanies "Infant" presents a blank-faced, domesticated Madonna nursing a swaddled, featureless newborn. Even in the context of Smith's minimal delineations of the human figure, this particular child is slight—dashed off in a scant two loops representing head and body. Indeed, the houseplant pictured on the adjoining table receives more distinguishing features than the baby. The image functions as a double-sided tabula rasa of the child's unformed mind awaiting impressions and experience, and as an undistinguished face onto which Smith's readers project their often unacknowledged conceptions of early childhood.

"Nourish Me on an Egg" straddles Romantic, Victorian, and modern constructions of childhood through a boy with intimations of mortality. Challenging the doctrine of children's innate innocence handed down from Rousseau, the poem presents a child demanding breakfast, beer, and seduction:

> Nourish me on an egg, Nanny,
> And ply me with bottled stout,
> And I'll grow to be a man
> Before the secret's out.
>
> (*Collected* 135)

This tyke desires "stout" masculinity but apparently lacks the requisite manliness to lift the bottle himself, as it appears larger than his torso in the drawing. Caught between desires for nourishment and over-consumption, Smith's child formulates a "secret" plan for his maturation that will hasten and stunt his development. The boy seeks sexual experience, a meaning Smith underscores with diction (*ply me*) and Nanny's buxom figure. But the boy's repetitive speech reflects a stunted imagination; each stanza begins with the same line, and each contains a similar-sounding line about the corrupting beverage. At one level, then, the poem counters Baudelaire's formulation of the child's heightened perceptiveness as a state of perpetual inebriation: "The child sees everything as a novelty; the child is always 'drunk'" (36). Like "Bog-Face," this poem raises the specter of the sickly Victorian child in the final stanza. Here the boy asks Nanny to stop crying and "close my eyes in sleep"—a phrase with sexual and deathly implications. The drawing depicts him sitting in bed while attending Nanny sheds a tear nearly as large as her eye, tweaking modern advertising's "gentle expression of anxiety about the ill child" in pitches for medicine (Kline 102). Smith's tense scene conveys frustration: the boy looks angry, while Nanny appears reluctant (see figure 2.5).

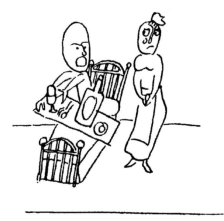

Figure 2.5 Stevie Smith's drawing for "Nourish Me on an Egg"

Readers must decide if her hand-wringing results primarily from the child's unruliness, forwardness, or imminent demise.

Smith gives another Freudian twist to the dynamics of boys and their caregivers in "The Last Turn of the Screw," one of her last child-centered poems. Spoken by young Miles from James's *The Turn of the Screw* (1898), the poem not only extends the novelist's unresolved questions about children's capacity for corruption, but also continues Smith's quarrels with Coveney's *Poor Monkey.* "The Last Turn of the Screw" offers a fuller characterization of its child speaker than the other poems I have discussed in this chapter. Like "Nourish Me on an Egg," it dramatizes a boy's decision to reach beyond his years in seeking manhood. Like "Papa Love Baby" and "Infant," it assumes a reader who will take issue with the speaker's view on children's fundamental nature and their process of acculturation.

Positioned at the threshold of the Century of the Child, *The Turn of the Screw* combines tropes of the ghost story with the discourse of Child Study, voicing the diary of a young governess assuming her first position in an isolated manor. She has sole charge of young Miles and his little sister, Flora, because their uncle is away and has asked to remain undisturbed. As the governess begins to hear strange sounds and perceive that the children bear a premature taint of forbidden knowledge, the novel recounts her frantic determination to ward off the corruption of the prior influence—and her increasing horror that her efforts are too late. "For," as Smith writes in her review, "Miles and Flora know evil and love it" ("Angels" 49). In many ways James's novel reads like a parody of Child Study. The well-meaning governess compulsively observes her young charges, delighting in their beauty and making "constant fresh discoveries" about their dispositions (30). Unleashing an array of enriching activities, she "overscored their full hours" in suffocating fashion so that the trio "lived in a cloud of music and love and success and private theatricals" (62, 63). She becomes aware that the children have been performing the very images of wholesomeness that she sought to instill—and that she can protect them no more than she can alter their already formed characters. Even more distressing, Miles dies shortly after she presses him to reveal the secret source of his corruption, which presumably took place on the premises.

In Smith's responses to the novel in her review of *Poor Monkey* and her poem "The Last Turn of the Screw," she highlights the limited perceptions of childhood shared by James's narrator *and* his critics. The review takes issue with Coveney for agreeing with critical consensus that the already fallen Miles is also "the victim of the Governess's cruel pursuit" ("Angels" 49; Coveney 166). Smith shares neither such critics' nor the governess's credence in children's inherent goodness. Rather, she approves of James's cagey positioning of Miles "a hairsbreadth this side of corruption and with ears agog for it," finding this portrayal superior to the "protested innocence" of modern fiction's "more fashionably vaunted children"—like McCullers's Frankie in *Member of the Wedding* ("Angels" 49). In effect, Smith argues, the governess and critics silence childhood by focusing so relentlessly on its potential for violation. In his recent assessment of James in the context of erotic innocence, Kevin Ohi imagines telling a story about childhood that is "not fueled by the panicked disavowal of eroticism," a story that allows the possibility of "hearing what Miles has to say before smothering him with protection" (152). Smith had already fashioned such a story in her poem, which gives desire and volition to Miles and assigns innocence to his governess.

Written the same year as her review of Coveney, "The Last Turn of the Screw" grafts her own interpretation of Miles onto the deliberate gaps in James's novel. The poem creates a discourse on Child Study that turns on the boy's manipulation of competing influences. Like the speaker of "Papa Love Baby," he claims a degree of agency in his development that challenges readers' credulity. Smith begins this process in the poem's first line, which disputes the novel's famous ending:

> I am Miles, I did not die
> I only turned, as on shut eye
> To feel again the silken dress
> Of my lovely governess.
> (*Collected* 440)

The poem opens a space for Miles's version of the encounter through the ambiguity of his cagey phrase *I only turned.* He compares it literally to shifting the position of his head so that he comes into fuller contact with her bodice, a meaning Smith reinforces with the drawing immediately to the right of this stanza. (In it, we see Miles embracing the governess with his eyes closed and her right hand on his cheek; his expression appears more dreamy than ill.) Miles's telling phrase also activates rich connotative meanings that foreshadow the way Smith will explore cultural mythologies of childhood. *Turning* can indicate that young Miles switched sides in a conflict, shifted away from his original path, or transformed into something else. From this point on, the poem explores each possibility as it moves from the couplets in its opening stanza to freer form and more conversational, adultlike diction.

As with James's novel, Smith's poem positions Miles between the competing influences of the governess and the ghost of Peter Quint, the dubious manservant who died before her arrival. Reacting to each with initial "squeamishness," the boy soon relishes their near-suffocating attempts to turn him from his prior state, because each adult furthers the boy's own agenda. Rather than being in Quint's clutches, Miles asserts that he willfully kept the servant close while "there was still some rotting to go on / In my own heart." He claims that he was already a man by the time he "lolled on Lady's lap," having incorporated Quint's "knowledge" so that it is "half myself by now." As for his "sweetly fatheaded" governess, she brings him close to "Virtue" only through her loveliness in the "silken dress." Moreover, she proves her genuine innocence by losing her fascination with Miles once he sheds his air of shadiness through a studied form of innocence. It is here that the boy miscalculates and finds himself vulnerable to this loss—even though it adds to his worldly knowledge. Smith underscores this final turn in the off-rhyming couplet "strange/pain" that ends the poem. And yet Miles will continue to protect his governess by feigning the guise of "a mere boy" so she can keep her illusions (*Collected* 441, 440, 442).

Miles had higher expectations of his addressee, but finds himself having to ward off objections to the poem's unconventional view of children's original nature—and their capacity to refashion it. Standing in for Coveney, another commentator on James, or any invested reader of the novel, this unvoiced interlocutor interrupts Miles at the poem's crux. For here the boy broadens the implications of his own story to childhood more generally:

> Some children are born innocent, some achieve it,
> You scowl; that doesn't fit with your philosophy?
> Can you by choosing alter Nature, you inquire?
> Yes, my dear sir, you can; I found it fairly easy.
> (*Collected* 441)

The disagreeable addressee "scowls" at Miles not only for taking innocence so lightly, but also for even suggesting that such a presumably innate thing can be acquired. Although Smith's poem responds to contemporary readers of *The Turn of the Screw,* its addressee reflects the attitudes of the novel's cultural moment. For nineteenth-century Americans, Karin Calvert points out, "children were pure and innocent beings, descended from heaven and unsullied by worldly corruption"; thus, losing this fundamental innocence "was akin to the loss of virginity, and the inevitable loss of childhood itself was a kind of expulsion from the Garden of Eden" (79). By *willing* this fall to happen and hastening its transformative turn, Smith's Miles disables the underlying innocent/experienced hierarchy that has lent conceptual coherence to literary childhood for three centuries. That Smith anticipates contemporary readers who harbor nostalgia for such views reinforces her sense that modern portrayals of childhood had regressed since James.

By engaging with James through the discourse of Child Study, Smith places her representations of childhood in the cultural center. The poems I have discussed here do not simply resist or reinscribe, parody or pastiche conventional figurations of the Romantic, Victorian, or modern child. Smith echoed Blake and reactivated his more experienced children through her indifferent tykes and cynical babes—even as she decried her peers' neo-Romantic portrayals of innocent childhood. She infected some child speakers with real or imagined illnesses while reanimating others. And she inflected child-centered poems with Freudian overtones even as she rejected his theories of psychosexual development. Unencumbered by familial connections to children, Smith operated through a discursive relationship to children's culture. She explored the cultural meanings of childhood not only through literary tradition, but also through material artifacts of childhood and images from popular culture. Recirculating variations on the child through a dynamic mise-en-page, Smith's signature style can hardly constitute an oppositional practice from the margins.

Revisiting Smith shows that the discourse of childhood is more than something for women's poetry to simply expel or embrace. Editors of pioneering poetry anthologies were well aware that the nineteenth-century poetess—a literary minor—still colored some readers' perceptions of the work they recovered and promoted. And yet the woman-poet-as-child remained a vexing figure for these editors as they began to plot the field of women's poetry studies. In *Without Adam: The Femina Anthology of Poetry* (1968), which includes three of Smith's poems, Joan Murray Simpson feels compelled to reject girlish default settings for women's poetry, declaring that it does not have "some kind of pink ribbon round it to distinguish it from the work of men" (18). Smith herself was cognizant of such "awkward" associations and objected to her inclusion in the anthology ("Poems" 180). In stark contrast to Simpson, the editors of *Psyche: The Feminine Poetic Consciousness* (1973) claim that women poets identify strongly with childhood because it is in many ways more fitting than "adult" stances:

> They also speak more often through the voice of the child than through the personas of mother or lover, perhaps because society enforces a childlike passivity and dependence on women. Like children, they are uncertain of the future and want to know not only Who am I? but more important, Who am I to become? (Segnitz and Rainey 18)

In other words, in its vulnerability and liminality the child parallels women's outsider status within patriarchy. While there is certainly some validity to this incarnation of the woman-poet-as-child, it borders uncomfortably on the girlish images of Smith I surveyed at the beginning of this chapter. And at its heart, the wide-eyed child of *Psyche* bears vestiges of Romantic innocence.

The flip side of this image—the rebellious child—inflected the psychoanalytic turn of feminist literary criticism in the 1980s and 1990s. We see this figure in *Naming the Waves: Contemporary Lesbian Poetry* (1989). In making her selections, Christian McEwen detected "the voice of a child" in recent lesbian writing that amounted to "something like a children's crusade" as poets began "to speak up, to try to make their voices heard over the confident pronouncements of the grownups" (xv). Feminist psychoanalytic critics drew on Julia Kristeva's influential theory of semiotic discourse (the repressed language of the pre-Oedipal infant) to recast allegedly "childish" aspects of women's poetry (especially linguistic playfulness) as strategies for subverting signification itself. In this model, which proved vital to recovering neglected figures, women poets operate as linguistic outsiders to the patriarchal symbolic order. Gertrude Stein (nicknamed "the Mother Goose of Montparnasse") and Edith Sitwell proved especially ripe for semiotic readings because their avant-garde styles can seem nonrepresentational. Kristevan approaches have not proved as successful with Smith's more accessible signature style, which, as we have seen, operates through the rhythms of popular verse and the look of children's literature. Smith's work unpacks and recirculates the cultural meanings of childhood, prompting us to acknowledge the lingering effects and limitations of the woman-poet-as-child. In *The Children's Culture Reader,* Henry Jenkins cautions against viewing children as Rousseau's "'gender outlaws' or cultural rebels" because doing so would place the child outside of culture (30). The same stakes hold for women's poetry studies when we impose an imperative for subversion that restricts not only the poet's subject and stance but also her range of formal innovation.

CHAPTER 3

Uneasy Alliances: Gwendolyn Brooks, *Ebony*, and Whiteness

Although Gwendolyn Brooks and *Ebony* magazine emerged from the same Chicago neighborhood and published their first volumes in 1945, previous critics have avoided linking America's first black Pulitzer Prize winner with its first black picture magazine. At first glance this dissociation seems fair enough. Many of Brooks's best-known poems give searing depictions of South Side poverty and scathing critiques of the white beauty standard. By contrast, the covers and lead stories of postwar *Ebony* featured wealthy entrepreneurs and glamorous celebrities, while several of its advertisements promoted skin bleachers and hair straighteners. Yet despite such obvious differences, their cultural proximity invites us to reconsider the poet in light of the popular magazine. Brooks appeared in several issues and knew key people on *Ebony*'s staff. The editors recommended her debut volume, *A Street in Bronzeville* (1945), in a promotion for the *Negro Digest* Bookshop. The magazine's first photographs of Brooks accompanied 1949 articles about back poets and the magazine's open house for its new building. Although Brooks's postwar presence in the magazine never matched that of Richard Wright and Langston Hughes, she did appear as a noted writer and minor celebrity.[1] She was among the celebrities who revealed "What Women Notice About Men" in 1950 and who picked their top heroes in 1953—the same year *Ebony* declined her proposal to prepublish *Maud Martha* with accompanying photographs (Kent, *A Life* 110). *Ebony* cited Brooks in annual reports on "Negro Progress" in 1953 and 1956, and included her in a 1960 article about success stories that also featured Lena Horne. Before publisher John H. Johnson started *Negro Digest* and then *Ebony, Jet,* and *Tan,* he and Brooks met through the local National Association for the Advancement of Colored People (NAACP) Youth Council. The poet would become close friends with managing editor Era Bell Thompson, who wrote many of *Ebony*'s editorials during the 1950s; three of the editorials invoked Brooks as a symbol of black achievement in the contexts of Mother's Day and black history. Between 1945 and 1960, Brooks emerged as a major figure with three volumes of poetry and a novel, while *Ebony* became the most widely read black periodical in the world.

Most pertinent to my analysis are key convergences that shaped the poet's and the magazine's postwar signature styles: both negotiated cross-racial audiences in a segregated society, both were accused of subscribing to whiteness, and both made whiteness visible in their texts. *Ebony* claimed a white readership "way up in the thousands" by 1952 ("Backstage" [1952] 12). Brooks not only had a large white readership, but also worked with a white editor at Harper & Row. Combined with her use of modernist techniques, this uneasy alliance has raised "troubling questions about her essential "'blackness'" for later critics, as Houston A. Baker points out; her early work strikes some as embodying "white style and black content" (21). Indeed, a significant consensus holds that Brooks "whitewashed" the poetry she wrote before 1967, to borrow Suzanne Juhasz's term (149).[2]

If early Brooks appeared to beat white modernism at its own game, *Ebony* embraced "beating white capitalism at its own game," as Bill V. Mullen puts it (201). Like its predecessor *Negro Digest,* the magazine reflected Johnson Publishing's inflection of "Lift while climbing" as "a racialized economic liberation cycle" (Doreski 91).

Indeed, in 1952 *Ebony* touted the clout of America's "15-billion dollar market" of black buyers ("Time" 116). Some of *Ebony*'s early readers accused it of promoting whiteness. For example, one black reader complained that the magazine interpreted black progress through "association with white people," while another decried the implicit message that "success comes with a fair skin."[3] Brooks herself recalled that the audience at the 1967 Fisk University Writer's Conference considered *Ebony* a "race traitor" (*Report* 84). And yet the "white" label grossly oversimplifies the cultural contexts that shaped the poet's and magazine's portrayals of both whiteness and race relations. Neither would have found startling the academy's later discovery that whiteness needs critical scrutiny. The magazine, in fact, republished its special issue on whiteness in book form, titled *The White Problem in America* (1966).

Brooks operated as both a cultural outsider and insider during her postwar career, which was shaped in part by "her adventure with the white liberal critical consensus," as Kent puts it (*A Life* 77), and her interactions with her white editor at Harper & Row, Elizabeth Lawrence. In her careful study of Brooks's reception, Zofia Burr points out that both her editor and white reviewers perceived her race relations texts as a form of literary trespass because they presumably go "beyond her own legitimate poetic terrain" of representing African Americans for the more "'reportorial' domain of social issues" (113–14). Moreover, as Kent reveals, Lawrence asserted some editorial control over Brooks's portrayal of whites by claiming that they lacked the originality and "freshness" of her portrayals of African Americans (*A Life* 109). Given the cultural meaning of *fresh* as dainty, contained femininity in numerous advertisements for feminine hygiene products (some of which appeared in *Ebony*), we cannot ignore the gender implications in this pointed comment. Doubly suspect, Brooks was being cited for unladylike conduct as well as inappropriate material; she was not writing "nice" poems about race relations. The poet's literary foothold often paralleled that of "African-American women's outsider-within positionality in power relations," to borrow from sociologist Patricia Hill Collins (8).[4]

As we shall see, Brooks's poems about cross-racial encounters reflect this freighted social space.

Like *Ebony,* Brooks also operated as a cultural insider through her role as one of the nation's key interpreters of race relations—especially in depicting the uneasy alliance between the black middle class and liberal whites. It is here that the poet and magazine intersect most fully by making whiteness visible and minoritizing its presence. Brooks wrote white characters into her poems about race, and *Ebony* published a section of white readers' letters to the editor. Wielding whiteness with a flourish in their postwar signature styles, Brooks and *Ebony* gained the rhetorical advantage by honing their tonal dexterity. Through strategic images, formats, and modes of direct address, they controlled their respective white readers' vantage points of cross-racial encounter. Maintaining these uneasy alliances proved crucial for the US civil rights movement and for postwar presidential politics; thus Brooks's and *Ebony's* participation in this joint venture was not simply a counter-discourse, but central to the national conversation about race.

Throughout the postwar years the term *liberal* would signify both a white ally in racial progress *and* an impediment to it. *Ebony's* editorials often invoked "the growing army of sincere, honest and understanding whites" who would join African American "battlers against bigotry" ("And a Child" 28). These rank-and-file liberals would take their place alongside popular leaders such as Eleanor Roosevelt and Frank Sinatra. Yet even as *Ebony* asserted that African Americans drew strength from white allies, the titles of these editorials often cast doubt on the whole enterprise: "Can the Negro Trust His White Friends?" (1946), "Are All Whites Prejudiced?" (1953), "Are White Friends Dangerous?" (1954). My focus on liberals is not meant to imply that their politics were the only option for African Americans seeking social change. Yet by 1944 "liberalism had become the default mode of black cultural politics" (Mullen 70). Liberals would figure prominently in the poet's and magazine's portrayals of race relations because, as C. K. Doreski explains, "the discourses of race and liberalism . . . were unable to maintain their boundaries in relation to a larger and national public" during the postwar period (93). Moreover, liberal critics were a key factor in Brooks's postwar status as a "favored Black woman poet," as Burr points out (121). My discussion of Brooks will center on the black/white interactions that shape her most controversial postwar poetry, all of which appears in her *Selected Poems*. Although these texts rarely circulate in women's poetry anthologies, feminist critics building on key work by Maria Mootry, Hortense Spillers, and Claudia Tate have rightly returned some of them to women's poetry studies (these critics include not only Burr, but also Kathryne Lindberg and Lesley Wheeler). Significantly, popular artifacts such as zoot suits and the Black press anchor this span of poems. In discussing *Ebony* I will draw from photo-editorials about race relations as well as from relevant letters by black and white readers. Reading these materials through one another reveals the flexible ways that Brooks's artful forms pressured the rigid dualities of US racism. Increasingly, her work called into question the efficacy of liberal allies in the aftermath of the Dixiecrat defection, Emmett Till, and the Little Rock Nine.

How to Read a Zoot Suit

Brooks's and *Ebony*'s first volumes emerged during a publishing boom that expanded white audiences for African American writers, many of whom enjoyed popular success. The year 1945 proved especially productive in marketing publications about black communities and race relations. Wright's *Black Boy,* published in February, became his second Book-of-the-Month-Club selection, ensuring another best-seller. In the same month, Ann Petry received Houghton-Mifflin's Literary Fellowship to complete work on *The Street* (1946). Journalist Ben Richardson published his first edition of *Great American Negroes* in 1945, and St. Clair Drake and Horace R. Cayton published their sociological study of Chicago's South Side, *Black Metropolis*. Fisk librarian Arna Bontemps found publishing success with *We Have Tomorrow* and *They Seek a City*. In August Harper brought out Brooks's *A Street in Bronzeville*.

By November the first issue of *Ebony* arrived on the newsstands, noting that New York publishers were "frantically grabbing at any and all manuscripts which touch on the Negro" ("Book" 24). Like the magazine, postwar black writers sought to counter exotic images from the Harlem Renaissance and to resist negative stereotypes in contemporary media. As *Ebony* put it, Hollywood continued to depict African Americans as "razor-wielding, watermelon-eating, eye-rolling, bandanna-clad menials," while the media presented them as pathological "slum dwellers, criminals, sharecroppers and zoot-suiters" ("Needed" 36; "Rogues" 62). Indeed, one of *Ebony*'s white readers spoke of a friend's "amazement" at seeing the magazine's articles on black businessmen and physicians, noting that both were victims of "'white' news censorship."[5]

Making a flashy, promiscuous zoot-suiter the centerpiece of her debut volume's longest poem would seem a counterproductive approach to combating racial stereotypes. Yet Brooks took this risk in "The Sundays of Satin-Legs Smith." According to Kent's biography, the poem supplied the longer, signature piece that Wright felt the manuscript needed (63). In her autobiography, Brooks recalls writing it after her white editor requested more "Negro poems" (*Report* 71–72)—perhaps with readers in mind like the white *Ebony* subscriber who relished the "exuberance that only the Negro seems to be blessed with."[6] It would be easy to oversimplify the poem as either "black" (Brooks's definitive poetic voice) or "white" (Brooks's concessions to her postwar white readership). But like her early career more generally, "The Sundays of Satin-Legs Smith" proves cagier in its rhetorical constructions—artful maneuvers designed to flush out the underpinnings of its readers' biases. Despite the poem's signature status in its volume—and critical stature in African American studies—it has not become part of the women's poetry canon.[7]

"The Sundays of Satin-Legs Smith" does not depict white characters, but addresses white readers through the rhetorical *you* they must share with middle-class black readers who have a closer vantage point. In effect, this strategic demarcation not only makes the ideology of whiteness visible, but also makes the poem's white readers emblematic of their race. While Brooks's portrait of a zoot-suiter shares *Ebony*'s agenda of "changing the false opinions that most whites have of us," as one black reader put it,[8] Brooks's speaker sometimes puts herself at odds with *Ebony*'s readership from the black middle class. As she presents Satin-Legs Smith to them and to liberals, she simultaneously re-creates and undermines the cross-racial coalition that was supposed to bring about desegregation. Previous interpretations tend to engage with only one component of Brooks's explicitly cross-racial audience. Mullen is foremost among the few who see Brooks targeting middle-class black readers, arguing that she attacks their bourgeois ideology (163). Most critics claim that Brooks targets white readers in a signature style that either subscribes to white aesthetics or attacks them. While offering important insights to the poem, such readings overlook the discursive complexity of its edgy *you*. Brooks interrogates her middle-class black readers' notions of respectability and her liberal white readers' fascination with black urban life, resisting their respective tendencies to view Smith as either a bad example or a representative figure. If we return "The Sundays of Satin-Legs Smith" to its postwar contexts, we can see that it casts early doubt on the uneasy political alliance reflected in Brooks's readership.

The poet restages the sartorial splendor of the era's zoot-suiter to make her focal figure a site of both cultural intervention and stylistic innovation. As he shuttles across the poem's "technique of a variegated grace," Satin-Legs occupies a shifting space between irony and sympathy, humor and seriousness, dandyism and defiance, black and white readers (*Blacks* 44). In the first section, Brooks bares Satin-Legs Smith by showing him at his bath, laying bare both the addressees' biases and the inherent instability of their coalition. Effecting irony and humor at his expense, Brooks opens with a view of Smith's posthangover toilette that parodies gentlemen's dressing scenes:

> Inamoratas, with an approbation,
> Bestowed his title. Blessed his inclination.

He wakes, unwinds, elaborately: a cat
Tawny, reluctant, royal. He is fat
And fine this morning. Definite. Reimbursed.

He waits a moment, he designs his reign,
That no performance may be plain or vain.
Then rises in a clear delirium.

He sheds, with his pajamas, shabby days.
And his desertedness, his intricate fear, the
Postponed resentments and the prim precautions.

Now, at his bath, would you deny him lavender
Or take away the power of his pine?
What smelly substitute, heady as wine,
Would you provide? life must be aromatic.

(Blacks 42)

This first *you* positions the poem's addressees in alliance through their education and middle-class values. They would appreciate Brooks's tony euphemisms for Smith's promiscuity ("inamoratas," "his inclination"), although black addressees would interpret his behavior as a class rather than a race marker. Addressing her cross-racial audience with the diction of "a 'talented tenth' class affiliate," as B. J. Bolden puts it (37), Brooks adds further mock grandeur to her protagonist through syncopated heroic couplets in the first four lines. While middle-class black readers might code Smith as foppish and white readers as exotic, both would agree that he is no gentleman.

Yet the poem's diction and cultural allusions will shift, along with its tone, when Brooks attempts to sustain her audience's temporary coalition and her own uneasy alliance with liberals. Her assonant phrase "clear delirium" straddles oppositions like all oxymorons, intersecting with her use of this device to pressure rigid social categories ("decently wild" and "sweet vulgarity").[9] At the end of this particular poem, Smith's current "inamorata" will contain "affable extremes" like "sweet bombs"—a South Side version of the era's bombshell. A more ambiguous technique than ironic

contrasts, oxymorons position Brooks's zoot-suiter somewhere between acceptable and unacceptable behavior. At this point the poem
unexpectedly addresses its readers with a collective *you,* assuming
that they would "deny" Smith the luxury of bath scents. What, we
should ask, is the audience's concern here? That he should spend
his scant money on less frivolous things? That he has exceeded the
bounds of respectability? That he (and perhaps the poem itself)
should be a better reflection of his race? The unity of Brooks's *you*
begins to splinter at this point.

The poem then launches its central issue—does its cross-racial
audience share anything other than bourgeois taste? For if "prim
precautions" are the only binding force, the coalition between the
black middle class and liberal whites is doomed. Brooks's speaker
baits her readers' preference for understated refinement by presenting a seeming non sequitur—Smith's status as a Southern migrant to Chicago: "But you forget, or did you ever know, / His
heritage of cabbage and pigtails" (*Blacks* 43). The Great Migration
to Northern cities in the 1920s and 1930s had a profound impact
on the South Side's demographics, exacerbating problems of in-
adequate housing and employment. Southern migrants prompted
social as well as economic anxieties. As Mullen notes, black
Chicagoans felt the need to "'civilize' the southern migrant," so
the *Chicago Defender* told newcomers how to conduct themselves
in public (45). Bronzeville biases against Southern migrants continued through the postwar era, prompting *Ebony* to note in an
editorial that Northern African Americans were "embarrassed" by
the migrants' "behavior, speech, and dress" ("Nobody" 68). Thus
Brooks's dividing *or* separates those black readers who may have
"forgotten" this social narrative from those white readers who
never knew or experienced it.

In her second and even more pointed address to this cross-racial
audience, the poem's speaker states that "there is little hope" to reform Smith's vulgarity "Unless you care to set the world a-boil /
And do a lot of equalizing things" (*Blacks* 43). These understated
yet pointed asides prove more ambiguous, as the lines could refer

to either racial or class equality. Yet ideologically speaking, liberals and affluent African Americans would have concurred in assigning social change *for those like Smith* to individual rather than structural means. Walter A. Jackson notes that postwar liberals saw racial inequality "in terms of the notion of 'prejudice'" on the part of individuals rather than racism on the part of institutions (98). While middle- and upper-class African Americans would have viewed racial inequality as a consequence of both, many of them would attribute Smith's lower-class position to his individual behavior. As Drake and Cayton explain in *Black Metropolis,* upper-class African Americans believed that the lowers "'don't know how to act,' or dress correctly, or spend money wisely" (563). In fact, some of Brooks's affluent black readers may have viewed Smith as contributing to racial inequality by presenting a "bad example" that confirms white prejudice.

After exerting rhetorical pressure on her readership's coalition and revealing class conflicts within black communities, Brooks makes her riskiest move by revealing Smith's status as a zoot-suiter. A culturally ambiguous signifier of black masculinity, the zoot suit drew strong reactions that broke across racial and class lines. It meant hip style to jazz musicians and young urban men; Cab Calloway sported a zoot suit in his stage shows. It meant criminality and ethnic excess to the white media, which gave inflammatory coverage of the 1943 "Zoot Suit Riots" between young Mexican Americans and white servicemen in Los Angeles. Wartime rationing of cloth made Latino and African American zoot-suiters seem like unpatriotic criminals to their white critics, so donning these oversized clothes and performing the requisite swagger was an act of defiance through style. Years before they became leaders of radical movements, Cesar Chavez and Malcolm X were zoot-suiters (Cosgrove 8–20). For many middle-class African Americans as well as for *Ebony,* the wildly colorful zoot suit reflected poor taste and demeaning stereotypes. Drake and Cayton note that "flashy clothes and plenty of liquor" mark the lower-class man's "style of living" in the Bronzeville of the mid-to-late 1930s (517). In 1948, an *Ebony* reader complained that advertisements for "extreme style clothes" would make African Americans "the laughing stock of the world."[10] An editorial from 1947 lambasted black nightclub entertainers who portrayed themselves as pimps, gamblers, and zoot-suiters. Because these clubs had white patrons, the magazine argued, such entertainers commit the "crime of portraying the colored American as a sex-crazed, switchblade-wielding, gin-drinking dialectician," thus holding back racial progress. This editorial's accompanying photograph depicted a "pop-eyed" and "beat-out zoot-suiter" ("No Biz" 42).

Brooks devotes considerable attention to Satin-Legs Smith's zoot suits, and here the poem's discursive dynamics grow more complex because of the zoot suit's plural meanings in postwar culture. Although the speaker maintains an analytical tone, she also positions herself a little closer to Smith by adopting a Southern migrant expression ("innards"). Smith becomes more ambiguous as the speaker's relationship to her reassembled audience becomes more vexed:

> Let us proceed. Let us inspect, together
> With his meticulous and serious love,
> The innards of this closet. Which is a vault
> Whose glory is not diamonds, not pearls,
> Not silver plate with just enough dull shine.
> But wonder-suits in yellow and in wine,
> Sarcastic green and zebra-striped cobalt.
> All drapes. With shoulder padding that is wide
> And cocky and determined as his pride;
> Ballooning pants that taper off to ends
> Scheduled to choke precisely.
>   Here are hats
> Like bright umbrellas; and hysterical ties
> Like narrow banners for some gathering war.
> (*Blacks* 43–44)

Brooks's descriptions give a mock grandeur to Smith's glorious "vault," which contains flashy clothes instead of refined jewelry or serving ware. Madison Avenue's postwar housewife donned low pumps and understated pearls as she polished her silver to the oxymoronic "dull shine" of respectability. As Elaine Tyler May notes, the white middle classes practiced "virtuous consumerism" that reflected home life and normative gender roles (12), and so for them Smith's consumerism marks poor taste and improper behavior. Yet his sartorial transgression offers a vibrancy that his observers lack; the poem is not simply what Kent calls a "criticism of hip black style" (41). Smith's attire is both outrageous ("wonder-suits," "hysterical") and menacing ("gathering war"), restrictive ("choke precisely") and enabling ("his pride"). Brooks's display of this wardrobe reflects her own "zoot-suit aesthetic," as Karen Jackson Ford points out, a "rhetorical extravagance" of "ornate locution" that rivals her character's indulgences "in perfumes and clothing" (348). At one level, Brooks's zoot-suiter becomes a flamboyant artist of limited means; his clothes and strut constitute "all his sculpture and his art / And all his architectural design" (*Blacks* 44). His childhood poverty and deprivations draw the speaker's sympathy, while his "squiring" of a dubious "lady" to Joe's Eats prompts more irony at his expense. Brooks's semiotic richness anticipates Ralph Ellison's zoot-suiters in *Invisible Man,* "men of transition" who disrupt the narrator's formulaic attempts to categorize them (440–41).

In the last section of the poem, Brooks uncovers the social prescriptions her audience would have for men like Smith and severs the temporary cross-racial alliance she has constructed. Reflecting her character's stereotypical carnal appetites, Brooks describes a "lady"-of-the-week whose unrestrained attire and manner promise immediate sexual gratification. According to Drake and Cayton, such "pursuit of 'pleasure'—direct and exciting—is a dominating feature of lower-class life" (608). Brooks recognizes that her readers—black and white—would censure Smith's "low" conduct and aimless pursuits:

> He had no education
> In quiet arts of compromise. He would

> Not understand your counsels on control, nor
> Thank you for your late trouble.
> (*Blacks* 47)

In other words, middle-class African Americans and liberal whites would urge Smith to improve his condition through education and religion, containing his zoot masculinity within respectable boundaries. As the poem has shifted from questions of taste to questions of morality, the implied audience becomes more paternalistic in its view of Smith. But the speaker no longer shares this perspective, noting sarcastically that her addressees need not "trouble" themselves any further on Smith's behalf with their belated and ineffectual concern.

Dislodged from her disapproving audience, the speaker utters the poem's final *you* from the vantage point of a neighborhood insider who patronizes a local diner:

> At Joe's Eats
> You get your fish or chicken on meat platters.
> With coleslaw, macaroni, candied sweets,
> Coffee and apple pie. You go out full.
> (The end is—isn't it?—all that really matters.)
> (*Blacks* 47)

This communal rather than adversarial "you" dismisses white readers from the speaker's discursive triangle, anticipating Brooks's eventual turning away from them in 1967. Given the status of "The Sundays of Satin-Legs Smith" as the volume's signature piece, this maneuver proves highly significant. The poem has provided a sumptuous feast of rhetorical and popular styles, but its white readers ultimately do not partake of the plenitude. In the poem's culminating vocal shift to lyric utterance, Smith expresses desire for the "honey bowl" of his lady's body. Released from inspection, he *will* "go out full" at the end of his week, unconcerned with his interpreters' difficulties in determining whether or not his respite from "shabby days" justifies his means of pursuing happiness.

Through the uneasy alliances between its black and white readers—and between the speaker and each group—Brooks's poem expresses doubt that postwar race relations can be repaired. It prompts readers to consider how far they are willing to go to bring about race equality. Should black and white readers mobilize on behalf of Smith and his ilk or only on behalf of those who subscribe to middle-class values? Drake and Cayton note that when black Chicagoans of the upper and middle classes spoke of "'advancing The Race,' what they really mean is creating conditions under which lower-class traits will eventually disappear and something approaching the middle-class way of life will prevail in Bronzeville" (710). We see the same attitude in a black reader's letter to *Ebony* from 1946, which blames kitchenette tenants for their squalid living conditions: "You cannot help a person that is too lazy to help himself. They are nothing but poor black trash." While several black readers would dispute this letter, others defended its position that "some of our people . . . will not try to help themselves."[11] As with Brooks's poem, *Ebony*'s early volumes show how cross-racial alliances often come at the expense of cross-class alliances within black communities.

If Brooks's black readers recognized the poem's class markers and made social distinctions within black communities, her white readers were more likely to attribute class-specific behavior to race alone—even if they were potential would-be allies. As *Ebony* explained, bad examples troubled liberal "racial do-gooders" who insisted that Negroes be "winged angels" ("Backstage" [1947] 8). When presented with a less-than-innocent figure such as Smith, such readers would likely revert to racist stereotypes about immorality. One white reader accused *Ebony* of promoting "irreligious, immoral selfish living" through advertisements for liquor and other forms of "indulgence," fearing the magazine would be a bad influence on her black maid. A paternalistic white reader who claimed to "really *know* the Negro" advised *Ebony* that "it must never glamorize the seamy side" of black life, suggesting that it publish images of "some fine, black school teacher" or "choir girl" instead of women with provocatively raised skirts.[12] Such unabashed letters from white readers give us a sense of the challenges Brooks faced in addressing her own readership. As Toni Morrison states in a striking rhetorical question, "What happens to the writerly imagination of a black author who is at some level always conscious of representing one's own race to, or in spite of, a race of readers that understands itself to be 'universal' or race-free?" (xii). Brooks straddled both positions in her postwar career.

The poet's second volume, *Annie Allen* (1949), emerged at a pivotal point in the nascent civil rights movement. The President's Committee on Civil Rights had issued its report at the end of 1947, instilling hope among many African Americans that the nation's highest powers would finally face the issue of race relations. Yet less than half a year later, an *Ebony* editorial disputed its effectiveness: "President Truman's project seems doomed to take its place on the bookshelves beside dozens of others sponsored by well-intentioned foundations and philanthropists who have devoted millions to studying the so-called 'Negro problem' but accomplished virtually nothing basically to improve the Negro's status in the nation" ("Do Do-Gooders" 46). Truman's desegregation of the armed forces in 1948 seemed to offer another promise that civil rights legislation would move forward, but the Dixiecrats' defection from that year's Democratic Party convention dampened this prospect. Liberals were proving uncertain allies in uncertain times, yet only the liberal wing of the national power structure seemed receptive to civil rights reforms. Bolden notes that as African Americans worked to "accelerate the pace of gaining social equality, so Brooks's poetry adopted a parallel tone to reflect those changes" (112). Reading these texts alongside *Ebony* helps us see how the poet presented cross-racial contact in the face of the Truman presidency, the lynching of Emmett Till, the 1956 presidential election, and the Little Rock Nine.

Urban Explorations in Black and White

In *Annie Allen* Brooks began portraying white people more directly, holding them up to cross-racial inspection to make whiteness visible rather than an unmarked social and representational default setting. Valerie Babb explains that "because it is a created identity, whiteness is sustained through hegemony, a complex network of cultural creations including, among other things, literature, museums, popular music, and movies" (4–5). Whiteness is also constructed through practices of everyday life such as dining out or making tea—as Brooks shows in "I love those little booths at Benvenuti's" and "Beverly Hills, Chicago." Paradoxically, these poems bring whiteness into the open by placing it in contained spaces (a South Side restaurant and a Hyde Park home, respectively). Brooks's use of ungendered collective pronouns such as *they* and *these people* reinforces the two poems' explorations of white privilege—and whiteness itself—by making vaguely embodied white characters emblematic of their race. "I love those little booths at Benvenuti's" and "Beverly Hills, Chicago" also question the prevailing liberal assumption that *contact* between the races would counter bias and further equality; *Ebony* tended to concur with this position. As Michael Omi and Howard Winant note, the University of Chicago's Sociology Department had shaped discourse about race since the 1920s, especially in the form of Robert E. Parks's "race-relations cycle" of "contact, conflict, accommodation, and assimilation" (10). Brooks's two poems challenge this model by prompting readers to ask if the foundational "contact" stage is even possible, while a third ("Men of careful turns, haters of forks in the road") assails the gradualism inherent in Parks's model and in postwar liberalism more generally. In the latter poem, Brooks draws on dysfunctional gender roles to figure American race relations—a strategy she will repeat in one of her poems about Emmett Till.

"I love those little booths at Benvenuti's" shifts the focus of *Annie Allen* from the heroine and her community to the white power structure that surrounds, researches, legislates, and attempts to define it. In this poem Brooks parodies the propensity to "study" African Americans and "discover" presumed characteristics. Less ambiguous than the shifting rhetoric of "The Sundays of Satin-Legs Smith," this poem's polarizing "they" designates white customers who have ventured into a Bronzeville restaurant so they can gaze unabashedly at the neighborhood patrons. Contemporary poet Phyllis McGinley certainly understood the racial meanings in Brooks's depiction, referring to the outsiders as "curious Aryans" in her review of *Annie Allen* (qtd. in Burr 119).[13] The "I" in Brooks's title not only comments ironically on the white customers' enthusiasm for their pursuit, but also voices their presumption of an insider's position. Reversing dominant sociological and ethnographic practice, Brooks makes these would-be experts on "the Negro" her object of study:

> They get to Benvenuti's. There are booths
> To hide in while observing tropical truths
> About this—dusky folk, so clamorous!
> So colorfully incorrect,
> So amorous,
> So flatly brave!
> Boothed-in, one can detect,
> Dissect.
>
> (*Blacks* 126)

In their minds the white urban explorers have entered a veritable jungle of exotic inhabitants. Thinking that they are hidden in the booth like hunters in a blind, they expect to have their stereotypes confirmed: namely, that the "dusky folk" are gaudy, hypersexual, childish, spiritual, and dirty. The paired feminine rhymes *clamorous/amorous* stick out as excessive, even slightly ridiculous, underscoring these assumptions—and those who hold them— as out of place. While the white observers perceive the restaurant's black inhabitants to be only "flatly brave," they will fall bravely flat in their endeavors by the end of the poem.

Brooks conveys their intrusion with aggressive diction ("dissect," "stab their stares"), playing ironically on their belief that black patrons would carry knives. The white observers "lean back in the half-light" of their blind, listening to their jukebox selections in a subterfuge of interracial understanding (*Blacks* 126). They grow bored and resentful when Benvenuti's fails to provide them with black exotica:

> They stare. They tire. They feel refused,
> Feel overwhelmed by subtle treasons!
> Nobody here will take the part of jester.
>
> The absolute stutters, and the rationale
> Stoops off in astonishment.
>
> (*Blacks* 127)

These white urban explorers undergo an experience that Thompson would describe in an *Ebony* editorial: "the shock of finding that, shorn of his stereotypes, the Negro is a normal, living and breathing American" ("Some of My Best Friends" 154). Lacking data for their hypothesis, Brooks's exposed characters have failed as amateur ethnographers. The "subtle treasons" that undo them pressure social categories in the face of unstable race relations, like the oxymorons in Brooks's other postwar poems. Treason is hardly subtle, and neither is their "analysis." These observers want to have it both ways: to "detect" yet remain blind, to intrude yet be welcomed. Unable to "step outside" of their whiteness, as Lindberg points out (287), they "feel refused" not only because they find the local clientele rather unremarkable, but also because they are unremarked for braving the urban jungle. None of the people they observe seems graced by their presence; the younger waiter walks past them "with straight haste" while the older one is "amused" (*Blacks* 127). The poem has exposed a one-sided "encounter" devoid of any contact.

Brooks would prove more pessimistic than *Ebony* about partnering with liberals, but her postwar poems shared the magazine's agenda of educating liberals about their privileged position in America's racial hierarchy. In a companion poem to "I love those little booths at Benvenuti's," Brooks reverses dynamics and presents Bronzeville residents venturing into the upscale, mostly white neighborhood of Hyde Park. But unlike their white counterparts who can enter black spaces, the urban explorers in "Beverly Hills, Chicago" must remain in their cars and keep moving. Brooks schemes the poem from their perspective through a first-person, plural voice (*we*), representing the white residents through their possessions, habits, and the distancing rhetoric of *these people, them,* and *they*:

> The dry brown coughing beneath their feet,
> (Only a while, for the handyman is on his way)
> These people walk their golden gardens.
> We say ourselves fortunate to be driving by today.
>
> That we may look at them, in their gardens where
> The summer ripeness rots. But not raggedly.
> Even the leaves fall down in lovelier patterns here.
> And the refuse, the refuse is a neat brilliancy.
>
> (*Blacks* 128)

Through Brooks's loaded phrase "say ourselves fortunate," the poem's black explorers acknowledge their ability to at least access the neighborhood's stately streets, while commenting sarcastically on their lack of the residents' good fortune. The "handyman" is the only African American who gains access to the property, but his temporary presence is displaced through synesthesia ("brown coughing"). As the wealthy white homeowners stroll through the idyllic world of their "golden" grounds, those in the car find excess even in the "brilliancy" of the trash, which recalls the trashy flamboyance that liberal and black middle-class readers perceived in Satin-Legs Smith. Because the poem loosens its ballad stanza (a popular form) with variable line and sentence length, as well as flexible rhythm and rhyme, these images of embellishment stand out—especially within Brooks's otherwise conversational, everyday diction.

The most compelling (and instructive) difference in these urban explorers and their white counterparts at Benvenuti's is that the Bronzeville residents' cross-racial gaze turns back on themselves in a way that the white explorers' does not. This poem's most vivid descriptions occur when, barred from following the wealthy into their stately manors, the black observers nonetheless know of the privileged life that takes place there. Because whiteness operates as an unacknowledged social default setting, Brooks strategically represents it through negation, translating a long-standing practice of Anglo-American sophistication (afternoon tea) to the everyday life of Bronzeville:

> We know what they go to. To tea. But that does not mean
> They will throw some little black dots into some water and add
> sugar and the juice of the cheapest lemons that are sold,
>
> While downstairs that woman's vague phonograph bleats,
>   "Knock me a kiss."
> And the living all to be made again in the sweatingest physical
>   manner
> Tomorrow. . . . (*Blacks* 128)

The assonant off-rhyme *mean/bleats* underscores the social incongruities Brooks invokes through her images of visceral kitchenette living, which follow the black observers into "Beverly Hills" and prevent even a temporary, vicarious escape into a world of leisure. The ellipsis signals the collective speakers' turn toward reflection on racial inequality as the driving factor behind this class disparity, returning to the larger idea of America's more and less *fortunate*:

> Nobody is furious. Nobody hates these people.
> At least, nobody driving by in this car.
> It is only natural, however, that it should occur to us
> How much more fortunate they are than we are.
> (Blacks 129)

The black observers adopt a position of moderation while reminding the addressees that some African Americans take a more radical stance against white privilege. Unlike the previous poem, this one attempts to repair the coalition with liberals by appeals to common sense. In measured tones, the collective speaker thrice employs the phrase "it is only natural" to mark the racial and economic dispari-ties observed from the car. But Brooks soon abandons this project, ending abruptly with the black explorers' exit and self-directed re-sentment: "We drive on, we drive on. / When we speak to each other our voices are a little gruff" (*Blacks* 129). *Ebony*'s explorers operate in the fashion of Michel de Certeau's everyday tacticians, "vigilantly mak[ing] use of the cracks that particular conjunctions open in the surveillance of the proprietary powers" and turning such "'opportunities'" to their advantage (37).

Three years after Brooks published *Annie Allen, Ebony* published an editorial on white flight to the suburbs that also contrasted kitch-enette living with Hyde Park. By this time the Supreme Court had struck down restrictive covenants, forcing the University of Chicago to reverse course and allow African Americans of means into its Hyde Park properties. Pointing out that "Negroes, too, appreciate and love beautiful homes," the editorial argues for "interracial community organizations" rather than white panic as the best solution to urban crime and substandard housing. Like Brooks, the magazine points out that most black Chicagoans cannot escape their living conditions. *Ebony* also reveals how some African Americans bend the unequal dynamics of cross-racial observation to their advantage: "They ride slowly through lily-white sections (preferably with a car filled with children) and openly appraise the homes while fearful whites quake as their car goes by." Turning the Sunday afternoon drive into an amusing new "sport," these drive-by explorers gaze at white subur-banites with willful intimidation instead of self-disparaging resent-ment—an alternative view of cross-racial inspection that enriches our understanding of Brooks's poem ("Will U.S. Cities" 90).

Brooks ends *Annie Allen* with a more fundamental dismantling of Parks's race-relations cycle in "Men of careful turns, haters of forks in the road," one of her more controversial and cryptic postwar poems. Kent contends that it "loses dignity," while Spillers claims that it "appears to verge on self-hatred" (Kent, "Aesthetic Values" 43; Spillers 231). By contrast, Henry Taylor finds the poem full of "considerable power," Claudia Tate asserts that it "declares" black women's pain and affirms sisterhood, and Betsy Erkkila sees a "protest against the white/male social order" and call to action (Taylor 265; Tate 151; Erkkila 205). Critics even disagree over the identity of the poem's speaker: the volume's heroine Annie Allen, Brooks herself, black women, or African Americans more generally. I see the poem not so much as an interracial love affair, which Spillers contends, but rather as what Louis E. Lomax terms "the strange affair between the white liberal and the Negro" (44). Specifically, Brooks plays on the dynamics of Renaissance courtly love poems to critique postwar liberals' courtship of the black vote.

Departing from *Ebony*'s military metaphor of liberals as allies in an interracial army, Brooks domesticates them as an abusive member of a dysfunctional relationship. The "men of careful turns" lack bold decisiveness, standing uncertainly before a road less traveled. By contrast, the feminized black speaker knows and demands what she seeks:

> Men of careful turns, haters of forks in the road,
> The strain at the eye, that puzzlement, that awe—
> Grant me that I am human, that I hurt,
> That I can cry.
>
> Not that I now ask alms, in shame gone hollow,
> Nor cringe outside the loud and sumptuous gate.
> Admit me to our mutual estate.
>
> (Blacks 139)

Unlike the collective black speaker in "Beverly Hills, Chicago," this one lays claim to white privilege both in terms of "Anglo-American literary tradition," as Wheeler argues (104), and full participation as a citizen. Indeed, Brooks chose to read this poem for a radio feature on her life in the "Destination Freedom" series (Kent, *A Life* 87). Yet the voice also speaks as a woman wronged by the kind of violence hiding behind smiling promises, like the abused wife of an alcoholic who denies his lapses into brutality. In a risky conceit that perverts the language of courtly love poetry, Brooks dramatizes her comparison by having the speaker recoil from this volatile embrace:

> And to love you
> No more as a woman loves a drunken mate,
> Restraining full caress and good My Dear,
> Even pity for the heaviness and the need—
> Fearing sudden fire out of the uncaring mouth,
> Boiling in the slack eyes, and the traditional blow.
> Next, the indifference formal, deep and slow.
>
> (*Blacks* 139)

Brooks refashions the courtly convention of figurative dismemberment in which the smitten lover enumerates the virtues of his beloved's facial features. Brooks's speaker wants to refashion cross-racial partnership on equal terms, rejecting outsider-within status and demanding full participation. The poem exposes liberals' pathological "need" for and simultaneous rejection of African Americans, likening this schizophrenia to a batterer's destructive cycle of attraction and repulsion. Instead of bidding his lady to give into his sexual desire as does the Renaissance lover, the postwar liberal wants his dark lady to give up on her desire for civil liberties.

Troping on the chivalric "courtesy" of courtly love poems—as well as popular notions of "courteous" race relations—Brooks presents postwar liberals as disingenuous in their overtures toward African Americans. As *Ebony* would state in a 1957 editorial, African Americans were no longer "fooled by sweet talk and empty promises" ("Penny" 96). Brooks's poem exposes the ways that liberals often masked the unequal power relations in their cross-racial alliances with polite talk about gradualism:

> (Now cruelty flaunts diplomas, is elite,
> Delicate, has polish, knows how to be discreet):
>   Requests my patience, wills me to be calm,
>   Brings me a chair, but one with broken straw . . .
>
> (*Blacks* 139–40)

Brooks brings a new technique to bear on representing whiteness: assigning liberals a voice with which to implicate themselves. The "men of careful turns" know how to "'sugar up our prejudice with politeness'" while maintaining "'the line'" between races—an ironic twist of Robert Frost's popular epigram that good fences make good neighbors. In their extended speech, which dominates the latter half of the poem, the liberals equivocate about "'the properness / Of things'" and the wisdom of "'our fathers'" (*Blacks* 139–40). Ultimately, Brooks's poem implies through its courtly conceit and liberal rhetoric that any alliance with liberals is structurally flawed. But it specifically reflects liberal Democrats' postwar courtship of the black electorate. As a 1957 *Ebony* editorial would put it, this vote had been "up for grabs" since the 1932 election, when African Americans "deserted a deceased Republican emancipator for a living Democratic provider" ("Penny" 56). Significantly, the latter affiliation positions them as wives dependent on a breadwinner; there is more than an uncanny convergence with the gendered dynamics of this postwar poem.

"Men of careful turns" serves early notice that the honeymoon between African Americans and liberals is over. The poem shifts pronouns in its famous final lines, dropping the individualized "I" for a collective voice:

> Rise.
> Let us combine. There are no magics or elves
> Or timely godmothers to guide us. We are lost, must
> Wizard a track through our own screaming weed.
> (*Blacks* 140)

One could argue that Brooks's plural pronouns address potential constituents of an alternative cross-racial coalition. But I see a shift toward a solely black audience that proves more akin to her poem about Satin-Legs Smith. The "screaming weed" positions this poem's new African American collective outside the "sumptuous gate" of the manor—but on their own terms. Brooks reinforces this at the formal level by nestling these assonant words at the end, breaking from the poem's loose pattern of ending sections with couplet rhymes. Her emergent *we* casts off any form of codependency with a dubious provider.

Brooks gives an acerbic portrayal of cross-racial charity in her much-discussed "The Lovers of the Poor," published in *The Bean Eaters* (1960). As Doreski notes, the poem signals the poet's "disengagement with liberal philanthropic agents" (127), a position that parallels *Ebony*'s misgivings about liberal largesse. In the poem, white women from "The Ladies' Betterment League" visit a South Side tenement to bestow money on its inhabitants. But the shock of poverty's abundant dirt, odor, and children prompts them to remove themselves and "their clean, their pretty money," taking care that their skirts "graze no wall" in their hasty departure. Again Brooks employs oxymorons to interrogate social categories: the white women's benevolence becomes a "loathe-love" that is "barbarously fair" (*Blacks* 351–52, 349). The latter phrase rewrites the courtly "fair lady" image of white women, something Brooks interrogates further in her poems about Emmett Till's lynching. Brooks's white ladies harbor a profound ignorance in their horrified realization that "good breeding does not blossom in tenements," as an *Ebony* editorial noted in 1949 ("Do Negroes" 52). If the white explorers in Benvenuti's err in expecting African Americans to conform to freakishly exotic stereotypes, these ladies err in expecting them to conform to Dickensian notions of "the very very worthy / And beautiful poor" (*Blacks* 350). And like the liberal addressees in "The Sundays of Satin-Legs Smith," these do-gooders conflate class with race. Kent points out that Brooks was inspired to write the poem after "two white women of considerable social pretensions from the North Shore" came uninvited to her house to see what she looked like; the poet had been subject to unannounced visits from curious whites since 1949 (*A Life* 89).

If Brooks offered white readers parables of their race's misbehavior, *Ebony* provided them with primers of race relations— guidelines for conduct they would not find in Emily Post's latest

Blue Book.[14] The magazine's first editorial on this subject, "Etiquette of Race Relations," appeared three months after *Annie Allen*. As ironic as many of Brooks's poems, it targets those liberals who, having "discovered the Negro in their midst," become "uncomfortable, newly tolerant zealots anxious to show that . . . well, they can appreciate some black folks." To help them avoid the "racial traps" of whiteness, the editorial instructs them to avoid "'credit-to-his-race' talk." It even offers a photograph of singer Marian Anderson to assist with such reprogramming, declaring that her internationally renowned talent is "a credit to no one" but herself and her country. Reversing the tired formula of paternal liberals and childish African Americans, the editorial urges the latter to be patient with their white allies because they are "still-unweaned innocents" (78). *Ebony* takes stronger issue with whites' slow learning curve in "Educating Our White Folks," casting more doubt on the efficacy of the uneasy alliance. Grown weary of foot-dragging gradualists, the editorialist writes that African Americans are now "impatient with patience and fed up with white ignorance." Richly ironic, this photo-editorial appears opposite a still of Uncle Remus from *Song of the South* (1946). Because of white Americans' failure to advance their thinking, *Ebony* argues, they place the additional burden of racial education on African Americans who must walk "the tight rope of race relations" like the speaker of Brooks's "Men of careful turns" (98). In a 1958 editorial that addresses affluent whites' new reality of sharing neighborhoods with African Americans who are their "economic, educational and cultural equal," *Ebony* returns to the primer model by offering whites a twelve-point "elementary guide to better race relations." Several instructions remind liberals that African Americans can see through disingenuous courtesy and false affiliation: "Do not pretend that you like a Negro if you do not"; "The Negro does not want to be treated 'extra nice' or 'extra lenient' because he is a Negro"; "Do not try to impress him by telling him about other Negroes that you may know." Digging deeper into the contradictions of liberal ideology, the editorialist (most likely Thompson) offers correction for a more curious behavior: "Do not get so carried away with your new-found tolerance that you believe Negroes can do no wrong, white people do no right" ("How to Treat" 94). Thompson and her editorial staff could see evidence of these attitudes from letters that white readers sent to *Ebony,* such as an extraordinary one from 1946: "As a white man, I suppose I do not suffer as much as the Negro in America, yet on the other hand, I spend about half of my time being ashamed of my race"—hardly the best course of action for effecting social change.[15] Like her friend Brooks, Thompson exposed liberal myths of "polite" race relations in texts designed to make white readers uneasy, interrogating their postwar alliances with middle-class blacks.

Emmett Till and Little Rock

In the aftermath of the 1955 lynching of fourteen-year-old Emmett Till—and the acquittal of his murderers—*Ebony* and Brooks assessed the white power structure of rural Mississippi. The Till case had strong links to Chicago, not only because it was Till's hometown, but also because key witnesses relocated to the city after the trial. Moreover, Chicago's influential black press gave the lynching much local and national publicity. *Ebony* and Brooks situated their portrayals of this cataclysmic event in the Southern social fabric rather than in the grisly murder itself, making counterintuitive turns toward whiteness to portray Till's death as a portent of change. For female reporter Cloyte Murdock, "the pattern of life in Mississippi" was set by the myths of white superiority and a tenant farming system that reinstituted master-slave dynamics in a new guise (91–92). For Brooks, "the pattern" was set by myths of white womanhood and continued through a misplaced ideology of chivalric romance—a dynamic she had explored in "Men of careful turns."

In her article "Land of the Till Murder," Murdock assesses the social and economic forces that fuel racial tensions in the Mississippi Delta. She focuses on the region's poorest black and white inhabitants, noting that each endures the nation's lowest living standards for their respective race. But rather than make a cross-racial alliance with black sharecroppers along class lines, the poor white nurtures a peculiar race hatred: "The Negro is his opiate and his panacea as well as the object of his derision. However poor the white man is, he has this buffer, this cherished fiction of inborn superiority, to place him in his mind above the Negro. He does not wish to see the colored person attain rights and opportunities equal to his" (95). This form of dependent hostility resorts to lynching even if the perpetrators are not among the Delta's poorest whites (as was the case with Till's murderers, Roy Bryant and J. W. Milam). Just as Murdock reveals the violent underpinnings of whiteness, Brooks reconstructs the mentality of the woman in whose name Till was lynched (Carolyn Bryant).

For Brooks, the Till murder was triggered by inherited myths of "pure" white womanhood, the women who believed them, and the men who reenacted them. Consequently, she portrays the lynching and trial as a metonym for this larger "composition" or "pattern" of whiteness (*Blacks* 335). Her poem strikes at the heart of Southern chivalry, revealing the contradictions of a culture that allowed the murder of a child to "protect" a mother. The poem's title both links and separates rural Mississippi with urban Chicago under the common denominator of motherhood: "A Bronzeville Mother Loiters in Mississippi. Meanwhile, A Mississippi Mother Burns Bacon." While each mother violates the rules of her socially prescribed role under segregation and domesticity, respectively, the key word *meanwhile* signals a fundamental division that should prevent readers from aligning them as equal victims under white patriarchy. Brooks breaks taboo by voicing the white mother's consciousness, entering figuratively the inviolate body of Southern white womanhood. From the opening lines, the poet situates her social analysis of a cataclysmic event in the South's fictive script of chivalric romance, in which white women are fair ladies and white men their valiant gentlemen:

> Herself: the milk-white maid, the "maid mild"
> Of the ballad. Pursued

> By the Dark Villain. Rescued by the Fine Prince.
> The Happiness-Ever-After.
>
> (*Blacks* 333)

Emmett Till unraveled the fabric of this myth with his youthful innocence, refusing to fit his prescribed role of "Dark Villain"; this dissonance prompts the Mississippi Mother to reevaluate the romance and her presumably innocent role in it. Similarly, her husband no longer fits his role as "Fine Prince." He becomes "ridiculous" in his rush to "hack down" a boy, hysterical in his hatred of the "meddling" Northern press, and brutish as he slaps his toddler at breakfast. While he clings to his belief that "Nothing could stop Mississippi," his wife awakens to the possibility of an alternative domestic and social order (*Blacks* 335, 336). Ironically, her conscience emerges most fully during the kiss that typically ends stories of rescued princesses:

> She did not scream.
> She stood there.
> But a hatred for him burst into glorious flower,
> And its perfume enclasped them—big,
> Bigger than all magnolias.
>
> (*Blacks* 339)

As Mootry concludes in her detailed analysis, the white mother "now fully comprehends that . . . the myth of the benign, patriarchal magnolia'd South must end, for the sake of women, of African Americans, and of society itself" ("Tell It Slant" 185). And yet the poem gives no indication that she—or any woman in her position—is capable of taking on such a task. Gertrude Reif Hughes argues persuasively that the white mother remains "caught within the killing romance" of the now-discounted ballad, still locked in her role (193). Although the poem ends by invoking the ballad's "last bleak news," Brooks has denied it ballad *form* to reinforce her overarching idea of a broken social pattern.

She returns to the historical grounding of the murder and trial in the short poem she placed immediately afterward, "The Last Quatrain of the Ballad of Emmett Till" (which employs a staggered quatrain form). This title reframes the disintegrated ballad of Southern chivalry, making the Bronzeville mother (Mamie Till Mobley) its central figure. Unlike the Mississippi mother, "Emmett's mother" is not confined to a kitchen, but occupies an ambiguous "red room" that fuses with Brooks's culminating image of prairie fire: "Chaos in windy grays / through a red prairie" (*Blacks* 340). While the bursting flower of hatred signified the Mississippi mother's emotional response, the chaotic prairie suggests a larger change that will be powerful and unpredictable. Murdock's article in *Ebony* ends with a parallel image of uncontainable social transformation: "progress and change are knocking at Mississippi's door, turning the key, and cannot be held back" (96). *Ebony* and Brooks saw Till's lynching as an event affecting all US citizens—black and white, Southern and Northern.

Despite the publicity surrounding the Till case, the issue of civil rights did not figure prominently in that year's presidential election. The year 1956 proved to be an especially fraught time for the national alliance between African Americans and liberals. Although the latter largely agreed that the trial and verdict had made US democracy a travesty in the court of world opinion, their eyes were on the prize of the White House. Liberal politicians reasserted gradualism as the means to achieving this end. Putting on hold their courtship of black votes, they began to woo Southern whites with a "go slow" approach. Democratic candidate Adlai Stevenson softened the party's civil rights rhetoric, aided by a speech writer who was among the nation's most influential liberal thinkers, Arthur Schlesinger, Jr.[16] *Ebony*'s June issue of 1956 noted that yet another prominent liberal—Hodding Carter—had joined "the flight of the liberalists to the cover of gradualism" ("God's Dilemma" 86). Even Eleanor Roosevelt, whom *Ebony* had deemed African Americans' best white friend, seemed to abandon the cause. She threatened to resign from the NAACP board when the organization did not rally behind Stevenson and his platform. Angered by the candidate's foot-dragging—and that of his fellow northern liberals—NAACP executive secretary Roy Wilkins maintained an uneasy public alliance with them out of political necessity (Jackson 105). *Ebony* would give Stevenson an unenthusiastic endorsement. In a postelection article, Carl Rowan termed the presidential contest as one between "the 'known devil and suspected witch' of 1956" (126).

In the fall of 1957, the school desegregation crisis in Little Rock, Arkansas, proved to be another pivotal event in postwar race relations. Although the local school board had formulated and approved an integration plan in compliance with *Brown v. Board of Education,* Governor Orval Faubus ordered the National Guard to bar African American students from Central High School. Rowan reminded *Ebony*'s readers that Faubus had "masqueraded as a liberal" before he secured political power by embracing segregation (123). Liberals were becoming not only untrustworthy, but dangerous. In response to Faubus's action, a reluctant but outraged President Eisenhower ordered federal troops to Little Rock to ensure the students' safe passage into the school. Images of armed soldiers, angry white mobs, and besieged black students circulated more widely and cross-racially than did coverage of the Till case. These young African Americans who endured threats and harassment became known as the Little Rock Nine. *Ebony* sent reporters and photographers to the scene, and Brooks drew on such media images for her final attempts at race relations poems.

Ebony's response to Little Rock was conflicted about the efficacy of cross-racial alliances. In his article "What Faubus Did for the Negro," Rowan asserted that the governor's action helped African Americans by providing "a setting in which Negro youngsters could walk heroically" and by forcing Eisenhower to abandon his moderation. Moreover, he argued that Little Rock would prompt shocked and conscience-stricken white citizens to confront segregationists and fight their agenda (123–24). The editorial "God's Angry Men" linked the Little Rock Nine to Till's lynching, asserting that such displays of "racial hate and brutality" galvanized

African Americans to protect their children and demand justice. But unlike Rowan, the editorial staff disputed the need for white allies, declaring that the black citizen "cannot dump his burdens on the lap of the Lord and the liberals then sit down to await results" (66). For Thompson, who had now become *Ebony*'s managing editor, the event ushered in a new era of black self-determination.

Brooks's response was "The *Chicago Defender* Sends a Man to Little Rock," published in *The Bean Eaters*. More widely anthologized than "Men of careful turns," this race relations poem has similarly vexed its relatively few critics. Brooks's Little Rock poem was praised by her white editor for its compassion, but criticized by some white reviewers for making too much social commentary. A larger gap occurs between black critics, who fault the poem for universalism, and white critics, who perceive it as a singular attack on their race. Kent considers it among Brooks's "least effective" in addressing postwar race relations (*A Life* 141). These reactions stem not only from the poem's use of description rather than argumentation or direct condemnation, but also because of its emphasis on everyday life.

More influenced by journalism than the previous poem, "The *Chicago Defender* Sends a Man to Little Rock" departs from Brooks's usual role as participant-observer of Bronzeville because it presents a simulated ethnography of Southern whites. Like her poem about Emmett Till, this one wrests the burden of representation from African Americans, offering a kind of ethnographic equity at a time when African Americans had been "surveyed, interviewed, analyzed and studied to death," to quote an editorial published shortly after the Little Rock crisis ("Penny" 56). Most of Brooks's poem inventories the banal activities comprising white Arkansans' daily life:

> In Little Rock the people bear
> Babes, and comb and part their hair
> And watch the want ads, put repair

> To roof and latch. While wheat toast burns
> A woman waters multiferns.
>
> (*Blacks* 346)

These certainly seem like trivial incidents in a world where trouble exists only in the occasional burnt breakfast. (The poem's form underscores this mundane impression with a string of adjacent, exact end rhymes that structure its opening stanzas.) But in the context of Henri Lefebvre's postwar theory of everyday life—which asserts that even the act of purchasing butter reveals a French woman's "life, class, and the sum total of . . . the nation and its history" (1:57)—Brooks's strategy allows her to unmask the latent capacity for racist violence lurking beneath social surfaces. Designating white Arkansans as "the people," a phrase inflected strongly with American nationalism, the poem shows them singing hymns in church, watching baseball, and attending an outdoor concert. They answer telephones and find numerous other ways to "be polite." For Lefebvre, such everyday practices constitute a "human raw material" that "reveals and disguises the deepest of realities, both implying them and concealing them" (1:189). Brooks's reporter-speaker concludes that "there is a puzzle in this town" because of such ordinariness, but then brings the poem's delayed event to bear on his cross-racial observations:

> And true, they are hurling spittle, rock,
> Garbage and fruit in Little Rock.
> And I saw coiling storm a-writhe
> On bright madonnas. And a scythe
> Of men harassing brownish girls.
>
> (*Blacks* 348)

The reporter also witnesses "a bleeding brownish boy." This dramatic shift to images of racist violence clashes with the innocuous images of everyday life, jarring Brooks's readers as well as her persona. The routine activity of walking to school has become a site of violation and, ultimately, social transformation.

Critical consensus holds that Brooks's closing couplet reflects a misguided, universalist position that Little Rock's white mobs are only human, after all: "The lariat lynch-wish I deplored. / The loveliest lynchee was our Lord" (*Blacks* 348). But her lines prove more ambiguous—and more culturally grounded—than that. By circling back to the everyday image of churchgoing, this infamous ending should make readers uneasy with its sinister irony. Moreover, the poem is hardly reassuring in having its reporter claim that white Arkansans are "'like people everywhere,'" an ironic reversal of postwar civil rights rhetoric that positioned black citizens as ordinary Americans. Brooks casts her poem in the persona of one who would not have been immune from the violence he witnessed. Black newsmen were kicked and beaten in Little Rock, and images of these attacks circulated widely. The photograph accompanying *Ebony*'s Little Rock editorial, for example, showed the harassment of *Tri-State Defender* reporter Alex Wilson ("God's Angry Men" 67). After being threatened, Wilson was battered in the head with a brick and ridden piggyback as he lay injured. When we consider this context, Brooks's allusions to lynching and Christ's crucifixion hold the disquieting possibility that the poem's speaker may be next. Like the editorial about Little Rock, Brooks's poem disputes conventional appeals to law-and-order that liberals thought sufficient to end racist violence.

Brooks's skepticism about partnering with liberals began earlier and proved more profound than *Ebony*'s, forming a consistent theme in her first three volumes. Putting these poems in dialogue with the magazine makes clearer the complex negotiations that each performed as racial ambassadors, a perspective with renewed relevance in the wake of John H. Johnson's recent death. The poet and magazine corrected demeaning stereotypes of African Americans and challenged those who held them. Postwar readers' responses reveal the profound impact of this cultural work. In 1946, a white reader lauded the magazine for "convincing our nation that as a group the Negro people are not conventional, not types." In 1953, a black serviceman wrote that *Ebony* combated white prejudice through its "difficult role of intelligent interpreter for the largest racial minority in our country."[17] In 1962, white reviewer Harvey Curtis Webster declared that Brooks's "poems about the Negro dilemma today seem her best because they help me and others to identify as we must" (19).

All of these readers agreed that white Americans needed considerable help to understand race relations. The poems I have discussed here continue to perform this function in the classroom, often prompting uneasy responses from a generation of American literature students more accustomed to humorous presentations of whiteness and racial etiquette such as satirist Christian Lander's *Stuff White People Like* (2008) and comedian Nick Adams's edgier *Making Friends with Black People* (2006). In navigating their cross-racial audiences, Brooks and *Ebony* brought the battle for new racial meanings into their texts by offering alternative images of black and white citizens. Omi and Winant have asserted that "the upsurge of racially based movements which began in the 1950s was a contest over the *social meaning* of race" (96). Thus, racial politics and popular culture contribute as much as modernist influences to the much-remarked difficulty of Brooks's postwar poetry. In light of these contexts, we need to acknowledge the discursive complexity of poems that mirrored black and white citizens' attempts to observe and interact with one another—through the media, cross-racial coalitions, and everyday life.

We should also acknowledge the curious status of Brooks's signature pieces about race relations and whiteness in the women's poetry canon.[18] The poems I have discussed remain largely absent in women's poetry anthologies, which foreground her poetry about motherhood and domesticity. Indeed, "The Mother" is the clear editorial choice, from Florence Howe's *No More Masks!* (1973) to Eva Salzman and Amy Wack's *Women's Work* (2008). Germaine Greer makes the poem metonymic for Brooks in her *101 Poems by 101 Women* (2001). And yet despite editors' strong preference for motherhood poems, "A Bronzeville Mother Loiters in Mississippi. Meanwhile, A Mississippi Mother Burns Bacon" and its companion poem fall under their radar.[19] Erlene Stetson draws heavily from *Annie Allen* for her Brooks selections in *Black Sister* (1981), but omits poems from its final section (which includes "I love those little booths at Benvenuti's," "Beverly Hills, Chicago," and "Men of careful turns"). Poems about postwar race relations are more likely to appear in survey anthologies of modern or modern American poetry.[20] What might account for such dissonant reception in venues through which Brooks's poems renew their negotiations with cross-racial readerships?

One clue lies in the emergence of women's poetry studies itself. Appearing the same year as Howe's groundbreaking anthology, Barbara Segnitz and Carol Rainey's *Psyche: The Feminine Poetic Consciousness* (1973) departed from *No More Masks!* by foregoing Brooks's motherhood poems for more socially oriented ones. To my knowledge, theirs is the only collection of poems by women that includes "The *Chicago Defender* Sends a Man to Little Rock," even giving it considerable attention in the introduction. But neither this poem nor its companions pass down the editorial line. I see at least two factors behind this critical absence. The first of these involves a key split in Brooks's larger reception that Mootry has outlined: the Black Arts Movement's downplaying (or even erasure) of her gender versus feminist critics' recovery of her as a "woman writer writing about women" ("Down the Whirlwind" 10). Not surprisingly, then, the majority of women's poetry anthologies that emerged in the 1970s and 1980s emphasize female characters such as Annie Allen, "Jessie Mitchell's Mother," and the "Bronzeville Woman in a Red Hat." Second, Brooks's race relations poems do not fit the second-wave model of women's poetry as a counter-discourse that answers back to a racially unmarked patriarchy. The poems I have discussed are designed to expose whiteness. Privileging gender provided her postwar liberal readers with a way to deflect this edge, as Burr explains: "Her status as a woman is often seen to 'humanize' her, transforming the experiences she deals with in her poetry into the basis for a (white) reader's comfort and identification" (121). We can see an uncanny parallel in the introduction to *Psyche*. Attempting to defuse "The *Chicago Defender*" by stressing its "purely human connection which transcends the issue of color," the editors place the poem in their larger narrative about Brooks's fundamental concerns with "decent human values" and "the universal values of art" (32–33). Intentionally or not, such readings attempt to re-erase whiteness, reconstructing precisely the kind of cross-racial coalitions that Brooks's postwar poems called into question. Recovering and reactivating this vitally central work not only extends our understanding of women's protest poetry, but also restores Brooks's artful maneuvers through a society of white privilege as a public intellectual.

CHAPTER 4

Everyday Ariel: Sylvia Plath and the Dream Kitchen

Our sense of Plath rests largely on how we perceive her relationship to domesticity. Did it hasten or delay her death? Did it thwart or release her poetry? Recent popular reassessments of her legacy foreground the poet's motherhood and cooking. The Plath photograph featuring a "triptych of values—mother, children, daffodils," as Anita Helle puts it (190), has now superimposed itself over the swimsuited young siren invoked in reviews of *Unabridged Journals* (and in Ryan Adams's song "Sylvia Plath").[1] The poet's baking drew prominent attention in Christine Jeffs's film *Sylvia* (2003), prompting reviewer Anthony Lane to declare that "if Sylvia's icing is anything to go by, we might have gained a rival to Betty Crocker" (206). Invoking America's current doyenne of domesticity on a television biography about Plath, Kate Moses quipped that the poet "out-Martha'd Martha Stewart" during her final years (interview). More recently, *The Sydney Morning Herald* headlined Plath as "The Wife and Mother Who Baked Poems" (Baird). This afterimage of Plath as domestic goddess is not limited to popular culture. Several contemporary poets rely on Plath to reclaim the household for their own work. For example Craig Raine, initiator of the so-called Martian school of domestic poetry in Britain, invokes *Ariel* in a poem about attending to his young children (20). And in *Sweeping Beauty: Contemporary Women Poets Do Housework* (2005), the first words of the first poem are "Sylvia Plath" (Gemin 1).

But Plath does not wear an apron so easily in the standard accounts of her career that shape both women's poetry anthologies and feminist criticism.[2] Since the publishing success of nineteenth-century poet Felicia Hemans, male critics have often invoked the *domestic* label to trivialize or otherwise denigrate poems by women. For the most part, editors of women's poetry anthologies see themselves with little choice but to either jettison domesticity as essentially unpoetic or to concede it as an essential component of womanhood—especially in assessing poems by white women.[3] Either way, domesticity figures as a transparent and banal set of practices that can distract one from becoming a major poet. We see this cultural narrative in the introductions for two landmark American anthologies published a decade after Plath's death—*Psyche: The Feminine Poetic Consciousness* (1973) and *No More Masks!* (1973). The first banishes "domestic schools of verse" in their efforts to kill off "the Lady Poet" (Segnitz and Rainey 15). Florence Howe articulates a more vexed response in the second, hailing women poets' images of their "daily lives" and kitchen work while also celebrating their ability to finally "look past domesticity both into their own selves and toward the mountains outside" (Howe 14, 30). And yet one of Plath's signature poems about domestic relations—"The Applicant"—appears in these very anthologies, as well as in *Salt and Bitter and Good* (1975) and *The Bloodaxe Book of Contemporary Women Poets* (1985). Several of Plath's poems about motherhood are sprinkled across these and other women's poetry anthologies of the 1970s, 1980s, and 1990s. So while "domestic arrangements took up a great deal of space in her writing," as Tracy Brain rightly points out (59), editors seem to lack a language for acknowledging that emphasis without appearing to diminish Plath's literary status. Maura Dooley distills this domestic dilemma in her introduction to a collection of women poets of the 1990s: "Write about blood, babies, the moon and jam-making and be a 'Woman Poet'; or, cut out half of your experience of life and get taken seriously" (13). Undoubtedly, some would claim that the popular notion of "having it all" cannot apply to women poets—an assumption with key implications for Plath studies.

Commentators on her work often reach an impasse when determining the degree to which domesticity hindered or helped her literary ambitions—especially for her poetry. In the Plath section of her *Bloodaxe* anthology, for example, Jeni Couzyn declares unequivocally that "babies do not combine with poetry" (147). Reviewing Plath's *Unabridged Journals,* Zoë Heller separates the poet from "a fake, *Ladies' Home Journal* Plath" (30), echoing Linda Wagner-Martin's earlier diagnosis of her *"Ladies' Home Journal* syndrome" (32). *Conflict* is the driving word in Wagner-Martin's portrait of a woman torn between marriage and writers' markets, dishes and diction. In her wider discussion of Plath and women's magazines, including America's postwar bible of domesticity, Jacqueline Rose modulates Plath's dilemma into one of shifting desires, hybrid discourses, and "ideological ambiguity" (173–76). Significantly, neither of these important analyses considers the fact that Plath published a *poem* in *Ladies' Home Journal.* This blind spot reflects a long-standing critical bias that domesticity is a more appropriate domain for her fiction. Intentionally or not, the views of all these critics and editors share certain assumptions: (1) domesticity may be a staple of women's poetry, but it is not the stuff of poetry per se; (2) "serious" women poets figure domesticity only in terms of conflict or critique; (3) domestic poetry is first and foremost a poetry of personal experience.

But the cultural work of *Ariel* involves far more than Plath's bringing new experiential layers and emotional registers to domestic poetry. She did not simply inflect motherhood with ambivalence or turn the American dream kitchen into what Sally Bayley distills as a "domestic horror show" (199). The larger discursive framework surrounding Plath's lived experience of domesticity was a heterogeneous one that occupied the public sphere. It exceeds the dualistic conceptions we see in so many accounts of the poet's career, as well as the influential model of "the divided self" that has shaped women's poetry studies since the 1970s.[4] The postwar discourse of domesticity that Plath brought into her late poetry included not only the three C's (childrearing, cooking, and cleaning), but also the intersections of housewifery with art, advertising, technology, and myth. These varied images and inflections are best distilled in women's magazines, especially in *Ladies' Home Journal* because it departed from its peers by publishing poetry—including work by literary figures such as Edna St. Vincent Millay, Marianne Moore, Adrienne Rich, May Sarton, and Maxine Kumin.[5] In fact, *Ladies' Home Journal* often bested more literary magazines in giving space to women poets; Sarton's work appeared there five times during the 1950s. Plath explained to her mother that the magazine provided her with "an Americanness" she felt compelled "to dip into," and she read it during her final years in England (*Letters Home* 433). Rose argues that the *Journal* and similar women's magazines do not articulate "a monolithic conception of their own project or of the culture which they serve both to reflect and produce" (176), while Nancy Walker asserts more recently that they "reflected an on-going debate about how domesticity could and should be defined" (16). Many of Plath's most anthologized poems traffic in the richness of this popular discourse, which hardly constitutes a unitary cultural script that she simply accepted, countered, or parodied. Indeed, one of her major contributions to contemporary poetry was revealing domesticity as a pliable and compelling source. For Plath did not just write domestic poetry; she reinvented it.

In 1958, the same year that Plath published a poem in *Ladies' Home Journal,* anthologist Louis Untermeyer praised women poets who had "lifted the ordinary round of women's everyday into the extraordinary" (27); his position reinforces the fundamental separation between domesticity and transcendence that we find in most commentary on women poets. But Plath's signature work taps an extraordinary dimension *within* domesticity, a quality it shares with Henri Lefebvre's and Roland Barthes's postwar assessments of everyday life (theories that draw, respectively, from women's magazines and household products). Indeed, some of Lefebvre's characterizations of what he termed "the women's press"—his metonym for the everyday—could serve as blurbs for *Ariel*: "Rich in surprises, inhabitable and densely inhabited, this feminine world has no closure" because "in it we find survivals, superstitions, rituals, myths and modern mythology" (2:81; 1:99). Plath began to turn toward a similarly expansive vision of domesticity in the late 1950s, concurrent with the second edition of Lefebvre's *Critique of Everyday Life* (Volume 1) and Barthes's *Mythologies*. While the poet was working Lysol into the title poem of her first volume, Barthes worked through the mythological meanings of soap powders, liquid cleansers, and margarine. Indeed, the theories of everyday life that emerged in tandem with her career can help us to rethink the issue of Plath and domesticity. Through these theories we can see how *Ariel* presents a new model of domestic poetry by tapping the rich ambiguities and strange images of the everyday.

Operation Lysol

In 1956, the year H.D. was completing her alternative myth of Helen, Plath had not yet tapped everyday mythologies to fashion her alternative style of domestic poetry. Lefebvre published the second edition of *Critique of Everyday Life* that same year. He cites in his foreword a journalist's reaction to a postwar American trend that was making its way to Europe: "'Kitchens are becoming less like kitchens and more like works of art'" (1:6). The Museum of Modern Art displayed a special exhibit of Tupperware in 1956, praising its beautiful yet functional design.[6] But Plath was not quite convinced that household objects could further the art of her poetry. In his edition of her *Collected Poems*, Ted Hughes plots 1956 as the turning point of Plath's career; the year that they married, it marked for him the beginning of her mature work. Significantly, it was the year that Plath began to work domesticity into her poems. "Black Rook in Rainy Weather" begins this cultural work by "contemplat[ing] explicitly the process of poetic inspiration," as Jo Gill puts it (97). Initially, the poem follows literary convention in looking outside and upward for a source, at one point Americanizing Thomas Hardy by desiring "some backtalk / From the mute sky" for motivation. Then it turns counterintuitively to consider a "minor light" closer to home, one that may

> Lean incandescent
>
> Out of kitchen table or chair
> As if a celestial burning took
> Possession of the most obtuse objects now and then—
> (Collected 57)

Plath's diction reflects the poem's ambivalent attitude toward domestic space: it is both "minor" and "persistent" like the kind of domestic verse that came before. In fact, the pattern of transverse slant rhyme (ABCDE) resembles a row from a basic cross-stitch sampler. Although the kitchen's "incandescent" light emanates from "obtuse" household objects, this domestic vision is no match for the "celestial burning" that powers a traditional aesthetic of transcendence. Plath has not yet let go of the Surrealist's belief that domesticity is insipid in and of itself, that art must liberate household objects from functionality so that they "ascended to a new level," as Marina Vanci-Perahim writes of Man Ray (17). At this point in her career, Plath is unsure that mere kitchen light can power her poetry, but by the time she configures the kitchen in "Lesbos," she will fashion a "fluorescent light wincing on and off like a terrible migraine" (Ariel 38). Indeed, that poem's "windowless" domestic space offers more than enough material for inspiration.

Kitchens and poetry would remain largely at odds with one another for Plath in 1958. In "Poems, Potatoes" she can see that the latter is useful raw material for culinary artists the way that stones are for sculptors. But when she perceives lines of poetry to be "sturdy as potatoes," she is expressing frustration that words are proving hard and inflexible in her hand—uninspiring foodstuff for innovation. And yet, paradoxically, the poem's clearest image of writer's block is the potatoes, even though its final stanza claims that their "knobby browns" remain "unpoemed, unpictured" (*Collected* 106). Plath has not yet found the domestic plasticity that will make potatoes hiss in "Lesbos," although her poems will keep making forays into the kitchen.

In "The Ghost's Leavetaking," Plath brings domesticity into momentary contact with the supernatural so that "our meat-and-potatoes thoughts" take on "the nimbus / Of ambrosial revelation." Inspired by Paul Klee,[7] who influenced the Surrealist movement, this 1958 poem re-creates his cryptic figure from "Departure of the Ghost," placing it within the speaker's household moments before dawn; it is perched "at the outermost / Fringe of mundane vision." Plath both separates and merges her poem's "two worlds," the mythic and the mundane, reflecting a poet intrigued by domesticity but still unsure if it can hold up to sustained attention. The poem's frequent breaks from iambic pentameter and opaque rhyme scheme subtly reinforce this overarching tenuousness. In her opening stanzas Plath contrasts Klee's "oracular ghost" with the "ready-made creation / Of chairs and bureaus and sleep-twisted sheets." These manufactured household objects can become mysterious "hieroglyphs / Of some godly utterance" only in the presence of spectral figures that emanate from the supernatural and the unconscious (*Collected* 90). In her essay on domestication, Rachel Bowlby reminds us that these realms conjoin in "the house of Freudian psychoanalysis," a domicile disturbed "by the presence of ghosts" (77). The haunted house of Plath's poem does offer "access to an uncanny and contradictory interior world," as Steven Gould Axelrod states in his Freudian interpretation (77). And yet "The Ghost's Leavetaking" also reflects Plath's increasing artistic investment in the interior of the home itself. She domesticates Klee's figure by transforming its parallel curves and foldings into "a knot of laundry," fashioning an "upraised" hand from a "bunch of sheets." The stanza repeats the word *sheets* as a second pair of end rhymes, and Plath echoes it in her penultimate stanza. Plath had tucked Giorgio de Chirico's domestic image of darning eggs into her 1957 poem "The Disquieting Muses," interacting with his painting of the same name. But she writes domesticity into Klee's painting, even comparing one of its small suspended shapes to "a stellar carrot"—in effect superimposing a kitchen image over his abstract figuration of the sky (*Collected* 90–91). Here household objects no longer need to lose their everyday legibility to transport her poetry into another dimension. In the context of women's poetry, Plath's mixture of domesticity and modernist painting reverses the dynamics of Gertrude Stein's *Tender Buttons,* in which syntactic collage renders food items abstract—and often illegible. In the context of women's poetry studies, Plath's domestication of Surrealism constitutes a form of what Elizabeth Bergmann Loizeaux terms "feminist ekphrasis," in which the conventional male gaze of poems about visual art "can be exposed, used, resisted, and rewritten" (81).

The title poem for Plath's first volume, *The Colossus,* brings domesticity into a mythic landscape by tapping the talismanic power of branded household products. Composed during the same year that one of her literary idols, W. H. Auden, published a poem about his new American-style kitchen[8] in *The New Yorker*—and two years after "Operation Margarine" appeared in Barthes's *Mythologies*—"The Colossus" expands the scope of domesticity in Plath's poetry. Its female speaker assumes the task of rehabilitating a "pithy and historical" figure she addresses as "father." Both a decayed statue and a "littered" landscape, the father-colossus becomes a sprawling domicile in need of deep cleaning with "pails of Lysol." The speaker's labor to "dredge the silt," repair with "gluepots," and "mend the immense skull-plates" becomes monumental like the Colossus itself, an epic domestic undertaking that is deliberate and unending: "I shall never get you put together entirely" (*Collected* 129–30). Plath's verb choice of *mending* suggests Herculean efforts in needlework. These enlargements of domesticity reflect more than Betty Friedan's wry observation that postwar housewifery "not only expanded to fill the time available, but could hardly be done in the available time" (241). Paradoxically, Plath's Operation Lysol augments rather than diminishes the speaker's position in her poem. It also complicates standard readings of "The Colossus" that render the speaker as fully "enclosed in the kind of patriarchal history" that the father-colossus represents, as Sandra Gilbert puts it (interview). Straddling mythic and material meanings, as well as gender boundaries, Lysol extends the speaker's position beyond daughter-subordinate by heightening the effects of her housekeeping.

Plath makes another counterintuitive turn to domesticity, tapping mythologies as richly layered as her classical allusions to Zeus, Aeschylus's *Oresteia,* and the Colossus of Rhodes. As Barthes notes, liquid cleaners with the powerful agents of ammonia and chlorine signify "a violent, abrasive modification of matter," an "absolute fire" that makes household cleaning analogous to both alchemy and "making war" (36). They bring an epic, even apocalyptic, aura to housework. Magazine advertisements that Plath would have seen shaped and reflected these everyday mythologies. In 1956, for example, an ad from *Ladies' Home Journal* pitched Lysol as an indispensable soldier in the perpetual war against household dirt, grime, and odors: "Here's your shield, your defender, your ally" (157). In the graphics, the housewife splits herself into a platoon of miniature duplicates armed with mops, brooms, sponges, and dustcloths—a virtual domestic army that both blurs and reinforces gender roles. A 1957 ad from the same magazine declares that lethal Lysol "kills every disease germ it touches" (143). Touting a threat to germs that now "needs no poison label," an earlier ad from 1954 claimed a potency of "up to 30 times more disinfectant power than bleaches" (120). So the speaker's domestic campaign in "The Colossus" cannot be a gentle undertaking, despite the poem's act of mourning. When it wasn't waging war on household germs and dirt, Lysol shifted meanings toward more intimate domain—and less empowering mythologies for women. Advertisements in *Ebony* emphasized the product's use as a douche additive for hygiene and "feminine daintiness," claiming the postwar protection of being "secure in your marriage" (1950; 1953). Literally, Lysol turned domesticity inside/out. Surely Anne Sexton had this duality in mind when she wrote "Housewife," a poem in which the central figure is "faithfully washing herself down" inside a domicile with "permanent and pink" walls like a vagina (77). Plath brought Lysol into the American poetic lexicon a decade before Sexton incorporated the scouring powder Bab-o into her revisionist myth-making about Briar Rose; Plath was not a mad housewife but a poet of Madison Avenue. Her inheritors in *Sweeping Beauty* draw from their stockpile of cleaning products, from "Clorox bleaching my fingernails lady-white" to the "windows emitting their glorious scent of Windex" (Kennedy 73; Laux 84). In reaching for Lysol, Plath found a household item that could perform better than Klee's ghost: it fused the mythic and mundane, it made domesticity strange in broad daylight, and it did not leave the house.

An Extraordinary Everyday

In several poems from the early 1960s, Plath's extraordinary depictions of household objects, routines, and relationships would push her domestic poetry into the expansive domain of *Ariel*. It is here that her writing intersects most closely with the dynamics of Lefebvre's everyday life and with Barthes's everyday mythologies. In his first volume of *Critique of Everyday Life,* Lefebvre takes issue with philosophies and aesthetics of transcendence that devalue the quotidian world, asserting that the "so-called marvelous realm" of the Surrealists "operates only on the level of everyday life." He insists on the "something else *which is there* in everyday objects, not an abstract lining but something enfolded within which hitherto we have been unable to see" (1:115, 134). Such household items are captivating in and of themselves, needing no "liberation" from functionality or enshrinement within a gallery (a male cultural preserve during Plath's career). Moreover, they are already invested with mythic dimensions through their status as consumer goods. Lefebvre genders everyday life as a feminine world that proves analogous to the discourse of postwar domesticity that would underwrite Plath's signature style.

Women's magazines were of paramount importance to Lefebvre in formulating his theory of the everyday. He did not see the uniform, transparent, and simple discourse that Friedan saw in *Ladies' Home Journal* and its counterparts. Looking at *Elle*[9] from the position of a nontargeted reader, he perceived in its glossy pages that "the practical texts (such as recipes, menus, dress patterns) read like dreams, and that conversely the imaginary texts read in a practical fashion, in a perpetual toing and froing from one to the other, in a never-ending equivocation which reproduces itself indefinitely." While Lefebvre intersects with Friedan in seeing postwar housewifery as being "immersed in everyday life, submerged, swallowed up," he did not find women's magazines to be disconnected from "issues of current affairs, fashion, art, politics, and history"—although they could also offer a temporary escape from these things. Unlike the enclosed "Hall of Mirrors" that Friedan saw in American magazines' discourse of domesticity, Lefebvre's everyday was elastic and expansive (Lefebvre 2:13, 51, 84; Friedan 65). There are certainly problems with his gender formulations, especially with his elision of the everyday and the feminine through a fundamental ambiguity he sees in each. Moreover, his bamboozlement before the women's press sometimes betrays romantic longings for an essential femininity that interfere with his Marxist aims of social transformation. And yet despite his own feminine mystique, Lefebvre's sense of being a stranger to the housewife's world yields aesthetic implications from the strangeness he finds there. His everyday theory can move us beyond experiential models of domestic poetry (and psychobiographical approaches to them) without denying the fact that, by and large, women do experience domesticity differently than men. Lefebvre's theory also provides a mechanism for getting past the domestic/poetic opposition because of the heterogeneity he perceives in women's magazines: "It is a world where triviality does not exclude the extraordinary, where the physiological does not exclude high culture, where the practical does not exclude the ideal, and where these aspects never become disconnected" (2:81). In the pages of *Ladies' Home Journal,* the work of canonized poets and painters could appear alongside homemaking articles, romance fiction, advice columns, and advertisements. In the magazine's feature on Millay's new kitchen, Gladys

Taber links its well-wrought design to the poet's consummate sonnets in near-seamless fashion (56). Plath would engage in a parallel expansion of the everyday world, creating a recipe for a new kind of domestic poetry in the process.

Her *Ariel* poems often integrate their mythic extensions so that household objects, activities, and relationships become extraordinary while maintaining their domestic legibility. Marjorie Perloff has termed this aesthetic "Plath's peculiar ability to fuse the domestic and the hallucinatory" ("Icon" 283), a claim that one could also make about many advertisements for kitchen products in postwar women's magazines. In these everyday images, some of which I discuss at length elsewhere,[10] supernatural entities inhabited the housewife's kitchen—including the Jolly Green Giant, the genie in Wish-Bone salad dressing, and Elsie the Borden Cow. Reddy Kilowatt—a personified lightning bolt—sprang from suburbia's electrical outlets to power the dream kitchen, like a domesticated Zeus. Through these mythic assistants, as well as the kitchen "magic" of processed ingredients and modern appliances, daily food preparation is transformed into something commonplace and fantastic, artistic and automatic. Conveniently, the housewife did not need to transcend domestic space and labor to experience such strange visitations. Some of Plath's *Ariel* poems manifest a similarly supernatural dimension within domesticity. In "A Birthday Present," for example, the speaker senses a spectral presence as she works in the kitchen: "When I am quiet at my cooking I feel it looking" (*Ariel* 66). Mythic figures receive fuller incarnation in "Kindness," a poem that appeared in the first edition of *Ariel*. In it, "Dame Kindness" (complete with smoking rings) "glides" through the speaker's house like a friendly ghost or a good witch (*Collected* 269). Here the supernatural permeates the entire household. Steeped in modernist aesthetics and British sensibility, Auden had written that "ghosts would feel uneasy, / a witch at a loss" in the "all-electric room" of his Americanized kitchen in Austria (531). But as an American woman who came of age in the 1950s, Plath could incorporate homegrown specters into her poems—even staging them on bright linoleum, under fluorescent lights.

Cooking and other forms of food preparation would also open up Plath's discourse of domesticity. The era of decorative cooking and food sculpture pushed boundaries between housewifery and artistry, altering the conventional appearance of culinary creations. As Karal Ann Marling notes, "In the classic 1950s presentation, chicken à la king looked like Abstract Expressionist color drips applied to a dinner plate, so completely were its properties as food overwhelmed by its pictorial charm" (223). Plath took note of the "lush double-page spreads of Technicolor meals" in women's magazines, working them into the metonymic *Ladies' Day* kitchen scenes of *The Bell Jar* (21). Magazine and advertising layout, as well as food photography, often highlighted these discursive links. For example, facing pages of the December 1958 issue of *Ladies' Home Journal* pair "I Love to Eat . . . But I Hate to Cook" with a reproduction of *The Flower Boat* (by naïve painter André Bauchant[11]); the issue also includes Plath's poem "Second Winter." Through the color and arrangement of the article's illustrations, the layout creates a graphic match that sutures the domestic/artistic opposition. The article's author, a commercial artist and painter, reinforces the link through her statement: "I always design a meal as carefully as I do a canvas" (Davis 64). The comparison anticipates the *Journal*'s later article titled "Cooking to Me Is Poetry," written and cooked by Phyllis McGinley (who would win a Pulitzer Prize for her poetry). This rhetoric of food-art does not simply dress up drudgery or create a second-class tier of household artists; it pushes the meaning of food preparation into the heterogeneous dimension of the everyday.

Perusing food photography in the pages of *Elle,* Barthes saw "a cuisine of advertisement, totally magical," that constituted "an openly dream-like cookery" and "a fairy-land reality" (79). We see the same dynamic in *Ladies' Home Journal* not only in artistic food features, but also in the exotic appeal of ads for Asian food products. For example, an Orientalist ad for Chun King's canned goods rerouted the evening meal from ordinary fare to a "menu magic bazaar" (94). Like Barthes, Lefebvre found that the allure of food in women's magazines constitutes a key ingredient in the marvelous realm of everyday life: "Cookery becomes a fairyland and fantastic stories are like recipes in a magic cookery book, flanked by articles on fashion and stories about the romantic agonies of a famous star or an oriental princess" (2:84). Such odd mixtures of seemingly disconnected elements make everyday domesticity an intriguing aesthetic for Plath, one she could tap for her signature poems. Her *Ariel* volume combines "romantic agonies" with domestic labors and mysterious veiled women. In "Fever 103°" the bedridden speaker regurgitates her lover's attempts at soup, yet still acquires an exotic glamour; "glowing" like a Japanese lantern, "smokes roll" from her "like Isadora's scarves."[12] The speaker of "The Bee Meeting" dons a "fashionable" Italian hat and "black veil" to witness the smoking of a hive that will eventually source her household's honey, the elixir of "Wintering" (*Ariel* 78–79, 81).

By the time Plath writes "Cut" in 1962, staple foods like potatoes and onions no longer signify obtuse images of writer's block; instead, they are portals to an extraordinary realm where the poet can showcase her signature style. In this poem's "departure from the domestic routine," the speaker cuts her finger in the kitchen— unleashing not only blood but also a profusion of metaphors that constitutes "a 'celebration' of verbal dexterity," as Susan Rosenbaum points out in her tour-de-force reading (140–41). At one level this arterial flow becomes a *l'ecriture feminine* in red ink, but it greatly expands the biographical and biological contours through which critics tend to read Plath's famous "blood jet" metaphor. "Cut" creates mythic characters that outperform any kitchen sprites lurking in cans, bottles, or appliances:

> Little pilgrim,
> The Indian's axed your scalp.
> (*Ariel* 25)

Plath also compares the speaker's injury to a "turkey wattle / Carpet" that "rolls" out of "the heart." As this flow continues it becomes "a million soldiers"; Plath makes them "Redcoats," of course (*Ariel* 25). Exercising the art of metaphor-making with flamboyance, the poem performs a red magic act that creates more startling effects than the earlier poems about pregnancy ("Metaphors" and "You're").

"Little pilgrim" echoes John Wayne, while the "Indian" invokes Hollywood's historical sense. Like the Redcoats, these figures from Westerns also invoke the violence of American history. Langdon Hammer has called the poem "an hallucinatory fantasy that links the sword of war and the cooking knife," and yet violence is an inherent part of food preparation (156). As food critic Betty Fussell writes in her memoir of postwar domestic life, a woman enters the kitchen prepared to "do battle, deploying a full range of artillery—crushers, scrapers, beaters, rousters, gougers, grinders . . ." (4). So *Ariel*'s kitchen was hardly anomalous in giving mealtime adventures a menacing edge. Plath not only joins such culinary actions with centuries of combat, but also grounds her soldier-sprites in postwar domesticity. Her opening phrase ("What a thrill") taps the rhetoric of appliance ads that promise kitchen ecstasy, while the "pink fizz" and "pill" suggest household medicines. Even the blood flow becomes a carpet. In the final stanzas Plath brings gender equity to the world of strange visitations, mutating the bleeding thumb into a girl in a babushka and then into a "dirty girl" (*Ariel* 25–26). Hysterical and historical, quotidian and theatrical, violent and witty, the poem reflects Lefebvre's sense that American writers "have been able to open their eyes to what is nearest to them—everyday life—and to find themes in it which amaze us by their violence and originality" (1:235). Although Lefebvre does not assess women writers in his analysis and, in fact, seems suspicious of them, Plath's late poems may offer the most powerful contemporary example of literary art through everyday means.

Mechanized Marriage and Femineering

Like the discourse of domesticity that shaped *Ladies' Home Journal* and other women's magazines, many of Plath's domestic poems mix technology with nature and romance. Lefebvre notes that in postwar society, the "partly technicized" configuration of everyday life "has not created its own specific style or rhythm" because "unconnected objects (vacuum cleaners, washing machines, radio or television sets, refrigerators, cars, etc.) determine a series of disjointed actions" in the home. The art of integrating these disparate appliances into a daily rhythm could prove as challenging for domestic poets as it was for housewives. Bringing automated technologies to bear on technologies of gender, the American dream kitchen was the prime site through which these tensions were heightened or resolved. Modern appliances functioned as a "techno-social" aspect of gender formation, to borrow from Teresa de Lauretis, and they could add new tensions to romantic relations (3). In "Words heard, by accident, over the phone," "An Appearance," and "The Applicant," Plath merges household technology with the discourse of romance, often drawing on advertising rhetoric to both expose and suture domestic discontinuities.

Although the first of these poems does not appear in either version of *Ariel,* Plath composed it during the prolific year in which she wrote most of the volume's poems. "Words heard, by accident" employs "a style of excess that had already become Plath's trademark in *The Colossus,*" as Karen Jackson Ford comments in her analysis of Plath's strategic violations of poetic decorum (126). At the same time, the poem escalates the figurations of domesticity in her writing from the late 1950s. In a 1957 journal entry, Plath recounted her new husband's ineptitude with American household technology: "Ted using coffee percolator wrong, making poisonous brew, milk boiling over, mislaying percolator directions" (*Unabridged* 301). The passage reflects how the proliferation of household gadgets called into question the traditional "maleness" of mechanical mastery, yielding new gender configurations. In "Words heard, by accident," Plath uses the automatic coffee maker to distill domestic ruptures caused by her inadvertent discovery of her husband's affair (Assia Wevill called their home). As Ford notes, the poet's strategic use of the verb *percolate* joins with other household words "in uneasy combinations" that force "images to come together in new ways" (131). Mutating appliances anchor images of the poem's dysfunctional gender relations, mixing the mechanical and the biological as Plath pushes domestic space into an alien terrain. She transforms the offending telephone into an errant coffee maker through which the caller's words ooze out in a muddy rush, "Thick as foreign coffee, and with a sluggy pulse." This mud jet disrupts domestic routine and coherence so that nothing in the household operates as it should. "O god, how shall I ever clean the phone table," the speaker exclaims, as the "muck" keeps "pressing out of the many-holed earpiece." In the final lines Plath merges the domicile with the set of a postwar science fiction movie; the telephone "withdraws its tentacle" and the speaker's heart is forcibly impregnated by percolating "spawn" (*Collected* 202–03). Some alien-induced, hybrid form of future offspring has landed in the house. Unlike her poetic inheritor Raine, Plath needed no Martian observer to make telephones strange.[13]

"Words heard, by accident" borrows from advertising rhetoric by reflecting marital relations through household appliances, while it counters Madison Avenue's tendency to smooth over potential domestic conflicts through new technologies. For example, a 1956 Bell Telephone ad in *Ladies' Home Journal* pitches housewives' need for a kitchen phone with a hypothetical switching of gender roles: "Madam! Suppose you traded jobs with your husband?" The central image depicts a beleaguered man wearing a business suit; he holds a crying baby in one hand and a stack of dishes in another. In the background, an aproned woman relaxes on the phone at an office desk. Reinventing the kitchen as a home office, the ad copy recommends purchasing another telephone to resolve the tensions in its gender-bending images. While the housewife would still be attending to dishes and babies even with this new appliance, the advertising image is not exactly a mystification or an act of trickery. For it makes visible her multifunctioning capacities by displacing them onto the opposite gender. And the husband crosses gender stereotypes by appearing at his wit's end (215).

In 1958, Plath was considering the possibility of a story that reconfigures domesticity by animating appliances and switching their roles. In her journal notes for "Changeabout in Mrs. Cherry's Kitchen" (published posthumously as "Mrs. Cherry's Kitchen"), she imagines that "shiny modern gadgets" and appliances have become "overspecialized" and wish to perform other tasks. Drawing on the supernatural dimension of the everyday, Plath envisioned having "fairies or equivalent" come at midnight to perform the "change-about" so that the refrigerator can store clothes, the dishwasher can cook, and the iron can make waffles. "Complex, perhaps, but possible?" she wondered (*Unabridged* 304). Indeed, how far can one push the boundaries of personification, functionality, and gender roles in the postwar dream kitchen while maintaining the legibility of its push-button technology? I believe these were key questions for Plath as she reinvented domestic poetry through cultural tropes in which spouses and appliances could become interchangeable assets.

Plath fuses romance and technology in "An Appearance," which her daughter Frieda Hughes considers one of the earliest poems to manifest "the distinctive *Ariel* voice" (xii). Plath's title reflects the blending of supernatural and material elements that shape her everyday aesthetic. The poet crosses gender boundaries with her male speaker of this domestic love poem, voicing his amazement at a wife he describes as a refrigerator, a typewriter, and a watch; her mechanical transformations are more mutable than those of the baby in "Morning Song," whom Plath compares to a "fat gold watch" (*Ariel* 5). Abandoning similes for the immediacy of metaphor, "An Appearance" first presents the wife as an animate refrigerator, complete with "blue currents" of electric circuitry and a feline "purr" in her mechanical heart. Her dazzling smile "annihilates" her adoring husband. When he ponders the nature of their procreative love, he figures it through the rhythmic action of a sewing machine: "Is this love then, this red material / Issuing from the steel needle that flies so blindingly?" (*Collected* 189). Like the poem's opening line, this one builds intensity through its assonant long *i*—the sound of ascent in so many of *Ariel*'s domestic transformations. Plath's tropes of redness, blindness, and a pierced heart play on romantic imagery, recalling her macabre valentine in the earlier "Two Views of a Cadaver Room." But here she does not need to depart from domestic space to make love strange.

Plath's key verb *issuing* links the cloth flowing under the needle with the couple's future progeny ("a dynasty"), which will be clad in the housewife's creations ("little dresses and coats"). Thus Plath mechanizes not only the woman but also romance, heterosexual re-production, and art; the male lover is woven into "this red material" to become part of the poem's mechanical processes. These technologies of gender and sexuality link with Plath's overlay of fallopian and radio tubes in her *Ariel* poem "Lesbos," which figures marital and reproductive malfunction. Her mechanized housewife also intersects with the rhetoric of magazine advertisements for sewing machines. For example, a 1955 ad in *Ladies' Home Journal* hailed the new Elna as "not a machine," but "the world's greatest home-maker"—complete with "magic discs" in its "Magic Brain" that made sewing "easy as playing a record" (211). The bold-face copy echoes René Magritte's famous painting "Ceci n'est pas une pipe," continuing domesticity's discursive links with Surrealism. In "The Courage of Shutting-Up," from *Ariel,* Plath turns to technology for figuring the speaker's thoughts and emotions as automatic responses. There are "black discs . . . of outrage" behind her lips as "the discs of the brain revolve," and the "tattooist" wields a needle that traverses the same "groove," "over and over" like a sewing machine (*Ariel* 45). But in "An Appearance," the merging of human/mechanical yields ecstatic domestic relations. The poem has answered its self-reflexive question of what "to make" of the delirious "contradictions" in its imagery (*Collected* 189).

Surely Plath had in mind the full-page magazine ads for kitchen appliances when she engineered the extraordinary everyday of her *Ariel* poems. Blending the mundane with the miraculous, copywriters extolled the marvels of ranges and refrigerators as *fabulous, magic, stunning, sensational, thrilling.* In a 1951 ad for Murray ranges, Lilliputian wives gaze in wonder at colossal ovens, assisted by tiny men who give them a "Cook's Tour" of domestic adventure (89). By the mid-1950s, as Juliann Sivulka notes, appliance manufacturers promoted "sophisticated new push-button gadgetry designed to activate unseen machinery" instead of the "obvious labor-saving benefits" of their products (246). For example, the housewife in ads for the Caloric Ultramatic range claimed that the product was "So AUTOMATIC it almost thinks for me," while Frigidaire hailed the power of the "Thinking Panel" on its oven (Caloric 191; Frigidaire

1957). Using these mysterious machines could usher in more mythic assistants such as the Magic Chef man and Lux's Minute Minder Man. In an ad campaign for the latter product, an oven-timing device, a smitten housewife confesses: "I'm in love with the man in my Automatic Range!" (6). Roland Marchand's observations about earlier American advertising prove relevant in this context as well: the "'re-personalization' of life" in these appliance ads entails "a tacit recognition of an unvanquished public propensity for animism—the belief that all objects are alive" (358). Such animations allow space for the supernatural in an increasingly technological society, joining mechanical and mythic dimensions.

"The Applicant," one of Plath's widely anthologized poems, portrays the impending marriage of a robotic woman and needy man, exposing the contradiction of repersonalizing mechanical marriage through a discourse that "evacuates personal intimacy," to borrow Deborah Nelson's phrase (30). In her 1962 broadcast for the BBC, Plath explained that the poem portrays a "marvelous product" pitched by "a sort of exacting super-salesman" (qtd. in *Collected* 293). Indeed, its housewife-machine combines good looks, superior technology, and motherly ministrations into a "living doll" that "works," offering the convenience of one-stop shopping for a feminized male consumer. As she did in "An Appearance," Plath effects a change-about in the housewife's form, but here she also alters the man's *gender*: he takes on female functionality by shopping for home appliances. Ironically, the salesman-turned-marriage broker faults the applicant for not being needy *enough,* as if pushing the relentlessness of Rosser Reeves's hard-sell technique past the point of negotiation. Initially he refuses to deal because the applicant does not appear to be "our sort of person." Seeking the requisite proof that "something's missing" in his prospective customer, the speaker asks if he wears

> A glass eye, false teeth or a crutch,
> A brace or a hook,
> Rubber breasts or a rubber crotch . . .
>
> (*Ariel* 11)

Note how his grotesque questions imply that a model wife is the ultimate prosthesis for men (and domiciles) with missing parts. Indeed,
Plath's images of surgery and gender-bending prosthetics present a
freakish image of young men on the marriage market, reversing the
hetero-normative rhetoric of postwar marriage expert Paul Landis:
"Except for the sick, the badly crippled, the deformed, the emotionally warped and the mentally defective, almost everyone has an
opportunity to marry" (Miller and Nowak, 154). In the economy
of "The Applicant," only men whose "crotch" has become some
kind of "crutch" make suitable husbands—a point Plath reinforces
through the consonance of her end rhyme. Naked and empty-
headed, the applicant's "last resort" for attaining wholeness is to
purchase the amazing housewife-machine and "marry it, marry it,
marry it" (*Ariel* 12). The triple repetition that Plath employs here—
and throughout *Ariel*—coincides with Reeves's masterful pitches
for miracle products like Anacin, which promised "fast Fast FAST"
relief to housewives suffering from nervous tension. Indeed, Plath's
applicant crosses gender boundaries by losing control of himself,
even crying in public (a "change-about" in normative masculinity).

His mechanical bride-to-be proves to be a more complex construction in Plath's poem. A hybrid construction, this feminized
"it" straddles boundaries between woman and machine, active
and passive. A less surreal figure than the appliance-wife of "An
Appearance," she does the thinking for her apparently brainless
user, but she also responds automatically to his voice commands.
She will outperform and outlive her "alarmingly defective" husband, as Janice Markey puts it (85), but she will also die of grief
when he is gone (becoming, in effect, a machine that cries). Even so,
she will outlast any appliance on the market because she occupies
a domestic place outside of planned obsolescence, a technological
cycle that overwrites the hetero-normative cycle of reproduction. In
similar fashion, Plath's signature style straddles categories by embracing some domestic tropes while calling others into question.

Some of the advertisements from postwar women's magazines
show that "The Applicant" was not unique in figuring household

appliances as mechanical spouses. Many of them went far beyond the Elna campaign in their everyday animations. Frigidaire pitched its "Sheer Look" refrigerators and ovens of the late 1950s as "stunning beauties" that were both "glamorous" cooks and intelligent machines (1956 advertisement). The rhetoric of these ads merged a model appliance with a model woman wearing an evening gown and opera gloves. By holding up her gloved hands in a right angle, this model evoked the glamour of Marilyn Monroe and Dior's "New Look" as she mimicked the "sheer" corners of Frigidaire's new streamlined design. But women were not the only mechanical spouses in women's magazines. A 1950 advertisement for Gibson refrigerators presented its miracle product as a model husband—a "Good Provider" and "true *help mate*" whose thoughtfulness and adaptability will enrich the housewife's daily life. (This particular ad appeared in *Good Housekeeping,* another magazine that Plath considered a market for her fiction.) As with "The Applicant," the sales pitch equates marriage with appliance shopping: "It's like getting MARRIED—you should get well acquainted first!" Comparing the features of individual products becomes analogous to weighing the differences between eligible men; after all, "you and it are going to live and work together for a good many years." Like Plath's poems of mechanized love and marriage, these ads present masculinity and femininity as interchangeable parts of modern appliances. Gendered relations between consumer and product, husband and wife, become more fluid in these everyday texts of technological wonders and home miracles. It was, after all, the era of the "femineered" kitchen—International Harvester's term for its line of colorful refrigerators keyed to match individual home décor (advertisement). A conception of domestic design that blends conventionally female and male attributes, *femineering* also suggests the hybrid constructions that Plath created with the tool kit of her signature style, in effect redesigning domestic poetry.

While one could argue that these advertisements comment ironically on the postwar housewife's insularity, even Friedan notes that the housewife's postwar role of managing household machinery could prompt her to view her husband as "the latest new appliance" she had to run smoothly (157)—another reversal of conventional gender relations. As the prime consumers for the home, housewives exercised considerable buying power in postwar American society. Elaine Tyler May points out that between 1945 and 1950, "consumer spending increased 60 percent, but the amount spent on household furnishings and appliances rose 240 percent" (165). Lefebvre saw the housewife figure as "the total woman" who "becomes everything because she does everything"—she even "produces and directs consumption" (2:82). So we cannot say that the housewife lacked agency or that her daily chores, magazine reading, and household shopping were trivial pursuits.

The Jet-Woman: Transcendence at Home

Conventional understandings of hetero-normative domestic poetry center on the idea of women's confinement within the home, contrasting this position with men's greater mobility beyond it. In postwar literature and popular culture, the housewife-breadwinner relationship distilled this dynamic, with the latter figure appearing most frequently as a suburban commuter in a gray flannel suit. And yet the era's mythic everyday housewife attained a vertical level of mobility that he lacked—she could fly at home. This most miraculous form of femineering manifests itself in magazine ads for household products that transported the everyday practices of housekeeping without leaving domesticity. We can see a parallel dynamic in *Ariel* poems that perform what Susan Van Dyne calls a "self-propelled ascension" (118), a key element in Plath's signature style. In the famously ambiguous endings to "Ariel," "Fever 103°," and "Lady Lazarus," she fashions home-powered levitations that shift her mechanical housewife into a new mythic figure—the jet-woman.

Barthes's *Mythologies* includes an essay on "The Jet-man," postwar harbinger of a hybrid masculinity that occupies an ambiguous middle space between adventurous "pilot-hero" and the posthumanist condition of suspended motionlessness. Jet-propelled aviation, Barthes theorized, produces a new paradigm of frictionless flight, one in which "an excess of speed turns into repose." While the jet-man remains mythic, he loses the traditional "romantic and individualistic elements" of his propellered predecessor (72–73). Professional rather than reckless, the jet-man is mobile and confined, "glamorous" and uniformed. The professionalized, high-flying housewife of Madison Avenue exhibited similar qualities. Her glamorous uniform included aprons, pearls, and pumps; her coiffed hair never mussed. But unlike her male counterpart, she sometimes sprouted wings. And she could even fly with her eyes closed.

In a double-page ad from an issue of *Ladies' Home Journal* published the same year as *Mythologies,* Jet Bon Ami cleaner allows women to "fly through housework"—combining the mechanical and spectral dimensions of the everyday (see figure 4.1). Powered by "the magic of this new waterless method" of cleaning, the housewife mimics airplane flight with her outstretched arms.

Her relaxed legs convey the effortlessness of her ascent, while her closed eyes convey a semiconscious state. She has no fear of flying. The trope of the jet-woman appears fairly often in *Ladies' Home Journal* ads of the mid-to-late 1950s. In a 1955 ad for River and Carolina Rice, for example, an aproned housewife becomes a femineered Hermes with winged pumps. The housewife becomes a flying angel in a 1959 ad, transformed by Sucaryl artificial sweetener. Baker's Angel Flake offers a delirious (and apparently contagious) form of domestic transcendence in a 1956 ad captioned: "Everybody's Going Coconutty." Frosted cake slices become wings that transport this jet-woman through the clouds, and yet her ascent remains within the everyday world of the dream kitchen. The literal jet-woman flies again in a 1958 ad for Junket Quick Fudge Mix; what "hauls" her "through air" is a fresh tray of treats (*Ariel* 33). In all of these images, the woman's smile and closed eyes render ambiguous her degree of control over her movement. She ascends only when she is alone, needing neither husband nor children to experience this form of domestic bliss. And yet even as the jet-woman flies solo, she maintains the trappings of her home.

Figure 4.1   Bon Ami© advertisement from *Ladies' Home Journal* (1957)

Like their mythical counterparts in advertising, Plath's jet-women tend to retain some level of normativity even as they levitate in their respective poems' culminating lines. These *Ariel* poems do not figure domesticity as extensively as the others I have discussed, but their moments of ascent nonetheless depend on contact with everyday life. The speaker of "Ariel" may leave behind "the child's cry" as she gallops on horseback, but she ends her ride by flying into a sun Plath figures as a "cauldron"; as Diane Middlebrook suggests, this culminating image can signify a "cookpot of poetry" (645). The delirious speaker of "Fever 103°" anticipates an ascent past the world of bedsheets and chicken soup, and yet she ascends into a space of roses, cherubim, and ambiguous "pink things"— images that, at one level, recall the nursery wallpaper in "Morning Song." Even the "red hair" of Lady Lazarus can suggest a domestic transformation powered by a home visit from Miss Clairol (*Ariel* 33–34, 80, 17).

In linking Plath's Ariel poems to a magazine discourse many would regard as antithetical to her poetry (or even to women's poetry more generally), I do not deny the more singular aspects of her signature style. But I am recovering a key component of this style that is mainstream, not "extreme." As we have seen, *Ariel* opens the home to strangeness and ambiguity, tapping popular sources such as *Ladies' Home Journal* and advertising rhetoric to enable a domestic poetry that refashioned household objects and relationships. Like Lefebvre's and Barthes's contemporaneous analyses of everyday life, Plath's late poems are inherently heterogeneous in their construction of domesticity. The artistic, technological, and popular dimensions of their discourse exceed the models of conflict or opposition through which critics tend to view the poet's figurations of housewifery and home. Everyday Ariel cannot be contained within experiential or essentialist models of domestic poetry.

Ultimately these expansive qualities, rather than Plath's life or psyche, most distinguish her domestic poems from those of Adrienne Rich, Anne Sexton, and other contemporaries who drew on the dream kitchen and housewifery at crucial points in their careers. In Rich's breakthrough poem "Snapshots of a Daughter-in-Law," for example, the woman washing a coffee pot hears "chiding" angels that prompt her to look far beyond her kitchen window—where she envisions a world as disconnected from her own as Rich's literary quotations are from housework (35). Culminating in Simone de Beauvoir's figure of the liberated woman as a helicopter/bird from *The Second Sex* (1949), the poem blurs mechanical/natural boundaries to escape a domesticity Rich sees as experientially and aesthetically confining (de Beauvoir 764). Sexton depicts a more mythic form of flight in "Her Kind," a signature performance piece from her debut volume. Its speaker is "a possessed witch" who flies out at night to cook and clean for the elves in their caves (15–16). That is, she must leave normative domesticity and femininity to perform kitchen magic. Sexton's poem moves in the opposite direction of Plath's everyday Ariel, bringing domesticity into supernatural domain. Unlike "Snapshots" and "Her Kind," Plath's domestic poetry has a home pantry full of strange images and happenings; their speakers rarely need to leave the house to produce their special effects. And this fundamental difference hinges on Plath's ability to distill a wide field of her era's domestic discourse—one that combined the mundane and the surreal, the technological and the mythic, the literary and the popular.

Current reconfigurations of domesticity through The Food Network; HGTV; and celebrity-entrepreneurs such as Paula Deen, Rachael Ray, and Martha Stewart make it more difficult to view cooking and home decorating as uninspired (much less uninspiring) activities. If the field of women's poetry studies maintains vexed attitudes about domesticity, many contemporary poets draw inspiration from the postwar discontinuities that Plath worked into her everyday Ariel. Contributors to *Sweeping Beauty* present a vibrant, dynamic, and heterogeneous domesticity so that "housework is romanticized as often as it is shunned or satirized," as editor Pamela Gemin states (xxiv). In the introduction to *Sweeping Beauty,* Gemin praises Laura Kasischke for a "warping of the domestic landscape" that is reminiscent of Plath's poetry (xxii). We see this in Kasischke's "Dinner," which creates an eerie kitchenscape permeated with a "nuclear blue" dusk that "smogs up" from under the door, seeping through cracked walls "like laughing gas" (64). Such painful otherworldliness recalls the smoggy kitchen of "Lesbos," as does Dorothy Barresi's description of a refrigerator "so turquoise it hurts" in her poem "In Waking Words" (10). Inheriting Plath's penchant for mutating household objects, Faith Shearin fashions a kitchen "garbage bag" that "fills like some hungry lung" in her poem "The Sinking" (127). Like Plath's "Cut," Julia Alvarez's "How I Learned to Sweep" brings the violence of history to bear on domesticity; the poem counterpoints images of working a broom and watching television images of soldiers in Vietnam: "I swept all the harder when / I watched a dozen of them die . . . / as if their dust fell through the screen / upon the floor I had just cleaned" (2). Domesticity is not closed off from the outside world, but permeated with it. In "Coming Home," Elizabeth Tibbets extends Plath's figurations of mechanized love by making the couple's Frigidaire function as a third party in their romance: they "pause / in the newness of the refrigerator's light" as the moonlight throws "a sheet on the kitchen floor" (140). And like her predecessor, Tibbets borrows Madison Avenue's script of falling in love with appliances. Elizabeth Alexander and Natasha Sajé provide the anthology's most extensive invocations of Plath. Alexander brings the poet herself into the domicile of "The female seer will burn upon this pyre," where she becomes a mythic figure. Plath rolls the speaker's hair and sets it aflame with her words; she is a stylist and a sorceress. Like her own Lady Lazarus, this Plath proves a tough act to follow with her "flat, American belly," her "stack of typed poems on her desk," and "a freshly baked poppyseed cake" in her kitchen—a perfect blending of household perfections (1). If Alexander makes Plath a domestic amalgam for poetic inspiration, Sajé captures the poet's protean domesticity. Her "Song of the Cook" comes from a knife-wielding kitchen witch who can "excise hearts" and "turn silver spoons into rabbit stew." As the speaker stands on "a pink tiled floor" to wage her latest kitchen war ("snip," "whack," "chop"), her body becomes both manufactured ("my fingers are forks") and natural ("my tongue is a rose"). In the final stanza of ascent (complete with Plath's trademark sound of long *i* assonance), she rises on her "maple broom / into the night sky's steam," joining sky and simmering pot like the culmination to "Ariel" (114). Ultimately, Plath's gift to these inheritors is showing how domesticity can be a rich and pliable source for poetry. She came to see domesticity as a *text* layered in multiple inflections, stunning objects, shifting ambiguities. If Lefebvre and Barthes theorized the poetics of everyday life, Plath brought the everyday into her domestic aesthetic to make poetry a form of cultural analysis.

CHAPTER 5

Killer Lyrics: Ai, Carol Ann Duffy, and the Media Monologue

S ince their respective debut volumes of 1973 and 1985, Ai and Carol Ann Duffy have riveted readers with a dazzling array of characters that seem to have walked off the television screen or front page. Ai's literary lineup includes Hollywood icons such as Marilyn Monroe and James Dean, but she remains best known for her chilling portraits of remorseless batterers, child abusers, and serial killers. If Ai voices the desperations of America's Most Wanted, Duffy voices the disaffections of contemporary Britain. Her gallery of outcasts includes displaced immigrants and disillusioned wives, as well as disturbing psychopaths. Both poets' notoriety comes from their unflinching portraits of violent male characters in monologues hardwired with media discourse. Ai's poems can seem like random acts of lyric mayhem as their speakers wield an arsenal of "knives, axes, blades, or pitchforks," to cite from Carolyn Forché's response to *Killing Floor* (F2). If Duffy's signature characters are edgy, Ai's go over the edge. Although Britain's current poet laureate has not created as many violent characters as Ai, her voicing of a serial rapist-killer introduces "shockingly 'unpoetic' material into poetry," according to Ian Gregson (97). Like Ai, Duffy draws from sensational journalism and crime cases for her most notorious dramatic monologues; Duffy evokes the Yorkshire Ripper, while Ai voices the perpetrators of the Atlanta Child Murders and the JonBenet Ramsey murder.[1] Both poets' most violent characters tend to remain at large, threatening traditional assumptions about women's poetry. Labeled "extreme" by their critics, their monologues operate as killer lyrics.

The multivalence of my key term in this chapter is deliberate. Murderous, difficult, cool, *killer* refers to both the subject matter and the style of the dramatic monologues I discuss here. Most literally, the poems voice characters that kill their victims. Like crime scene photos or graphic films, these poems are hard to take.[2] They are also difficult to account for as women's poetry. In varying degrees, Ai and Duffy create speakers who perform hardened versions of cool masculinity, fashioning their identities through movies, music, and other forms of media. Moreover, their violent utterances violate poetic language. Crossing into presumed masculine territory, the poets present a different kind of outsider by depicting perpetrators who function as media commodities. In short, Ai and Duffy construct a mainstream extreme.

Character Counts

While dramatic monologue allows poets to cross gender, race, and class identities, reception history shows that character counts when critics judge such performances as women's poetry. Ever since Wordsworth wrote "The Complaint of a Forsaken Indian Woman," dramatic monologue has offered poets strategies for voicing characters outside their own social position. Presumably, writing through multiple personae allows women poets to move beyond restrictive expectations of subject matter, style, and voice—including the unwritten rule to articulate a confessional, experiential, and "feminine" self. Dramatic monologue also has the potential to disable "the gendered overmarking of lyric" itself as inherently "emotive, personal, descriptive, nonintellectual," functioning as another means of what Linda Kinnahan has termed "lyric intervention" (*Lyric* 2). Little wonder, then, that so many modern and contemporary women poets have embraced this lyric mode as "a strategy for self-protection" against gender bias, as Glennis Byron notes in her study of dramatic monologue (47). And yet at the same time it remains a fraught space for women poets because, paradoxically, it foregrounds their reception *as* women poets. Readers allow J. Alfred Prufrock to utter a dramatic monologue, but often turn Lady Lazarus's words into a vagina monologue. Voicing male characters would seem to avoid this problem, but interpretive biases within women's poetry studies as well as literary tradition have troubled the reception of women's dramatic monologues. As the field began to emerge, the preference for woman-centered poems led some to claim that women poets "rarely portray convincing male characters" and maintain an authentic poetic voice. Barbara Segnitz and Carol Rainey found such characters "remote and abstract" (19), but Ai's and Duffy's can prove all too present and real.

Dramatic monologue's double standard reaches back much further than second-wave feminism. Ai and Duffy refuse the rules that shape our fundamental understanding of the literary genre and conventional "womanliness." As Alan Sinfield explains in his survey of the genre, the belief in "sympathetic identification" with others as "the foundation of moral sensibility" compelled male Romantic poets to write from the perspective of underprivileged figures such as William Blake's chimney sweeper and little black boy (43–44). If the Romantics established the empathetic imperative by voicing the deprived, Robert Browning and his imitators voiced the depraved. A major influence on modern dramatic monologue, the Browning school preferred outsiders who were "criminals, madmen, and other misfits," as Byron points out, while his female counterparts preferred "prostitutes or fallen women" (65). In other words, women monologuists of the nineteenth century expressed empathy by giving voice to female victims. Through their killer lyrics, Ai and Duffy trouble the gender split that continues to shape their reception: they voice perpetrators rather than victims, and they do not cast clear judgment on their speakers. Nor do they quarantine these depraved, violent figures through stances of parody or critique, troubling our expectations of modern and contemporary women's monologues (although some of the poems do employ forms of irony). Moreover, such poems' media affinity can make them appear "complicit with the commodification of mass murderers and serial killers in our culture," as David Kennedy explains (223). Killer lyrics convey toughness rather than sensitivity. By performing these characters, Ai and Duffy do not act like women poets and thus forfeit the protective space that dramatic monologue would seem to offer.

These contemporary poets shift the genre's standard question of whether they empathize with their violent characters to whether they *should*. Duffy's "Human Interest" and Ai's "Penis Envy" are their least disturbing because these poems conform to at least some expectations of dramatic monologues—and women's poetry. Combining journalistic and literary tropes, they voice jailhouse confessions of men who murdered their betraying lovers. The poets situate the extremity of these actions within the cultural mainstream, writing as insiders well versed in the discourses of popular media. Duffy's poem from her debut volume predisposes us to identify with her perpetrator through its title. A feminized form of journalism, the human interest story conveys experience and emotions in ways designed to elicit sympathy. Like dramatic monologue, it employs direct address, telling details, and colorful speech to compel readers. "Human Interest" presents a character who recounts his feelings and actions in working-class vernacular, projecting a vulnerable toughness with lyric intensity:

> Fifteen years minimum, banged up inside
> for what took thirty seconds to complete.
> She turned away. I stabbed. I felt this heat
> burn through my skull until reason had died.
>
> (*Standing* 36)

Punning on imprisonment and distress ("banged up inside"), Duffy's opening line distills the interplay of heartache and violence that propels this poem. The short, clipped sentences that begin line

3 highlight Duffy's trademark terseness that Kinnahan likens to "soundbites" ("Now I am *Alien*" 208), layering media inflections with poetic lyricism. Like a murderer in a Browning monologue, Duffy's perpetrator is in turn credible and dubious in his attempts to justify the unjustifiable. His vernacular assertion, "I'd slogged my guts out for her," gives a physical credence to his professed love, while his detached report of finding a necklace from "the other bloke" corroborates his claims of betrayal. But his veracity crumbles when the poem emits the palpable jealousy that makes him lose all "reason" and believe that his beloved "stank of deceit."

Duffy discloses her character's crime of passion in a form hardwired for love—the Petrarchan sonnet. Its constricted lines well suit a speaker behind bars and "choke[d] / with grief." But the poet herself is less confined by the sonnet's prison-house, recasting it through media and replaying its cruel lady trope as a provocation to murder. Moreover, Duffy breaks the form's octave-sestet pattern into alternating four- and three-line stanzas to reinforce a lack of closure. The final lines neither resolve the speaker's dilemma nor cast a verdict on his character. In the penultimate line, the speaker's outburst of tenderness ("My baby.") clashes with his pathetic attempt to defend his beloved's character: "She wasn't a tart / or nothing." Duffy reserves the dramatic irony we expect from monologues for her final line, mitigating its punch with a cliché that insists on the murderer's inherent gentleness: "I wouldn't harm a fly, no joke." Duffy has explained that "often the most tragic or joyous moments are expressed in cliché," which raises at least the possibility that her character utters these words in all sincerity (Interview 75). Should we at least empathize with him for his loss and remorse, or condemn him for an inauthentic disavowal of his violence? His mixed feelings and modes of expression complicate our response to his character, as does Duffy's mixture of love poetry, dramatic monologue, and tabloid confession. Ultimately the title's degree of irony proves indeterminate. Nestled between complicity and critique, it evokes media constructions of murderers and other perpetrators of violence as "human interest" figures, acknowledging our daily appetite for their criminal confessions. As with her other killer lyrics, Duffy's refusal to cast a verdict on either her character or the media renders the poem suspect as women's poetry.

Ai's "Penis Envy" draws from television for its media inflections, presenting a cuckold's revenge story in the context of the 1991 Clarence Thomas hearings. It appeared in the volume *Greed* (1993), which replayed other media sensations such as the Rodney King riots and the Mike Tyson-Desiree Washington rape case. This poem voices an anonymous Gulf War veteran who strikes a position between psychotic killer and tawdry talk show guest as he recounts gunning down his wife and her lover with an AK-47. If Duffy's prison monologue portrays her most lyrical perpetrator, Ai's portrays one of her most dislikable. Indeed, we recoil from him at the start: "My wife deserved to be shot" (*Vice* 176). Ai brings us uncomfortably close to this ruthless character not only through direct address ("and I am telling you," "if you ask me"), but also through a straightforward, graphic description of the murders. Catching the adulterous couple unawares, the husband "aimed through the windshield" before moving to "the passenger side" and targeting the man's head: "A red mass / exploded like a sunburst" (*Vice* 176). Ai reserves the poem's only figurative language for describing the rival's death with a rapid-fire metaphor and simile, reinforcing her reputation as "the premiere American poet of gore," as Dana Gioia dubs her. The speaker draws us into her character's twisted thoughts, recalling that he opened the other man's pants to verify his wife's accounts of greater prowess, then considered "how easy it would be / to take two or three more people with me" (177). Sounds from the scene build intensity as the killer's own screams bleed into the approaching sirens. The conversational diction reads like a "sampling from the true crime genre," as Sue Russell writes in her review of the volume (153). This monologue's boastful murderer feels destined "to be a living example for other men, / who are only bluffing when they threaten violence" (177). We find ourselves suspended between repulsion and fascination with such figures, like viewers of daytime television's real people seeking their designated minutes of fame.

While "Penis Envy" puts us close to the action, it also employs distancing devices we do not find in Ai's more seamless—and chilling—performances. The monologue makes heavy use of dramatic irony to add humor to the horror, exposing Freud's most notorious theory as a fantasy between men. Catching his victims mid-tryst in the parking lot of "Hot Dog Heaven," the murderer discovered that his rival's "sad, shriveled" anatomy doesn't measure up to his wife's accounts of "foot-long" ecstasy. His weekly advice column "on relationships" for the prison newsletter defies belief. These ironic moments in the poem reinforce the underlying insecurity that drives the character's boorishness, rendering him as ridiculous as he is dangerous. But when he happens upon a copy of "this Othello play" in the library, the dynamics of Ai's poem become more complex. On the one hand the speaker reduces Shakespeare's tragedy to a tale of parallel lives, reinforcing his unintentional self-parody by calling it the story of "a guy" who loses face as well as his wife's faithfulness: "well, he kills her, but she made him." On the other hand Ai draws attention to the speaker's deeper affiliation with the protagonist by making it the poem's shortest line: "Othello's black" (*Vice* 176–78). It is here that the monologue links the culmination that follows with its central media figure, Clarence Thomas.

The poem's major turn occurs when the speaker identifies with Thomas because he perceives the new Supreme Court justice as a degraded black man with a "dick fixation." Here Ai reactivates the explosiveness of the hearings as a sensationalized event, which then Senate Judiciary Committee Chairman Joe Biden characterized as "the kerosene of sex, the heated flame of race, and the incendiary nature of television lights" (Boot 27). Thomas's former employee Anita Hill was summoned to testify about allegations of sexual harassment, which prompted parental advisory warnings before the broadcasts. Ai's cuckold killer applauds Thomas because he "stands tall" with men "born again from the fire of their ridicule," even if he did not gun down Hill as the unhinged speaker fantasizes he would have done. In the closing lines Thomas's most infamous moment superimposes itself over the speaker's double homicide, shifting his reported words into the dictum that if a humiliated man "finds some pubic hair / in his can of Coke," he "must ask, regardless of the consequences, / who put it there?" (*Vice* 178, 179). Overlaying her character with such a polarizing figure brings America's gender and racial conflicts to bear on dramatic monologue's central dilemma: determining truthfulness.

With their respective poems "Education for Leisure" and "The Kid," which gained them notoriety early in their careers, Duffy and Ai bring violence closer to home with portraits of hardened youth who wreak destruction on their households. In breaking from domestic confinement, each character also breaks through the page to engage readers with unnervingly intimate forms of address, turned loose by the poet to remain at large in our very midst. "Education for Leisure" presents a member of a generation destined for the dole under Thatcher's economic policies. Its first line is Duffy's most shocking: "Today I am going to kill something. Anything" (*Standing* 15). Echoing Gloucester's famous lines from *King Lear* ("As flies to wanton boys are we to th' gods, / They kill us for their sport"),[3] the psychotic speaker decides to "play God" and rub out a housefly, then moves up the food chain:

> I squash a fly against the window with my thumb.
> We did that at school. Shakespeare. It was in
> another language and now the fly is in another language.
> I breathe out talent on the glass to write my name.
>
> (*Standing* 15)

Duffy's sound-bite Shakespeare nestles within the speaker's edgy tirade against "being ignored," bored, and unacknowledged as a "genius." Comparing Elizabethan English to a foreign language reinforces the adolescent's alienation within a school system that deadens him to possibilities. (The *Lear* allusion and the speaker's violence have predisposed critics to assume he is male, a gendering compounded by Duffy's reputation for writing "extreme" poems about male perpetrators.)[4] Twisting the stereotype of youthful optimism, he announces that "today I am going to change the world. / Something's world" (*Standing* 15). He continues his domestic mayhem by flushing the goldfish ("I see that it is good"), wielding his limited power by eliciting fear in the remaining household pets ("The cat avoids me . . . . The budgie is panicking"). We are startled at "the indiscriminate nature" of the speaker's "hatred against the world," Stan Smith writes of the poem—a quality that also gives Ai's "The Kid" and "Hitchhiker" much of their menacing edge (157). Duffy's form reinforces the speaker's instability as paired end rhymes shift position and type across the four-line stanzas, loosening from overlapping exact rhyme in the first quatrain (*today/day*) to slant and off rhyme (*chain/town, half/cat*).

Faced with "nothing left to kill" in the household, the speaker reaches out to fellow humans for the recognition he craves. He telephones the local radio station and claims to be "a superstar." Bristling when the DJ "cuts me off," the speaker retaliates by grabbing the "bread-knife"—an implement that is both dangerous and domesticated. The angry youth exits the home and violates the fourth wall by accosting us in the final line: "The pavements glitter suddenly. I touch your arm" (*Standing* 15). The monologue leaves us wondering what prompts the speaker's disaffection to take this unexpected turn, and how Duffy views her character and his actions. Is psychological or economic instability the primary force in the character coming unhinged? Is his escalating violence a gratuitous means of grabbing readers' attention? How does it relate to the title's social commentary? Although "Education for Leisure" entered culture during the era of Thatcherism, it now intersects with media coverage of more recent concerns about the UK's social safety net: the growing ranks of sixteen- and seventeen-year-old "NEETs" (those neither in employment, education, or training). A teenage girl quoted by the BBC in 2008 revealed that her peer group was "just not doing anything with their lives, just sitting at home doing nothing"—a sign that they will likely remain unemployed over time ("18%"). Duffy's bored youth is hard to fathom because he straddles the boundary between being a representative and extreme figure; indeed, some critics see him as a serial killer in the making.[5] Ironically, "Education for Leisure" appears in two small collections of women's poetry for the British school system, but not in the more comprehensive *Sixty Women Poets* (1993) and *Modern Women Poets* (2005).[6] As if sensing the poem does not fit expectations for women's poetry, Duffy did not include it in her own selections for *Penguin Modern Poets Volume 2: Carol Ann Duffy, Vicki Feaver, Eavan Boland* (1995).

"The Kid," which appeared in Ai's aptly named volume *Killing Floor* (1979), ranks among her most extreme killer lyrics. Like Duffy's young perpetrator, its speaker shocks us not only by his actions, but also by his methodical disregard for dispensing with victims as he breaks more violently from domesticity. With no apparent trigger other than being asked to "help hitch the team," this fourteen-year-old boy murders his family and their horses and then strikes for the open road. The starkness of the monologue's rural setting magnifies the speaker's actions, inflecting the poem with the horrifying American gothic that distinguished much of Ai's early work. Distilling this static environment into an image of going nowhere, she first presents the young teenager circling the family truck and "hitting the flat tires with an iron rod" (36). He begins his bloodbath with his father, positioning us as accomplices to murder as he enacts it through the raw, visceral language of Ai's urgent present:

> I stand beside him, waiting, but he doesn't look up
> and I squeeze the rod, raise it, his skull splits open.
>
> (*Vice* 36)

Jarring us with his sudden springs into action, the boy seems to fast-forward through his first murder as he jumps across the comma separating his raised weapon and resulting gore. He "get[s]" his mother by taking advantage of her nurturing gesture, breaking her back when she attends to her husband. The boy changes weapons to complete the elimination of his family, laughing before he shoots his sister ("the one out back") while she clutches her doll. His detachment is almost as brutal as the rapid-paced murders themselves (*Vice* 36).

"The Kid" lacks the intervention of ironic humor we find in "Penis Envy" as well as an identifiable social issue like the one in "Education for Leisure." Because of the speaker's age, this poem amplifies Claudia Ingram's observation that Ai's characters "disturb by their ambiguity, seeming both innocent and evil" ("Mixed" 572). The boy occasionally veers from violence to vulnerability, most strikingly when he shoots his sister and then rocks her doll. His recollections of children's verse during his rampage reinforce his proximity to childhood; identifying himself as "Jack, Hogarth's son," he asserts he is "nimble" and "quick" like his nursery rhyme counterpart. Ai also gives these popular allusions an eerie irony as she plays with expectations: "Roses are red, violets are blue, / one bullet for the black horse, two for the brown" (*Vice* 36). Her double-edged title plays not only on the character's youth, but also on the mystique of baby-faced American outlaws like Billy the Kid. According to Byron, Ai's poem targets "the romanticisation of violence by the media," an interpretation that fits "The Kid" to the contours of critique, a preferred stance when women's poetry crosses the yellow tape of crime scenes (142). The speaker's desire to obliterate his origins and reemerge as a mythic figure certainly supports this reading. And yet I find that the monologue's culmination also triggers more demanding—and disturbing—responses from its readers. Compellingly, the boy takes his sister's doll, his mother's "satin nightgown," and his father's "best" clothes as he leaves the farm. Ai withholds his age until the closing lines: "I'm fourteen. I'm a wind from nowhere. / I can break your heart" (*Vice* 37); the poem's final image straddles literal and figurative meanings as its speaker forces sudden intimacy upon the reader. As it moves from a broken skull to our own broken hearts, "The Kid" ultimately enacts a harrowing of lyric itself.

Ai's "The Hitchhiker" and Duffy's "Psychopath" voice hardened cases, serial rapist-killers that prowl desert roadways and small town carnivals, respectively. Acting as desperately as their unsuspecting victims (women who mistake calculated charm for romantic overtures), these drifters inhabit poems that are killer lyrics in the fullest sense. They give graphic portrayals of assault and murder through speakers that perform deadly versions of cool masculinity, pulling us into proximities that "make neither easy nor pleasant reading," as Kennedy says of "Psychopath" (227). Mixing the extreme with the mainstream, each monologue inflects its violent utterances with a wide range of popular culture: hard-boiled fiction, Hollywood film, crime reportage, R&B, soul. This poetics of murder, media, and music presents a different style of excess than those featured in women's poetry studies (extravagant form, linguistic experiment, unrestrained protest),[7] so it troubles each poet's reception as a woman poet. While "The Hitchhiker" reinforces accusations that Ai's work as a whole is "obsessed with sex-and-violence" (Interview with Kearney and Cuddihy, 2), "Psychopath" remains Duffy's most notorious poem. The speakers remain at large, but the poems have been critically quarantined because these characters compel some to question the character of the poets themselves. As we shall see, the monologues' media saturation also adds lyric conventions to Ai's and Duffy's body count.

In "The Hitchhiker," from her debut volume *Cruelty,* Ai creates a ruthless version of "on the road" stories that pulls us directly into the murder. She frames its carnal killer with the heat exuding off pavement; the sidewalk where he hunts for women "burns" his shoes, while the "hot, soft asphalt" of his exit street "caresses" his feet. This monologue unfolds with the immediacy and speed of a James M. Cain novel, similarly reducing its protagonist to his most relentless drives as Ai fillets lyric down to its central nervous system. Within a mere fourteen of the poem's twenty-three lines, he accepts a woman's offered ride, signals his offer in exchange, and kills her with a switchblade. His "hands ache" as she "moves closer" to him in the car, but "somehow" he "get[s] the blade into her chest." Jarringly, he recalls the popular song "Everybody Needs Somebody to Love" while the woman dies:

. . . the black numerals 35 roll out of her right eye
inside one small tear.

(Vice 14)

Early in her career Ai stated her admiration for Cain's and Raymond
Chandler's way of "suspending you—of holding your breath while
their characters talk" so that "you don't breathe till they're finished" (Kearney and Cuddihy 5). In the case of "The Hitchhiker,"
the ambiguous word *ache* suspends us between the speaker's sensu-
ality and callousness; it could indicate his urge to kill, embrace, or
both. Clearly he hates women, but might he also hate a desire for
them? Ai often brings an "eerily voluptuous" feel to her depictions
of violence, as David Wojahn observes of her later volume, *Sin* (38).
I find that the language of sex and murder elide in Ai's poems in
ways similar to Cain's. In his signature novel *The Postman Always
Rings Twice* (1934), for example, the femme fatale commands the
drifter narrator to "bite me" and "rip me"—disturbing directives
even within the hard-boiled genre's misogynistic conventions (15).
Ai's speaker replays hard-boiled tropes in characterizing his interactions with his latest victim; he enters the car "grinning at a face I do
not like" and exits when her number is up. His surreal replacement
of the victim's last tear with "the black numerals 35" tallies her age
as well as his body count. Immediately after this climax he laughs
and snaps his fingers: "Rape, murder, I got you / in the sight of my
gun," mixing hard-boiled bravado with the desperado. Charming
and ruthless, he is the iconic American drifter of popular fiction,
Hollywood movies, crime reportage. Ultimately, Ai leaves open the
issue of whether her mimicry of such characters critiques or simply
perpetuates these popular images.

    If the poem's ventures into noir territory dehumanize both
characters, its allusion to a soul standard powers an underlying
emotional grid of loneliness and desperation. "Everybody Needs
Somebody to Love" links the speaker's act of murder with sexual
hunger, especially in Wilson Pickett's delivery of its lyric urgency:
I need you, don't you know I need you? . . . in the mornin', baby . . . in

the evening . . . in the midnight hour.[8] Making physical desire both palpable and painful, the song establishes a discomfiting connection between murderer and victim; Ai asserted that all the characters in her debut volume resort to "violence and sex as a way to express that desperation" attending loss (Kearney and Cuddihy 2). Ai's allusion to the song also serves as the closest the poem comes to revealing her desert drifter's consciousness; he claims to "think" its opening words. As we saw with the allusions to nursery rhymes in "The Kid," Ai's killer lyrics often substitute a popular archive for a psychic one, going against expectations of dramatic monologue by denying us direct clues for the motive behind her characters' actions. Duffy's poem will do both. As a consequence, her readers encounter a dynamic that several critics find even more unsettling than viewing violence at close range: being placed in a position to consider the possibility of empathetic identification.

"Psychopath," the most ambitious of these killer lyrics, also presents the fullest portrait of its speaker—a carnival worker that preys on teenage girls in dreary postwar towns. Hovering between internal and dramatic monologue, his utterance unfolds between scenes in which he views his reflected image through the lens of iconic Hollywood masculinity. Even more so than in "Education for Leisure," the poet puts her edgy signature style on display with her character's sound-bite sentences and punk demeanor. Within its eight-line units, the poem's jagged transitions from the street, the carnival, his childhood, and the bar simulate the jump-cut editing of music videos. Jukebox songs and tabloid celebrities round out the popular inflections of his character, making him an unstable blend of media, murder, and memories. In each key strand of the poem, female figures operate as trigger points for his shifting mood; his engagement with them heightens what Antony Rowland terms a "hysterical masculinity" that reflects and negates mass-produced fantasies of desire ("Love and Masculinity" 207). This murderer "zip[s] up the leather" to assume another performance of James Dean and Marlon Brando (*Selling* 28), and Duffy gets inside his skin to make ours crawl. Well aware of her double risk in simultaneously performing a murderer and media commodity, Duffy told Andrew McAllister that she set this monologue in the 1950s "so that it didn't come over as exploiting something that you would read in the newspapers" (Interview 70). She did not say that journalism was off-limits.

The poem's present tense happens on the carnival's final night, after he has disposed of his latest victim's body in "the dull canal"—a leveling allusion to *The Waste Land* and the Tunnel of Love. Disturbingly, it is through the violation of this first female figure that "Psychopath" most fully embodies its speaker. We first see him as he stops to "pose" his reflection between shop window mannequins and admire it: "Lamp light. Jimmy Dean." Projecting the era's rebel image of cool masculinity to attract his prey (and thus to "love" himself), he claims he can "do it / with my eyes" by imitating Brando. Duffy emphasizes the instability of this performance by jumping to an image of self-erasure: "Some little lady's going to get lucky / tonight. My breath wipes me from the looking-glass." As the monologue continues, the victim reanimates in his memory because he needs her to substantiate his manhood. Alive with the sexualized innocence of the 1950s, she was a "good-looking girl crackling / in four petticoats" that made him "feel like a king" (*Selling* 28).

Duffy paces these fragmented recollections with increasingly frenetic carnival rides and popular music to create an unsettling blend of normative and psychotic gender relations as her speaker slips into the teenager's fantasy of romance: "She rode past me / on a wooden horse, laughing, and the air sang *Johnny, / Remember Me.* I turned the world faster, flash" (*Selling* 28). John Leyton's 1961 hit foreshadows her fate; ironically, it is a sentimental recollection of a dead girlfriend.[9] In the controversial end of the monologue, the speaker utters a modified version of Little Richard's signature line from "Tutti Frutti" (1955)—"Awopbopaloobop alopbimbam"; in this context the song's delirious celebration of lovemaking is downright chilling (*Selling* 29). As Rob Jackaman points out in his study of contemporary poetry, the psychopath's "cool tone" and

Duffy's nonhierarchical arrangement of images make the murder and cultural allusions equivalents, contributing to the poem's "exceptionally unpleasant" nature (102, 103). But its most harrowing moments occur when the speaker recounts his explosion of violence at the young woman's insistence that his flirtations have crossed the postwar double standard of sexual containment:[10] "*No, don't.*" Perceiving this directive as "a right well-knackered outragement," he directs us to "imagine" something we would prefer not to, her final minutes: "One thump did it, then I was on her, / giving her everything I had. Jack the Lad, Ladies' Man." Duffy's serial killer injects more naturalistic descriptions of his assault than Ai's does, noting that his victim "lost a tooth" and was "dead slim" when he hid her body (*Selling* 29). He is ready to resume his fleeting performance of a screen rebel in the next town.

Duffy's psychotic character violates this "clean" girl not only to feel real, but also to repress memories of his sexual humiliations at the hands of "Dirty Alice" and his mother. In his pubescent attempt at seduction, Alice "flicked" his penis from his pants and "jeered"—preferring to use his hand instead. At a younger age he saw his mother with "the Rent Man" when he had returned home for his sandwiches, which "were near her thigh." He recalls running from the scene with the hysteria of Chicken Licken: "The sky slammed down on my school cap." This psychic archive not only adds depth to the psychopath's character, but also links him with his victim through the trope of betrayed innocence. Shortly after alluding to the nursery tale and her refusal to "say Yes" to his physical demands, he declares: "Easier to stay a child, wide-eyed / at the top of the helter-skelter" (*Selling* 28–29). These parallels—as well as our glimpses of the murderer's underlying vulnerability—place us in an uncomfortable position because "we are obliged to give consideration to attitudes which in other circumstances we would find repellant," as Sinfield points out in his survey of dramatic monologue after Browning. The character is ultimately a "frightening and sad creature," as reviewer Vernon Scannell notes. Like readers of "Porphyria's Lover" (and Duffy's

"Human Interest"), we are suspended "between sympathy and judgment" so that the poem is more than a contrast between idealized postwar gender roles and what Jane Thomas rightly terms their "logical and violent extreme" (Sinfield 44, 33, 5; Scannell 36; Thomas 132). Only another psychopath could condone the speaker's violence. And yet his psychological profile forces us to consider childhood experiences that border on mitigating circumstances, so that the monologue operates as "both accusation and exoneration," as Rees-Jones asserts (*Carol Ann* 23). Duffy's killer lyric places her in a double bind because taking no clear position on this character makes her suspect, while conveying empathy would seem downright criminal.

The poem's final section does not resolve these issues; moreover, Duffy throws a wild card into the monologue's mix of female figures. Becoming an image once more, the speaker stares into a bar counter mirror as his reflection "sucks a sour Woodbine and buys me a drink." His imitation of Bogie ("Here's / looking at you") continues the killer's fantasies of Hollywood cool; it also seems to threaten the reader, as Thomas notes (133), like the direct address in "Education for Leisure." Suddenly, he spots "a dead ringer / for Ruth Ellis" across the room. Platinum blonde like the era's bombshells, Ellis was a nightclub hostess who shot her abusive lover outside a pub; in 1955 she became the last woman executed in Britain. This media allusion brings to the text a lethal femininity that contrasts the local victim's innocence; like a noir femme fatale, her heavy lipstick "smears a farewell kiss on the lip of a gin-and-lime." Might she signal a potential threat to the serial rapist-killer, a reminder not only that he could not attract someone like her, but also that some women fight back? The speaker feels a "bang" in his skull that yields "a strange coolness" as the bar begins to close, anticipating the memory loss that will come when he is "elsewhere" tomorrow (*Selling* 29). But he will remain Duffy's most memorable—and riskiest—character. We rarely meet such ruthless speakers in lyric poetry—especially in women's poetry.

How Could She?

The critical conversation surrounding "Psychopath" tends to shift the issue of empathetic identification from the poet's skill to her ethics, reinforcing double standards for dramatic monologue that would restrict subject and stance. In his interview with Duffy, for example, McAllister's insistence that this murderer falls "outside whole barrels of morality" seems to implicate the poet along with her character, multiplying her most extreme speaker into an overpopulation of "rapists and psychotic hardmen" in Duffy's work (Duffy, Interview 70)—a characterization that would be much more fitting for Ai. Gregson and Neil Roberts reach curious moments in their otherwise insightful commentaries: each feels compelled to separate poet from speaker in a cross-gender dramatic monologue. Arguing that the central character is "caricatured" in a double-voiced parody, Gregson reassures readers that "Psychopath" releases them from "the feeling that they and the poet are complicit with the poem's speaker" because of our "sense of the implied author as a didactic feminist" (98–99). In other words, Duffy's status as Britain's most prominent woman poet intervenes to assume the role of judging her character on her behalf. Roberts asserts that the poet "subtly withdraws" from an already distancing title that is hardly subtle—as if attempting to remove even the trace of any guilt by association (38). Such interpretative interference reflects the degree to which *women's poetry* functions as a category through and against which Duffy must operate, even when she goes to extremes (like Ai) by writing killer lyrics that do not overtly judge their violent men.[11] Pushing back against the expectation that she should "write the kind of poetry that tells the reader that I as a feminist think that this guy should have his prick cut off because he was the Yorkshire Ripper," Duffy insisted that "if a male poet had written 'Psychopath' no one would have noticed it" (Interview 70).

While Duffy's killer lyrics prompt some commentators to exonerate her character, Ai's apparently prompt them to validate her gender. Anne Sexton's cover blurb for *Cruelty* states unabashedly that the volume is "all woman" as well as "all human," as

if anticipating readers' doubts that a woman poet would un-
leash such lyrics as "The Hitchhiker," "Recapture," and "Child
Beater."[12] In their respective reviews of *Killing Floor*, Forché and
Randall Albers underscore what they see as the essentially feminine aspect of Ai's poetry. "In counterpoint" to the heavy violence,
Forché notes, "there are images of women lifting their skirts, just
as darkness lifts its own, revealing the feminine, revealing daylight" (F2). Compensating for the volume's "surprising" number
of male speakers, Albers reminds readers that *Cruelty* gave voice
to "woman's pain"—and reflected "the importance of woman as
life-giver" (120). This insistence on the poetry's inherent "womanliness" mitigates the shock of Ai's graphic imagery, fitting it to
a softened version of second-wave feminism. Like Duffy, she has
acknowledged her frustration with readers' narrow views of poems
by women, defending her "serial killer stuff" as one strategy for
overcoming them (Interview with Morín, 9). Duffy notes in an
early interview that, paradoxically, some of these protocols come
from the same anthologies that played such a vital role in challenging traditional views of women's poetry: "For quite a long time . .
. we've been allowed certain areas of subject matter, like children,
what bastards men are . . . all these things that appear in late seven-
ties, early eighties women's anthologies" (Interview 72). Killer lyrics provide both poets with extreme measures for escaping topical
and stylistic constraints, but they also allow each to write in unexpected ways about the traditionally female domain of domesticity,
relationships, and even children.

Women's poetry anthologies have not accommodated these
poems, giving little (if any) space to Ai while embracing Duffy
at their expense. Editors who do include Ai tend to select either
female-voiced monologues or those that clearly distance themselves from their male speakers with irony and critique. In *Early
Ripening: American Women's Poetry Now* (1987), Ai's single poem
("The Prisoner") voices the female victim of an abusive relationship, reinforcing editor Marge Piercy's aim to gather poems "of
our times, our flesh, our troubles"(3). *The Extraordinary Tide: New*

Poetry by American Women (2001) includes an egomaniacal portrait of Branch Davidian leader David Koresh ("Charisma"), but omits any of the close range "deaths by axing, shooting, bludgeoning, strangulation, and *hara-kiri*" that have so arrested the poet's early reviewers—and continue to compel my students (Yenser 566). By contrast, Ai's choices for her volume of selected poems, *Vice* (1999), include all but one of her killer lyrics. Duffy's anthology editors tend to blunt the toughness of a "warrior queen of British verse," as Christina Patterson dubbed her (9). In *Sixty Women Poets* (1993), Linda France presents her as woman-centered, praising the poet's monologues for displaying an "impulse of empathy" she sees as "a traditionally feminine quality" (18). France's selections include two of Duffy's most widely circulating poems—"Standing Female Nude" (which voices an artist's model) and "Warming Her Pearls" (which voices a lady's maid). More recently, Rees-Jones's *Modern Women Poets* (2005) continues the trend of featuring Duffy's female characters while repressing her most violent poems; four of its six selections are monologues with female speakers. As with *Sixty Women Poets* (and the most recent edition of *The Norton Anthology of Literature by Women*), "Warming Her Pearls" serves as the lead poem. Duffy has, in fact, produced fewer killer lyrics as she continues writing, and yet she included "Psychopath" and "Education for Leisure" in her *Selected Poems* (1999). Significantly, "Psychopath" also appears in anthologies that foreground stylistic innovation: Bloodaxe's *The New Poetry* (1993) and *The Oxford Anthology of Modern British and Irish Poetry* (2001). Disturbing as they are, both poets' killer lyrics proved instrumental in honing an edgy style as well and clearing a space for postmodernizing the monologue.

Media Monologues: Women's Poetry Inside/Out

Ai and Duffy reinvent dramatic monologue not only by depicting violence but also by voicing their characters with media-speak: making it new by faking the news and other popular forms of journalism. Such *media monologues* are "traditionally inappropriate both to femininity and to poetry's high language," as Rees-Jones writes of Duffy (20); indeed, each poet's media affinity has raised almost as many eyebrows as her body count. Russell compares the effect of Ai's parade of characters to "watching a TV talk show without a host" (153), while Michael Lewis singles out Ai in his satire on being "a poet-entrepreneur" because she "can grab something off the front page, stuff it in a poem, and still hold her head high" (358).[13] Living in a nation with Poets' Corner and a long-standing laureateship, Duffy does not have to go as far as Ai to cross the literary line; Simon Brittan simply faults her for practicing "journalistic poetics" (qtd. in Michelis and Rowland, 1). More telling is Jackaman's link between "sensationalist language" in "Psychopath" and "language atrocities" in her poem about a headline writer, "Poet for Our Times"; it points to killer lyrics' collateral damage of violating poetry as they depictviolence (103). One could say the same of Ai's poem about a television journalist, "Evidence: From a Reporter's Notebook"—both monologues dissolve their speakers into the media discourse they produce. Fashioning a mainstream extreme, these poems from Ai's and Duffy's mid-careers focus on media constructions of scandal—the stuff that tabloids are made of.

Published in *Fate* (1991), Ai's "Evidence: From a Reporter's Notebook" voices a relentless television reporter ("Maggie") who pursues a "questionable rape" victim as her latest opportunity to beat "the competition" (*Vice* 125). The monologue intersects with the controversial Tawana Brawley case of 1987, in which a jury found false her allegations that six white men (including an assistant district attorney) sexually assaulted her; she had been found in a plastic bag scrawled with racial insults and smeared with dog feces.[14] Ai's speaker presents an insider's account of making a media sensation, reflecting a postmodern privileging of event over experience that renders Ai's title ironic. Like the "trash TV" talk shows that emerged in the wake of *Geraldo*'s debut in 1987, the reporter (and poem) sensationalizes its sordid details to "play off the outrage / and the sympathy of others." Maggie stalks into a hospital to interview her new victim, an underprivileged "protégée" who tells the seasoned reporter to "'write it down or somethin'" that she was racially harassed, beaten, bitten, raped, and smeared "between my legs" with her white attacker's spit. Maggie has learned to "make myself unclench" when she devours such horrifying details, rehashing and "reliving" them so that it is ultimately her own performance that fuels the news cycle of "front-page" and talk show appearances (*Vice* 125, 124).[15] If she could step outside the poem, this character could read Ai's most gut-wrenching poems without wincing. Ai's insertions of Maggie's extended dialogues with the woman (and her attending physician) give this conversational monologue an effect of live-action news-gathering. The characters become further entangled as Maggie "couldn't prove" her new "big winner" was lying, and "couldn't prove she wasn't." As they make the circuit "on Oprah / or on Donahue, facing the packed pews / of the damned and the saved," the reporter must face her "own night of degradation" and "graduation from the shit to shit" (*Vice* 126–128, 124). Along with her cited lyrics from "Brightly Beams Our Father's Mercy," a hymn about rescuing the drowning,[16] this spiritual rhetoric taps what Martin Conboy calls "the meta-narrative of personal redemption" that drives so much popular journalism (13–14).[17] The poem's culmination transforms the alleged spit into "the thick spit" of Maggie's "betrayal" of herself, her latest sensation, and her audience. And yet despite Ai's depictions of her reporter's manipulations, the monologue simulates as much as exposes tabloid media. It also breaks barriers between poetry and popular journalism by shifting briefly to iambic rhythms for its larger theme, the indeterminate nature of truth: "the lens with which we view the truth / is often cracked and filthy with the facts" (*Vice* 127). The lines apply equally to Maggie, Ai herself, and her readers.

If Ai "scours today's news" for scandalous subject matter (Seaman 1028), Duffy's "Poet for Our Times" invents tabloid headlines. Like "Evidence: From a Reporter's Notebook," this media monologue pushes against expectations of critique and parody by bringing sensation journalism to the center of its innovations. Although the poem does not depict physical violence, its dictum to "bang the words down" violates poetic decorum. The headline writer's brashness—"My shout"—is a barbaric yawp aimed at the masses, invoking the tabloid trinity of the British Royal Family, political scandal, and soap operas. Duffy's ungendered speaker holds forth on this "special talent" at a pub, boasting of his or her "punchy haikus featuring the Queen." Each stanza offers examples of this cleverness and verbal dexterity: "TOP MP PANTIE ROMP INCREASES TENSION. / RENT BOY: ROCK STAR PAID ME WELL TO LIE" (*Selected* 70). H. W. Fowler decried "headline language" in his classic *Modern English Usage* (1926), declaring that when it "begin[s] to corrupt literary style" the matter becomes "of public interest, and protest is legitimate" (242). When it enters the traditional iambic pentameter of English poetry, the stakes rise considerably; Jackaman asserts that Duffy's media-speak is "cheapening the poetic discourse" even if her poem "has a certain rough linguistic energy to it" (103–04). But there is nothing "rough" about Duffy's form of six-line stanzas that enliven their even-numbered lines with jaunty limerick rhythms (amphibrachs). The poem's punch line—"The instant tits and bottom line of art"—creates a seamless blend of iambic pentameter and tabloid wit. Most commentators on "Poet for Our Times" assume that Duffy adopts tabloid style strictly for purposes of satire. For example, Kennedy asserts that its "parodies of tabloid press obsessions" call into question a society that "regards such things as newsworthy" (228), while Gregson argues that Duffy "employs a simple direct style to attack simplification" (104). Clearly the poem does interrogate contemporary media, but I find its style more complex than either dualistic conceptions of poetic and media language or one-way models of parody. Recently, the *New York Times* elided poetic and tabloid language by pronouncing "immortal" the *Sun's* headlining of Prince Harry's nightclub scandal, which contains the internal rhyme "Stripper Jiggled . . . Prince Giggled" ("Tabloid"). Duffy's poetry is also known for its trademark sass—her diction often resembles the *Daily Mirror*'s "abrasive, populist political edge" (Conboy 127). She was Britain's de facto "people's laureate" long before assuming the official laureateship. If "Poet for Our Times" parodies tabloids (and it does), it ultimately parodies English poetry by breathing life into it. Duffy's jaunty headlines also introduce a mainstream form of excess into women's poetry: *l'écriture féminine* in bold caps.

The persistence of critical bias against media affiliation seems surprising given the fact that each poet became well established in the 1990s, when critics began to see a new proximity to media as one of contemporary poetry's definitive traits. Marjorie Perloff assessed "poetry in the age of media," cautioning that contemporary American poetry "is by no means . . . just a case of the 'sensitive' poet reacting against the 'vulgarities' of the media" (*Radical* 74). Introducing his concept of "poetry as media," Kennedy claimed that "self and experience are indivisible from the discourses of culture and the media" in British poetry since 1982 (18). And yet despite each critic's considerable contribution to studies of poetry and popular culture, even these accounts of media relations privilege the stances of irony and critique—the same default settings we have seen in conversations surrounding Ai's and Duffy's dramatic monologues. The poems I have discussed here stake a position between integration and interrogation, employing strategies that often prove much closer to pastiche than to parody. Fredric Jameson's key distinction between them in the context of postmodernism proves useful here. He asserts that while pastiche shares with parody "the imitation of a peculiar or unique, idiosyncratic style, the wearing of a linguistic mask," it proves ultimately "a neutral practice of such mimicry"—in part because "the norm itself is eclipsed" into "a neutral and reified media speech" (*Postmodernism* 17). Although both poets' forms of mimicry maintain a degree of satire that Jameson finds lacking in pastiche, they level mediaspeak and poetic language. Displaying the kind of "commodification, ambidexterity, and self-reflexiveness" that Kennedy observes in media-affiliated poetry (217), Ai and Duffy refuse the false dilemma of complicity or critique that drives our conceptions of women's—and contemporary—poetry. Turning women's poetry inside-out, these poets use front-page tactics to assert their position as cultural insiders, going to extremes in claiming the mainstream for their signature styles.

Key Notes: Manifesto for Women's Poetry Studies

Shopping for Images, Reimaging Shoppers

It's a steal. When women poets enter the storehouse of popular images and forms, they reconfigure a major metaphor in feminist criticism and theory: women's writing as an act of theft. We can trace it as early as H.D.'s invocation of the patron god of thieves in "Hermes of the Ways," in which he serves as a muse of innovation. In *Trilogy,* Hermes Trismegistus becomes a thief lord who instructs the speaker to *steal, plunder,* and *take* cultural artifacts to perform poetic alchemy (63). Through a mixture of materials, H.D. could widen the scope of her work—and women's place within it. For Alicia Suskin Ostriker, women poets must *steal the language* of patriarchal literary tradition to emerge from coded pilfering to bold revisionism. They steel themselves for their counter-poetics of appropriation and resistance, paradoxically assuming an inflexible position to render that tradition more pliable in their hands. Hélène Cixous links theft with woman's fundamental act of flight ("stealing away"), drawing on the doubleness of the French verb *voler.* Her manifesto of *l'écriture feminine* counters the master language with a revolutionary "laugh of the Medusa" to reject rather than revise; Cixous steals/flies to "depropriate" (*Feminisms* 356–57). In all three figurations of writing-as-theft, the woman poet operates as an outsider. She raids from a literary culture that excludes her, or she turns her back on it.

In popular parlance, of course, *it's a steal* means something quite different: the storehouse is practically giving it away. Smart shoppers are always on the lookout for such bargains. The poets I have discussed operate in parallel fashion, using freely accessible forms of popular culture to find essential elements for their signature styles. Out in the open, the woman poet finds a steal but commits no theft. To reconfigure a prevailing model is not to deny or reject it. In proposing a more consumer-oriented approach to women's poetry, I am not simply contesting the emphasis on women poets as cultural outsiders. And yet if one is always outside of a shifting canonical or consumer mainstream, she eventually has no place to go.

* * *

Entering his supermarket of images, Allen Ginsberg wandered its wide aisles of "neon fruit" and normative families to present himself as a nonconformist shopper. Covert and overt at once, this figure produces poetic language by sampling produce alongside Walt Whitman. The poets "possess" the latest trend of frozen foods (29). Paradoxically, America's ultimate icon of consumerism—the supermarket—becomes a site of inspiration for its iconic countercultural poet. Ginsberg's "shopping for images" anticipates Michel de Certeau's concept of the tactical consumer, which he figures as a housewife in the supermarket. A shopper who "confronts heterogeneous and mobile data," she looks for bargains (*steals*) to synthesize "their possible combinations with what she already has on hand."[1] In other words, she mixes new products with her ready repertoire of working materials. For de Certeau, the everyday practice of tactical consumption does not yield a "discourse" but rather a decision—"the act and manner in which the opportunity is seized" (xix). And yet he draws on the discourse of poetry to reveal an inherent creativity in consumer choice: through her tactics de Certeau's resourceful consumer "boldly juxtaposes diverse elements in order suddenly to produce a flash shedding a different light on the language of a place and to strike the hearer" (37–38). Thus the art of consumption sounds startlingly akin to the art of making a poem. If Shelley called poets the world's unacknowledged legislators, de Certeau calls consumers "unrecognized producers, poets of their own acts" (xviii). Given this network of literary and popular meanings, wouldn't women poets be the ultimate tactical consumers in modern and contemporary culture?

De Certeau's theory of consumption is ultimately one of resistance, so it can also extend feminist perspectives that view women's writing as a counter-discourse. And yet he describes the tactical consumer as one who "draws unexpected results" by practicing "an art of being in between" (30). Rather than being confined in this social location, she has maneuvering room to shuttle back and forth in her provisioning. There is no unitary mode of consumption, no strict compliance with or contestation of popular culture among women poets. As tactical consumers in the supermarket of images and forms, these poets do not limit themselves to the "correct" purchases or behaviors of either traditional or revisionist expectations. I imagine Stevie Smith peering at perambulators to round out her next sketch, while Plath looks for the mealtime magic of tomato sauce. Brooks considers the social meanings behind a package of Lipton tea. At the checkout stands, H.D. notices the star of the Met's *The Egyptian Helen* on the cover of *Time*,[2] while Ai and Carol Ann Duffy find front-page tactics in tabloid headlines.

Anthology Mythologies: Women's Poetry, Women's Magazines

Women's poetry anthologies are crossover texts that blur traditional boundaries between literary and popular culture. They also complicate traditional claims about marginality through their market viability. As poet and recovering anthology editor Carol Rumens acknowledges, "Let's say it loud and clear: anthologies of poetry by women sell" ("My Leaky" 26).[3] Bridging academic and mass-market publishing, these collections have made increasing use of graphic design and photographic images, yielding hybrid texts that can appear equally at home on a magazine rack or a library shelf.

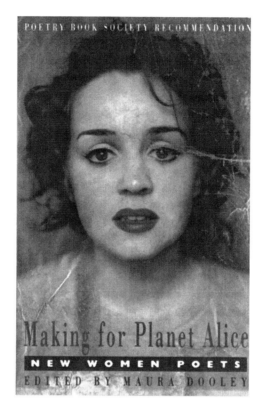

Figure 6.1   Front cover to *Making for Planet Alice* (1997)

For example, note how the striking cover to *Making for Planet Alice: New Women Poets* (1997) makes a literary fashion statement of edgy innocence (see fig. 9.1). Through such glossy incarnations, the women's poetry anthology becomes virtually indistinguishable from "the up-market version of the woman's magazine," Rumens declares, offering a parallel venue for female readers to peer into other women's lives, to confirm their own identities, to find role models ("My Leaky" 26). Presumably, such packaging detracts from the poetry itself, shifting the consumption of women's poetry from signature styles to stylish topics such as beauty, design, and relationships. But hasn't Anglo-American poetry always addressed these things? Although Rumens intends her analogy as a sign of limitation, I see it as a provocative means of expanding our sense of what—and *how*—women's poetry means. Like a rich mix of *Cosmopolitan, Vogue, O,* and *W.,* women's anthologies range across generations, topics, voices, and styles to present a spread of autonomous yet interwoven materials. The cultural proximity of women's anthologies and women's magazines does not reflect a one-directional flow of media into women's poetry. Nor is it only a matter of poets becoming magazine celebrities (as Edna St. Vincent Millay was for *Vanity Fair,* as Julia Alvarez is for *Latina*).[4] Rather, it is a mainstreaming of women's poetry itself through the mass market—a status with important implications for how we read *women's poetry* as a literary and conceptual category.

*   *   *

Does the *women's poetry* brand really render the work of individual poets into a "vaguely fashionable mass" of material ("My Leaky" 26), as Rumens contends? If *fashionable* evokes stereotypes of frivolous femininity, *mass* conjures up the specter of "mass culture[5] as woman" against which modernism articulated its masculinist mystique (Huyssen 44, 55). It was a mythology that either denied women's status as cultural producers or denounced them as producers of indistinguishable (and undistinguished) products. A man's poem might appear in a popular magazine, but a woman's poem disappeared into it. Despite postmodernism's project of calling such hierarchies into question—and the resulting revaluation of women artists and popular culture—responses to women's poetry anthologies can still become mired in the old morass of *mass.* I find the term *ambiguity* more suitable and useful for assessing the women's poetry anthology, a contemporary form that unsettles old gendered hierarchies of individual/mass, high/low, hard/soft. This signifier of difficulty has been a privileged term in modern poetry criticism since William Empson's classic

Seven Types of Ambiguity (1930). A necessary ambiguity also proves central to Henri Lefebvre's "feminine world" of the everyday, a foundational concept in cultural studies extrapolated from *Elle*. It is neither uniform nor predictable, but "a mishmash of the aesthetic, the ethical, and the practical" that reflects no "given feminine 'essence'" (2:81–82). One could say the same of a women's poetry anthology or of *Essence* magazine. Rather than driving a wedge between the signifiers *women* and *poetry, ambiguity* nestles them within overlapping domains of gender, literary history, and everyday life.

* * *

Take another look at the ambiguous *Planet Alice* cover, which might present a metonym for the anthology's contributors, for its readers, or for women's poetry more generally. Its design frames the close-up shot of a young woman between an endorsement from the Poetry Book Society and the highlighted subtitle "New Women Poets," blending the literary clout of the organization co-founded by T. S. Eliot with bold marketing claims of freshness. The cover also accrues a postmodern historical sense by resembling a found photograph, creased and smudged with paint to simulate everyday use. (The anthology is making it new by faking it old.) Of course, the cover's major signifier of newness is the figure of womanhood itself. Her look combines heavy make-up (ultra femininity) with an understated t-shirt (androgyny); her expression blends vulnerability with sass; she wants more and she has had enough. If Rumens saw a "pert, sensual, wounded little face" that projects a "banal" and sexist version of femininity ("My Leaky" 26), one of my male students saw a t-shirted Everywoman that makes women's poetry compelling and inclusive across gender lines—like the anthology itself. (One of the most persistent everyday myths about women's poetry is that it is for women only.) Chicly worn like distressed denim, the image seems to suggest that women's poetry travels comfortably in pocket and pocketbook alike.

Mythic meanings also contribute to the cover's ambiguity by linking it to two realms of popular fantasy. Through the anthology's title, the young woman acquires the aura of Alice in Wonderland, continuing long-standing associations between women's poetry and childhood that have accrued both positive and negative meanings. Through its title, "I am Marilyn Monroe," the cover image acquires conflicted connections to Hollywood glamour and its myths of fatal beauty. The woman in the image simulates Monroe's makeup but does not pull off her performance of a screen siren. Given the fundamental ambiguity of the image, determining what degree of irony (if any) we should assign it would prove difficult, as would determining the anthology's overall stance. Indeed, the cover to *Making for Planet Alice* functions as a conceptual Rorschach test for contemporary femininity and for women's poetry.

*   *   *

Alice is not alone. There are myths about women's poetry anthologies (womanhood-trumps-poethood being foremost), but there are also mythologies that these texts tap, perpetuate, and create. Indeed, a collection would seem incomplete—and to some even dubious—without Eve and Mary, Isis and Nefertiti, Helen and Marilyn. Through the mythic figures that often appear in their titles, women's poetry anthologies lend coherence to their rich ambiguities. *Without Adam: The Femina Anthology of Poetry* (1968) invokes Eve to recover the Maligned Mother, leaving her name unspoken so that she becomes Everywoman. *Psyche: The Feminine Poetic Consciousness* (1973) uses the Greek figure for soul to construct an essential, universal womanhood that anticipates the psychoanalytic approaches of second-wave feminism. If *Psyche* constructs an interior version of the Everywoman myth, *The Muse Strikes Back: A Poetic Response to Men by Women* (1997) renders its Greek goddess as Superwoman. She stands in for the woman poet who revises a gallery of female figures, continuing the myth that most women's poetry injects back talk between the line breaks. More ambiguous is the titular mythic figure of *Woman Who Has Sprouted*

Wings: Poems by Contemporary Latin American Women Poets (1988). Natural and supernatural like Plath's ascending women, she is bird and angel. *Sweeping Beauty: Contemporary Women Poets Do Housework* presents another Superwoman, the Domestic Goddess. Combining Grimm and Disney with the mythic 1950s housewife and Bree Van de Kamp, this ambiguous figure sweeps away one-sided assumptions about women poets and domesticity. She is also Everywoman wielding a broom and vacuum in a creative frenzy of good housekeeping. Everywoman and Superwoman: the twin goddesses of women's poetry and women's magazines.

Assessing the nature of literary and popular mythologies in the mid-1950s, the decade before contemporary women's poetry anthologies entered culture, Roland Barthes asserted that "there is no fixity in mythical concepts: they can come into being, alter, disintegrate, disappear completely" (120). They can also be suppressed. In an era of women laureates and female-majority campuses, the myths that long suppressed women's poetry no longer hold such sway.[6] But the literary and popular myths surrounding women's poetry anthologies are still very much with us, becoming part of the dynamics through which the category of women's poetry constructs, sustains, and renews itself.

Schema: Compass Points

Paradox 1: The central position of the outsider in women's poetry studies eventually reaches a point of impasse.

Paradox 2: Reclaiming the cultural center spreads the field.

Proposition 1: The outsider model of women's poetry yields outlier poets and poems that either subvert the mainstream in some ways but not others, or forego resistance altogether.

Proposition 2: Too many outliers can indicate a problem in measurement.

Question: How can we outflank the problem of the outsider while keeping it in view?

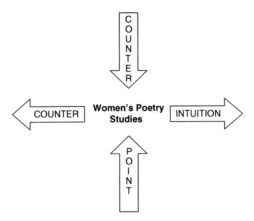

Going Wide: The Image-Text of Women's Poetry Studies

What would a new women's poetry studies look like? We can draw an important clue from Plath. The field's most iconic figure, her work has long been tethered to her life and psyche. "I am vertical," she began one of her later poems, "but I would rather be horizontal" (*Collected* 162). Given the legendary status of Plath's suicide and the poem's images of traversing and "lying down" in a landscape, readers can certainly make a case that it expresses her longing to return to the earth. But what happens when we shift the focus of the *I* from the poet and the meaning of *horizontal* from a prone corporeal body? What if the poem articulates its desire to be reoriented by stretching out its frame of reference? Read self-reflexively, "I Am Vertical" might offer instruction for reading Plath's work through the horizontal method of cultural studies and the "field of action" within each poem itself; William Carlos Williams proposed the latter model as a way "to expand the structure, the basis, the actual making of the poem" (291).[7] Plath's shifting placement of the *I* also suggests a change in orientation. After its initial appearances as the first or second word in a line, *I* begins to gravitate toward the center so that it is flanked on either side by images of the landscape, the sky. If the *I* appears diminished by occupying a panoramic horizontal frame, it also has more space around it, more places to go.

This horizontal perspective does not (indeed, cannot) erase vertical axes of meaning: the timeline of a poet's life and career, the matri-lineal line of women's poetry from Sappho, the line of literary tra-dition from Homer. But verticality does not dominate widescreen images—or widescreen modes of reading. Moreover, going wide is not going outside; it is harder to position women poets as outsiders in an extended scope of cultural meanings.

* * *

What I am calling for is not simply a matter of appending or "apply-ing" cultural studies to women's poetry or vice versa. For if cultural studies has been wary of poetry, it has paradoxically relied on what we commonly call women's culture—and the feminine itself—to generate theories and methodologies. "The women's press" provided Lefebvre with a metonym for everyday life (2:13), Greta Garbo's face captured for Barthes the mythology of Hollywood iconicity, the magazines *Jackie* and *Just Seventeen* anchored Angela McRobbie's analysis of youth culture.[8] Classic modes of cultural analysis often articulate a poetics of popular culture, such as Roland Marchand's iconographies of ad-vertising and Tania Modleski's study of Harlequin romances and soap operas. Such texts, which early advocates of cultural studies deemed the antidote to poetry and its institutional aura, are the same kind of materials I am reclaiming for women's poetry studies. Like poetry stud-ies more generally, this field has tended to assess popular culture in terms of ideology that writers must reject—thus raising the stakes con-siderably for women poets. If Wallace Stevens asserted that "the poem must resist the intelligence / Almost successfully" (250), too many of us still believe that a woman's poem must resist popular culture to be successful. But we have seen that it offers poets aesthetic inspiration as well as an ideological sounding board. As artful consumers, poets open their signature styles to the graphic and the glossy, the screen and the scene. Modern and contemporary women poets take popular culture into their work, and readers must take it into fuller account.

* * *

According to sociologist Pierre Bourdieu, literary fields *refract* (rather than simply reflect) the external "lines of force" that distribute "specific kinds of capital (economic, symbolic, cultural, and so on)" within them (216). In other words, the "social microcosm" of the field—and of the individual texts and figures that comprise it—compresses these wider configurations so that our work as literary critics involves reading through this necessary distortion. Turning this model toward the distillations of poetry, Rachel Blau DuPlessis unpacks the panoramic perspective that Bourdieu's field offers us:

> The use of poetic texts as indices or refractions of social and ideological materials does not necessarily depend on a work's being "occasional," or tied directly to a particular historical or political event, but depends on analyzing the interfaces of cultural materials with their ideological layers and historical allusions as these saturate texts and are specified within them. ("Social Texts")

This horizontal continuum situates the poetic line just as its patterns of rhythm and images do; together, they propel the poem through the process of how it means. As DuPlessis insists, culturally based approaches to poetry cannot flatten form into an ideological mirror; we must adopt "reading strategies to help mediate between what is said *in* poetry and what is said *as* poetry" (*Blue* 122). Despite the tendency to align poems by women with the vertical axis of confession, we must recognize that they are, first and foremost, widely invested productions.

I find the controlled distortions of anamorphic lenses a compelling analogue for rethinking the ways that women's poetry distills popular culture (and other components of its horizontal field). In CinemaScope technology, this "anamorphic squeeze" compresses a wide image onto standard 35-mm film, which is then projected through an adaptor lens to restore the image to its horizontally expanded aspect ratio (Hart). Poets produce similar creative compressions in their texts, and readers can restore the fullness of their cultural scope through widescreen approaches. Of course, poems maintain degrees of legibility even if we do not view them through this mode, but they can never be panoramic unless we do. (Bear in mind that viewing a widescreen film in standard dimensions reduces the image by up to 66 percent, reinforcing the tendency to focus only on the actions and emotions of central characters.) Gender cannot always be the focal point of the critic's gaze in the widescreen perspective of women's poetry studies, but it always occupies some portion of the larger frame.

*　*　*

What types of materials comprise what I am calling the *image-text* of women's poetry studies? For this wide field has become more visually oriented over the past fifteen years. According to W. J. T. Mitchell, "the term 'imagetext' designates composite, synthetic works (or concepts) that combine image and text," while "'image-text,' with a hyphen, designates *relations* of the visual and verbal" (89). Stevie Smith's illustrated poems would fall within the former domain, and all of the other poetry I have discussed within the latter. The image-text of women's poetry studies includes visual forms that inflect poets' individual works and signature styles. Some of these forms come from the traditional visual arts repertoire (drawing, painting, sculpture, photography, film), while others come from the popular arts and media (picture books, family albums, fashion and design, advertising, photojournalism, magazines, television, new media). Ekphrastic poems (and ekphrastic moments within poems) comprise a subset of this category; here the poet creates a verbal depiction/distortion of a real or imagined visual image within her text (such as Adrienne Rich's "Photograph of the Unmade Bed" and Rita Dove's *Museum* poems). Expanding the frame of women's poetry studies further, we must also include autonomous visual productions *by* women poets, (such as H.D.'s contributions to film and drawings, and paintings by Mina Loy, Elizabeth Bishop, and Plath) and corporate collaborations, such as Maya Angelou's line of greeting cards. The field's horizontal scope expands even more when we consider women poets as icons (Gertrude Stein, Edith Sitwell, Millay, Plath) and women poets' media relations (which include their appearances in anthologies, the press, television interviews and programs; Dove's appearance on *Sesame Street* and Angelou's recitation for President Clinton's inauguration are groundbreaking examples). Such horizontal expansions renew the field by recovering contexts that open possibilities for the next generation of women's poetry studies.

* * *

As literary studies become more interdisciplinary within reconfigured humanities departments, even poetry that does not adopt experimental or electronic form enters a discursive spectrum that is more visually and popularly oriented. Rei Terada observes that we now "talk about how lyric is, as it were, made of the same substance as other media and continuous with the fiber of a society" (196); in other words, isolationist approaches to poetry are proving more and more difficult to sustain. By tapping these contemporary literacies in the classroom, teachers of women's poetry can fashion pedagogies that challenge lingering stereotypes. DuPlessis locates two common assumptions that I find among my students: (1) a woman poet is an "angry woman, writing poetry" and (2) women's poetry foregrounds "certain themes of 'difference' involving women's experiences—menarche, menstruation, childbirth, kid life, sexisms experienced, incest" (*Blue* 63, 62). One of my female students distilled the latter as "the heavy, full-breasted category of women's issues," while another noted that some had questioned her decision to study "overly emotional" poems by women. We can dislodge these attitudes by restoring the poetry's intersections with other cultural discourses and by allowing student research to enter the widening field of women's poetry studies.

Because most women's anthologies are crossover texts, they remind us of the poetry's cross-currents with other cultural discourses. They also position women's poetry within a canon that is well established and widely expanding; since the time of *No More*

Masks!, the women's poetry anthology has proven an especially receptive venue for the work of emergent figures. Taking up residence in this canon and field does not mean settling for second-tier status or settling down—just as occupying the mainstream does not mean suspect or second-rate. Women poets still resort to resistance in their tactics, but their work often simulates as much as appropriates popular culture. The poets do not need to steal from this expansive and widely shared repertoire.

But they can steal our attention by confounding our expectations.

Notes

Introduction

1. See the excerpts from *Revolution in Poetic Language* and *Desire in Language* in *The Portable Kristeva*, especially pages 32–39 and 104–07.
2. As Deryn Rees-Jones notes in *Modern Women Poets* (2005), modern and contemporary women poets are often drawn to dramatic monologue, "a genre which highlights women poets' anxieties about their self-presentation and poetic determination" (19). Gill's critical survey also highlights contemporary poets' reworkings of the form, which has renewed prominence with the rise of Carol Ann Duffy.
3. Juhasz drew her title from Adrienne Rich's poem "Blood-Sister."
4. In 1980, Gilbert and Gubar continued to open the field with the special double issue of *Women's Studies* they co-edited, Women Poets.
5. Emily Stipes Watts's earlier *The Poetry of American Women from 1632 to 1945* conveys a similar sense that American women's poetry constitutes "an opening up, an extending" (8).
6. In Lacan's psycho-linguistic theory, subjectivity forms through the key transition from the Imaginary to Symbolic order. See Montefiore 97–112.
7. We see a similar position in Sharon Bryan's cross-Atlantic collection *Where We Stand: Women Poets on Literary Tradition* (1993).
8. See, for example, *A Dangerous Knowing: Four Black Women Poets* (1984), *Naming the Waves: Contemporary Lesbian Poetry* (1989), *Sisters of Caliban: Contemporary Women Poets of the Caribbean*

(1996), *Woman Who Has Sprouted Wings: Poems by Contemporary Latin American Women Poets*, 2nd ed. (1988), and *Yellow Pencils: Contemporary Poetry by New Zealand Women* (1988).

9. In addition to Frost's and Kinnahan's books, critical work in this key signature includes the collections *Feminist Measures: Soundings in Poetry and Theory* (1994), edited by Lynn Keller and Cristanne Miller; and *We Who Love to Be Astonished: Experimental Women's Writing and Performance Poetics* (2002), edited by Laura Hinton and Cynthia Hogue. Stein (joined recently by Mina Loy) replaces Emily Dickinson as the foundational figure for this branch of women's poetry studies, which focuses mostly on American poets. British avant-garde poetry began to receive more attention in portions of Vicki Bertram's edited collection *Kicking Daffodils: Twentieth-Century Women Poets* (1997). Recent work on linguistically experimental women's poetry has begun to question the lyric/experimental opposition. In *American Women Poets in the 21st Century: Where Lyric Meets Language* (2002), Juliana Spahr claims lyric as a site of innovation that "avoids confession, clear speech, or common sense" (2), intersecting with Kinnahan's identification of an "experimental feminist lyric" practice (xiii).

10. Held at Duquesne University, the Lifting Belly High conference was organized by Elisabeth Joyce, Linda Kinnahan, Elizabeth Savage, and Ellen McGrath Smith.

11. The poem is "Käthe Kollwitz."

12. The anthology title comes from Deryn Rees-Jones's poem of the same name, which appears in the collection.

13. For a provocative unpacking of *f*-words in the context of feminism and women's poetry, see parts 2 and 3 of DuPlessis's *Blue Studios*.

14. One finds notable exceptions in anthologies drawn from feminist periodicals, such as *A Fierce Brightness: Twenty-five Years of Women's Poetry* (2002), compiled from *CALYX Journal*, and *Poetry from Sojourner: A Feminist Anthology* (2004).

Chapter 1

1. The film's alternate title is *The Face that Launched 1000 Ships*.

2. Twentieth-Century Fox had ushered in CinemaScope with its 1953 biblical epic, *The Robe*.

3. For a useful discussion of how widescreen photography altered cinematic style, see "CinemaScope: What It Is; How It Works" on Martin B. Hart's website "The American WideScreen Museum." This unattributed article was originally published in *American Cinematographer* (March 1953), and includes shot sketches for *The Robe*.

4. Charlotte Mandel and Anne Friedberg brought to light not only H.D.'s participation in the avant-garde film collective POOL, but also her essays for its affiliate journal *Close Up*. POOL's best-known production, *Borderline*, starred Paul Robeson and featured H.D. This cultural work plays a large factor in critics' focus on avant-garde film. See Mandel's "The Redirected Image: Cinematic Dynamics in the Style of H.D." and Friedberg's "Approaching *Borderline*." Subsequent critics such as Susan Edmunds and Susan McCabe draw on montage in their analysis of H.D. and film; see their respective books *Out of Line* and *Cinematic Modernism*. For discussions of H.D. and popular cinema, see Mandel's "Garbo/Helen: The Self-Projection of Beauty by H.D.," Gallagher's "H.D.'s Distractions: Cinematic Stasis and Lesbian Desire," and Hopewell's "'The Leaven, Regarding the Lump': Gender and Elitism in H.D.'s Writing on the Cinema."

5. Invoking Georg Lukács, Jameson employs the concept of the form-problem to assess the rearticulation of earlier styles in reconfigured social conditions. See *Signatures of the Visible* (133) and *The Geopolitical Aesthetic: Cinema and Space in the World System* (33, 45, 133).

6. For example, the film's intertitles include monument dimensions and citations from Herodotus's account of Babylonian culture.

7. The heroine of *Helena* saves Hector from a lion by raising her arms heavenward, as if she invokes the gods. The extended sleeves of her diaphanous gown give her the appearance of a high priestess. She later rebukes Priam for asking her to do "ungodly things"—anticipating the heroine's rebuke of her ignoble husband in *Helen of Troy*. In the later film, Helen saves Paris from Menelaus's palace guards. Unless otherwise noted, all citations from the films and their promotional materials come from my own viewing notes.

8. Like H.D.'s epic poem, Erskine's novel focuses on Helen's life after the war, containing far more dialogue than action. *The Private Life of Helen of Troy* presents an utterly frank and logical Helen who is well aware of the dilemmas her divine beauty poses to herself and

others. But she disputes her reputation, blaming Menelaus for the war. Surprised that neither the Trojans nor Menelaus killed her, she attributes this "'ethically confused'" behavior to the double standard of peerless beauty: "'They always said I was beautiful, but the only effect I could notice was that they treated me as if I weren't a human being'" (45, 140). She also faults her bumbling husband for succumbing to her legend: "You didn't spare the woman you loved; you preserved me as an object of art!" (264, 147). In short, Erskine's Helen needs no Stesichorus or Euripedes to defend her, as she is more than capable of outwitting anyone she meets. Given the novel's international success and H.D.'s interest in historical fiction, she likely read *The Private Life of Helen of Troy.* The book was reissued in a Popular Library edition in 1952, becoming the original impetus for Warner Brothers' *Helen of Troy* (Pryor, 13).

9. For example, DuPlessis has assessed the ways that *Helen in Egypt* (as well as H.D.'s novels and later poems) mirrors the destructive pattern of thralldom in the poet's own relationships, stressing its capacity to leave "the wounded woman" in its wake ("Romantic Thralldom" 422). Focusing on popular romances such as Harlequins and soap operas, Modleski has critiqued the pattern of "feminine self-betrayal" that emerges from "the mystery of masculine motives," yielding a narrative system in which the heroine's "punishment miraculously turns into reward" (29, 31, 34).

10. For example, one head note links "the protective mother-goddess," Isis, to "her Greek counterpart, Thetis," helping the reader navigate H.D.'s tendency to merge deities from different cultures. Another head note overlays the Amun temple complex with ancient Karnak, Luxor, and Thebes (*HE* 13, 11).

11. Although Helen "is never an isolated character, but always a compound such as Helen-Achilles, or Helen-Paris or Helen-Thetis," as Dianne Chisholm points out (169), H.D. links her most consistently with Achilles—the poem's other half-divine, half-mortal character.

12. Grauman's Egyptian Theatre enshrined the ancient world with a scale and style rivaling even the most elaborate set constructions. Inscribed columns flanked its gigantic screen, with immense hieroglyphic designs forming rows across the top.

13. Achilles becomes enraged when Helen invokes his mother—a scene that anchors the poem's numerous psychoanalytic interpretations.

See especially Friedman (*Psyche Reborn*), DuPlessis ("Romantic Thralldom"), Chisholm, and Edmunds.

14. See *The Voyage In*, eds. Elizabeth Abel, Marianne Hirsch, and Elizabeth Langland.

15. For a good discussion of women, Orientalism, and film, see Ella Shohat's "Gender and Culture of Empire." She notes epic filmmakers' "visual fascination with Babylon's and Egypt's material abundance, emphasized through a mise-en-scène of monumental architecture, domestic detail, and quasi-pornographic feasts" (24). In this aesthetic, scantily clad women function metonymically as an exotic and accessible East.

16. Here Achilles also draws from cinema to make a graphic match between the ideal couple's "sea-eyes."

17. Even this more counterdiscursive component of H.D.'s poem intersects with popular epics. In a television spot for *Helen of Troy*, Warner Brothers presents an anachronistic scene of a modern reporter interviewing a Helen who disputes her legend. Outraged at being misperceived, the regal figure insists that "History lies" about her: "I am only the excuse for war, not the reason. My husband lusts not for his Queen, but for the treasures of Troy" ("Interviewing Helen").

18. My viewing notes.

19. Because Theseus "dogmatically, and one-sidedly, favors 'Greek' rationality," as Jeanne Larsen points out, he is the only major character that never appears in the poem's "ideal realm of 'Egypt'" (96).

20. H.D. misspells the star's name in her poem, although the possibility of a self-reflexive play on *form* is provocative.

21. In *Helen in Egypt* Amen serves as the poem's prime mover, a counterpart to the Amen-Ra figure in *The Walls Do Not Fall*. Here H.D. fuses Amen with the legendary king Proteus who, according to variant classical tradition, guarded Helen in Egypt while her phantom went to Troy *Amun* is now the standard spelling.

22. See pages 59 and 235 of *Helen in Egypt*.

23. H.D. figures the "caravel" that transported Achilles to Egypt in terms suggesting Khufu's solar boat, giving it "a great sun's outline" (*Helen* 22). For a good discussion of Egyptian-inspired films before and after the discovery of Tutankamun's tomb, see Lant.

24. H.D. also invokes the American West when she describes the Avenue of the Sphinxes in her story "Secret Name: Excavator's Egypt," part

of *Palimpsest* (1926). The main character, an American, imagines herself in "some Wild West show" as she rides "across strange fields where buffalo were grazing" (218, 235). H.D. and her compatriot writers and filmmakers used such images to construct an "American Nile," as Mary Ann Eaverly and I have discussed.

Chapter 2

1. Winner of the Queen's Gold Medal for Poetry in 1969, Smith is the only British poet ranked equally with Marianne Moore, Elizabeth Bishop, and Sylvia Plath in Fleur Adcock's *Faber Book of Women's Poetry* (1987). By 1991, Sanford Sternlicht notes, she was "the most widely anthologized modern British female poet" (2). Smith became a generative figure for British women poets who emerged in the late 1960s and early 1970s. Jeni Couzyn's *Bloodaxe Book of Contemporary Women Poets* (1985) starts with Smith, and Linda France's *Sixty Women Poets* (1993) declares a "post-1971" era of women's poetry to honor the year of her death (14).
2. These Smith-as-child-titles come from Arthur C. Rankin and Jessica Walsh. Rankin, Jack Barbera and William McBrien, and Sternlicht all refer to Smith as "Stevie" throughout their books.
3. The phrases come, respectively, from Severin's books *Stevie Smith's Resistant Antics* (1997) and *Poetry Off the Page: Twentieth-Century British Women Poets in Performance* (2004).
4. Nonfiction selections she reviewed included alphabet books, animal guides, and histories.
5. The poem's appearance in her debut volume contributes to this reception.
6. Sylvia Plath, a fan of Smith, would incorporate the same anapestic rhythm in "Daddy."
7. *Shen of the Sea* retells Chinese stories.
8. For a good cultural analysis of family photography in the context of art history and the popular imagination, see the chapter "Snapshot Families" in Anne Higonnet's *Pictures of Innocence: The History and Crisis of Ideal Childhood* (1998).
9. Sometimes Tim boards with an old boatman who forgets him upon departure. Tim's parents never seem to notice that he is away— sometimes for days.

10. Other critics have discussed Smith's interactions with Blake's *Songs of Innocence* and *Songs of Experience,* especially in her poems "Little Boy Lost" and "Little Boy Sick." See especially Catherine Civello's book *Patterns of Ambivalence,* Eleanor Risteen Gordon's essay "Daddy, Mummy and Stevie," Mark Storey's essay "Why Stevie Smith Matters," and Jessica Walsh's essay "Stevie Smith: Girl, Interrupted."

11. The quotation is from Wordsworth's poem "My heart leaps up."

Chapter 3

1. Brooks would not be the focus of an *Ebony* feature article until 1968. In 1971 the magazine published what the poet described as her "seven-page piece of verse journalism," titled "In Montgomery" (*Report* 186).

2. As Norris B. Clark notes, such critics see her style moving from "white" to "colored" to "black," a spectrum in which "white" signifies the craft and ironic detachment of her first two volumes (85).

3. Letters to the Editor, *Ebony,* July 1946, 50; May 1948, 8.

4. Collins generated her figure of the *outsider-within* from studies of black domestic workers in white households. For an excellent discussion of Brooks's *In the Mecca* that draws from Collins, see Kirsten Bartholomew Ortega's recent article in *Journal of Modern Literature.*

5. Letter to the Editor, *Ebony* August 1954, 9.

6. Letter to the Editor, *Ebony,* August 1946, 51.

7. Sandra Gilbert and Susan Gubar add the poem to their third edition of *The Norton Anthology of Literature by Women.*

8. Letter to the Editor, *Ebony,* May 1946, 50.

9. These oxymorons come from the poems "Obituary for a Living Lady" and "The Soft Man," respectively.

10. Letter to the Editor, *Ebony,* May 1948, 9.

11. Letters to the Editor, *Ebony,* May 1946, 50; December 1946, 50.

12. Letters to the Editor, *Ebony,* May 1947, 3; February 1949, 8.

13. In contrast, Kathryne Lindberg's reading of the poem emphasizes the white intruders' presumed masculinity (286–87).

14. Emily Post's updated edition of her *Blue Book of Social Usage* appeared in 1945.

15. Letter to the Editor, *Ebony* July 1946, 50.

16. Schlesinger published *The Vital Center* in 1949, the year of Brooks's *Annie Allen*.

17. Letters to the Editor, *Ebony*, May 1946, 50; May 1953, 10.

18. Surprisingly, Brooks is either absent or marginalized in British anthologies of Anglo-American poetry. She does not appear in Joan Murray Simpson's *Without Adam* (1968), Cora Kaplan's *Salt and Bitter and Good* (1975), or Diana Scott's *Bread and Roses* (1982). Fleur Adcock relegates her to three poems in *The Faber Book of 20th Century Women's Poetry* (1987), while Deryn Rees-Jones allots her but two selections in her more recent *Modern Women Poets* (2005).

19. "The Last Quatrain of the Ballad of Emmett Till" does appear in Gilbert and Gubar's third edition of *The Norton Anthology of Literature by Women* (2007).

20. For example, Jahan Ramazani's revised edition of *The Norton Anthology of Modern and Contemporary Poetry* (2003) includes "The Last Quatrain," while "The Lovers of the Poor" appears in Norton's 1988 edition. Cary Nelson's *Oxford Anthology of Modern American Poetry* (2001) includes "The Ballad of Rudolph Reed," inspired by the housing riots that often ensued when black Chicagoans moved into formerly all-white neighborhoods.

Chapter 4

1. "Sylvia Plath" is a track on Adams's chart-topping album *Gold* (Lost Highway Records, 2002).

2. For a provocative discussion of domesticity, "domestication," and feminist theory, see Rachel Bowlby's essay in *Feminism Beside Itself* (1995).

3. In her anthology *Black Sister* (1981), Erlene Stetson points out that the home has different social meanings in African American women's poetry. Because the house symbolizes "the historic quest by black women for homes of their own"—as well as women's quest "for a whole and complete identity"—domestic poetry in this context signifies "heaven, haven, home, the heart, women's estate, the earthly tenement, the hearth." Home also signifies geographies of the African diaspora (xxii).

4. See, for example, Howe's introduction to *No More Masks!*, the second chapter of Ostriker's book, and Jane Tompkins's "Me and My Shadow" in *Feminisms*.

5. Established male poets who appeared in the *Journal* during the 1950s include Richard Eberhart, Robert Hayden, Randall Jarrell, Galway Kinnell, and Theodore Roethke. While the majority of the magazine's poems tended to be more sentimental than the work of its more literary contributors, poetry was nonetheless a long-standing component of the magazine's discourse of domesticity. See my "Ariel's Kitchen."

6. For an excellent analysis of Tupperware, including its relationship to the modernist aesthetic, see Alison Clarke's cultural history.

7. For an overview of Plath's poetic responses to Klee and other modern painters, see Sherry Lutz Zivley's essay in *College Literature*.

8. Originally titled "On Installing an American Kitchen in Lower Austria," the poem would become Part VIII ("Grub First, Then Ethics") of Auden's sequence *Thanksgiving for a Habitat*.

9. Kristin Ross points out that *Elle*'s cofounder had worked for several magazines in the United States, and thus brought an American look to this exemplar of French women's magazines (79).

10. See my "Plath, Domesticity, and the Art of Advertising and "Ariel's Kitchen."

11. A popular artist whose work combined nature and mythic figures, Bauchant worked as a market gardener. His work was embraced by Parisian modernists in the 1920s, prompting Diaghilev to choose him as set designer for the Ballet Russes's production of Stravinsky's *Apollo*.

12. The volume's most Orientalized figure is the "enigmatical" bride of "Purdah," veiled behind her domicile's silken screens (*Ariel* 62).

13. See the title poem to Raine's *A Martian Sends a Postcard Home* (1979).

Chapter 5

1. See Duffy's "Psychopath," which sets the Yorkshire Ripper in the 1950s, and Ai's poems "The Good Shepherd, Atlanta, 1981" and "Star Witness."

2. Indeed, Steven Cramer claims that Ai wields a poetics "sensationalized into genre-flick dismemberment" (108).

3. The lines appear in Act IV, Scene 1 of *King Lear* (lines 36–37); see Bevington (1200).

4. Stan Smith, for example, states the monologue voices a "boy" (182). Although Jane Thomas acknowledges the poem's gender indeterminacy, she assumes that it constructs a "male subject" (134).

5. Michelis and Antony see Duffy's speaker as "a potential murderer" (9). Smith speculates further that the speaker was "an abused child," a shared trait among many serial killers (157).

6. See Green's and Baxter's school anthologies; Green's selection of Duffy's monologues is the most varied I have seen in any anthology. For the adult-oriented collections of women's poetry, see France's and Rees-Jones's anthologies.

7. For an excellent analysis of excess in women's poetry, see Ford. The introduction mentions Ai's shift from employing excess "as an oppositional strategy" to "a primarily stylistic one," a trend Ford sees in the work of contemporary poets (22).

8. Solomon Burke, the king of rock and soul, co-wrote and first recorded "Everybody Needs Somebody to Love." The Rolling Stones, Wilson Pickett, and the Blues Brothers did famous covers of the song.

9. For more information about the song's continuing resonance in the UK, see <www.johnleyton.com>.

10. I borrow the term *sexual containment* from the fifth chapter of Elaine Tyler May's *Homeward Bound*.

11. O'Brien notes that Duffy's depiction of "mad" characters hinges on this "deliberate detachment" (166).

12. Like "Star Witness," "Child Beater" voices a shockingly abusive mother.

13. The examples of critical responses to Ai's media affiliations are too numerous to cite in the text. Karen Kilcup contends that Ai's poetry "mirrors the paradoxical bloodshed and detachment of the six o'clock news" (11), while Molly McQuade's review of *Vice* finds a "labored literalness" in the monologues' "journalistic rehashing of national figures and events" (X4).

14. For more information about the Brawley case, see the *New York Times* online index.

15. Geraldo's first show featured former model Maria Hansen, victim of a face slashing arranged by a jealous ex-lover.

16. See #148 of *The Methodist Hymnal* (Nashville: The Methodist Publishing House, 1966).

17. For a discussion of Ai's violent poetics in the context of redemption and "regeneration," see Rob Wilson's recent book *Be Always Converting, Be Always Converted: An American Poetics* (Cambridge, MA: Harvard University Press, 2009).

Key Notes

1. De Certeau also employs the other sense of *steal* to theorize consumption: "Everyday life invents itself by *poaching* in countless ways on the property of others" (xii), a mode of tactical consumption he sees as both theft/not theft. See especially "Reading as Poaching" in Part IV of *The Practice of Everyday Life*.

2. The Met staged the American premiere of Richard Strauss and Hugo von Hofmannsthal's *The Egyptian Helen* in 1928. Soprano Maria Jeritza posed for the cover image for the November 12, 1928, issue of *Time*.

3. Rumens edited two women's poetry anthologies: *Making for the Open* (Chatto & Windus, 1985) and *New Women Poets* (Bloodaxe, 1990).

4. *Latina* named Alvarez its Woman of the Year for 2000.

5. As Huyssen explains, *mass* and *popular* have overlapping yet distinct meanings. The former term bears both the modernist meanings he assesses and the mistaken sense that mass culture arises *from* the masses, like traditional forms of popular art or folk culture (47–48). Postmodern inflections of *mass culture* sometimes use it to signal a flow in the other direction, a "culture industry" imposed from above *on* the masses (see Horkheimer and Adorno). Typically, the term *popular culture* places more emphasis on the consumer and constructs a more dialectical relationship between production and consumption.

6. In her introduction to the recent anthology *Women's Work* (2008), Eva Salzman notes that "women comprise two-thirds of the poetry-buying public and a majority of workshop attendees" (10).

7. In his 1948 lecture "The Poem as a Field of Action," William Carlos Williams called for a fundamental shift in poetic structure to better reflect the structural changes in scientific paradigms (Einstein's theory) and nationality (in this case, the American idiom).

8. See McRobbie's *Feminism and Youth Culture: From* Jackie *to* Just Seventeen. London: Macmillan, 1991.

Works Cited

"18% of 16–17s 'doing nothing.'" *BBC News.* July 19, 2008. Web. Nov. 2, 2010.

Abel, Elizabeth, Marianne Hirsch, and Elizabeth Langland, eds. *The Voyage In: Fictions of Female Development.* Hanover, NH: University Press of New England, 1983.

Adams, Ryan. "Sylvia Plath." *Gold.* Nashville: Lost Highway Records, 2002. CD.

Adcock, Fleur, ed. *The Faber Book of 20th Century Women's Poetry.* London: Faber and Faber, 1987.

Ai. Interview by Lawrence Kearney and Michael Cuddihy. *American Poetry Observed: Poets on Their Work.* Ed. Joe David Bellamy. Urbana, IL: University of Illinois Press, 1984. 1–8.

———. Interview by Thomas Q. Morín. *The Writer's Chronicle* 36.3 (Dec. 2003): 4–9.

———. *Vice: New and Selected Poems.* New York: W. W. Norton & Co., 1999.

Aizenberg, Susan, and Erin Belieu, eds. *The Extraordinary Tide: New Poetry by American Women.* New York: Columbia University Press, 2001.

Albers, Randall. Rev. of *Killing Floor,* by Ai. *Chicago Review* 30.2 (Spring 1979): 119–22.

Alexander, Elizabeth. "'The female seer will burn upon this pyre.'" *Sweeping Beauty: Contemporary Women Poets Do Housework.* Ed. Pamela Gemin. Iowa City, IA: University of Iowa Press, 2005. 1.

Alvarez, Julia. "How I Learned to Sweep." *Sweeping Beauty: Contemporary Women Poets Do Housework.* Ed. Pamela Gemin. Iowa City, IA: University of Iowa Press, 2005. 2–3.

"And a Child Shall Lead Them." Editorial. *Ebony* Dec. 1945: 28.

Ardizzone, Edward. "Creation of a Picture Book." *Only Connect: Readings in Children's Literature*. Eds. Sheila Egoff, G. T. Stubbs, and L. F. Ashley. Toronto: Oxford University Press, 1969. 347–56.

———. *Little Tim and the Brave Sea Captain*. 2nd ed. New York: Henry Z. Walck, Inc., 1955.

———. *Tim All Alone*. Rpt. New York, Henry Z. Walck, Inc., 1958.

———, illus. *Mimff-Robinson*. By H. J. Kaeser. Trans. Ruth Michaelis Jena and Arthur Ratcliff. London: Oxford University Press, 1958.

"Are All Whites Prejudiced?" Editorial. *Ebony* Jan. 1953: 72.

"Are White Friends Dangerous?" Editorial. *Ebony* Feb. 1954: 60.

Ariès, Philippe. "From Immodesty to Innocence." *The Children's Culture Reader*. Ed. Henry Jenkins. New York: New York University Press, 1998. 41–57.

Auden, W. H. *Collected Poems*. Ed. Edward Mendelson. New York: Random House, 1976.

Axelrod, Steven Gould. "The Poetry of Sylvia Plath." *The Cambridge Companion to Sylvia Plath*. Ed. Jo Gill. Cambridge: Cambridge University Press, 2006.

Babb, Valerie. *Whiteness Visible: The Meaning of Whiteness in American Literature and Culture*. New York: New York University Press, 1998.

"Backstage." *Ebony* Aug. 1947: 8.

"Backstage." *Ebony* Feb. 1952: 12.

Baird, Julia. "The Wife and Mother Who Baked Poems." *Sydney Morning Herald* Feb. 21, 2004, News and Features sec.: 35. *LexisNexis*. Web. Jan. 20, 2011.

Baker Jr., Houston A. "The Achievement of Gwendolyn Brooks." *A Life Distilled: Gwendolyn Brooks, Her Poetry and Fiction*. Eds. Maria K. Mootry and Gary Smith. Urbana, IL: University of Illinois Press, 1989. 21–29.

Baker's. Advertisement. *Ladies' Home Journal* Apr. 1956: 194.

Barbera, Jack. "The Relevance of Stevie Smith's Drawings." *Journal of Modern Literature* 12.2 (1985): 221–36.

Barbera, Jack, and William McBrien. *Stevie: A Biography of Stevie Smith*. New York: Oxford University Press, 1985.

Barresi, Dorthy. "In Waking Words." *Sweeping Beauty: Contemporary Women Poets Do Housework*. Ed. Pamela Gemin. Iowa City, IA: University of Iowa Press, 2005. 10.

Barthes, Roland. *Mythologies*. Trans. Annette Lavers. 1957. New York: Hill and Wang, 1987.

Baudelaire, Charles. *Intimate Journals*. Trans. Christopher Isherwood. London: Blackamore Press, 1930.

Baxter, Judith. *Four Women Poets*. Cambridge Literature Series. Cambridge: Cambridge University Press, 1995.

Bayley, Sally. "Sylvia Plath and the Costume of Femininity." *Eye Rhymes: Sylvia Plath's Art of the Visual*. Eds. Kathleen Connors and Sally Bayley. Oxford: Oxford University Press, 2007. 183–204.

Bell Telephone. Advertisement. *Ladies' Home Journal* Apr. 1956: 215.

Benjamin, Walter. "A Short History of Photography." 1931. Trans. Phil Patton. *Artforum* Feb. 1977: 46–51.

Bennett, Paula Bernat. *Poets in the Public Sphere: The Emancipatory Project of American Women's Poetry, 1800–1900*. Princeton, NJ: Princeton University Press, 2003.

Bernikow, Louise. *The World Split Open: Four Centuries of Women Poets in England and America, 1552–1950*. New York: Vintage, 1974.

Bertram, Vicki. Introduction. *Kicking Daffodils: Twentieth-Century Women Poets*. Edinburgh: Edinburgh University Press, 1997.

Bevington, David, ed. *The Complete Works of Shakespeare*. 3rd ed. Glenview, IL: Scott, Foresman and Company, 1980.

Blackford, Holly. "Apertures in the House of Fiction: Novel Methods and Child Study, 1870–1910." *Children's Literature Association Quarterly* 32.4 (2007): 368–89.

Blake, William. *Collected Poems*. Ed. W. B. Yeats. New York: Routledge, 2002.

Bluemel, Kristin. "The Dangers of Eccentricity: Stevie Smith's Doodles and Poetry." *Mosaic* 31.3 (1998): 111–32.

Bolden, B. J. *Urban Rage in Bronzeville: Social Commentary in the Poetry of Gwendolyn Brooks, 1945–1960*. Chicago: Third World Press, 1999.

Bon Ami. Advertisement. *Ladies' Home Journal* Oct. 1957: 36–37.

"Book Boom for Negro Authors." *Ebony* Nov. 1945: 24.

Boot, William. "The Clarence Thomas Hearings: Why Everyone—Left, Right, and Center—Found the Press Guilty as Charged." *Columbia Journalism Review* 30.5 (Jan.–Feb. 1992): 25–29.

Bordwell, David, and Kristin Thompson. *Film Art: An Introduction*. 2nd ed. New York: Alfred A. Knopf, 1986.

Bourdieu, Pierre. "Flaubert's Point of View." Trans. Priscilla Parkhurst Ferguson. *Literature and Social Practice*. Eds. Philippe Desan, Priscilla Parkhurst Ferguson, and Wendy Griswold. Chicago: University of Chicago Press, 1989. 211–34.

Bowlby, Rachel. "Domestication." *Feminism Beside Itself*. Eds. Diane Elam and Robyn Wiegman. New York: Routledge, 1995. 71–91.

Brain, Tracy. *The Other Sylvia Plath*. London: Longman, 2001.

Brantlinger, Patrick. *Crusoe's Footprints: Cultural Studies in Britain and America*. New York: Routledge, 1990.

Brooks, Gwendolyn. *Blacks*. Chicago: The David Company, 1987.

———. *Report from Part One*. Detroit, MI: Broadside Press, 1972.

Bryant, Marsha. "Ariel's Kitchen: Plath, *Ladies' Home Journal*, and the Domestic Surreal." *The Unraveling Archive: Essays on Sylvia Plath*. Ed. Anita Helle. Ann Arbor, MI: University of Michigan Press, 2007. 211–35.

Bryant, Marsha, and Mary Ann Eaverly. "Egypto-Modernism: James Henry Breasted, H.D., and the New Past." *Modernism/modernity* 14.3 (Sept. 2007): 435–53.

Burr, Zofia. *Of Women, Poetry, and Power: Strategies of Address in Dickinson, Miles, Brooks, Lorde, and Angelou*. Urbana, IL: University of Illinois Press, 2002.

Byron, Glennis. *Dramatic Monologue*. London: Routledge, 2003.

Cain, James M. *The Postman Always Rings Twice*. New York: Grosset & Dunlap, 1934.

Caloric. Advertisement. *Ladies' Home Journal* May 1952: 191.

Calvert, Karin. "Children in the House: The Material Culture of Early Childhood." *The Children's Culture Reader*. Ed. Henry Jenkins. New York: New York University Press, 1998: 67–80.

"Can the Negro Trust His White Friends?" Editorial. *Ebony* Aug. 1946: 40.

Chisholm, Dianne. *H.D.'s Freudian Poetics: Psychoanalysis in Translation*. Ithaca, NY: Cornell University Press, 1992.

Chun King. Advertisement. *Ladies' Home Journal*. Jan. 1954: 94.

Civello, Catherine A. *Patterns of Ambivalence: The Fiction and Poetry of Stevie Smith*. Columbia, SC: Camden House, 1997.

Cixous, Hélène. "The Laugh of the Medusa." *Feminisms: An Anthology of Literary Theory and Criticism*. Eds. Robyn R. Warhol and Diane Price Herndl. Rev. ed. New Brunswick, NJ: Rutgers University Press, 1997: 347–62.

Clark, Norris B. "Gwendolyn Brooks and a Black Aesthetic." *A Life Distilled: Gwendolyn Brooks, Her Poetry and Fiction.* Eds. Maria K. Mootry and Gary Smith. Urbana, IL: University of Illinois Press, 1989. 81–99.

Clarke, Alison J. *Tupperware: The Promise of Plastic in 1950s America.* Washington, D.C.: Smithsonian Institution Press, 1999.

Collins, Patricia Hill. *Fighting Words: Black Women and the Search for Justice.* Minneapolis, MN: University of Minnesota Press, 1998.

Conboy, Martin. *The Press and Popular Culture.* London: Sage, 2002.

Connor, Rachel Ann. *H.D. and the Image.* Manchester: Manchester University Press, 2004.

Cosgrove, Stuart. "The Zoot Suit and Style Warfare." *Zoot Suits and Second-Hand Dresses: An Anthology of Fashion and Music.* Ed. Angela McRobbie. Boston: Unwin Hyman, 1988. 3–22.

Couzyn, Jeni, ed. *The Bloodaxe Book of Contemporary Women Poets: Eleven British Writers.* Newcastle upon Tyne: Bloodaxe Books, Ltd., 1985.

Coveney, Peter. *Poor Monkey: The Child in Literature.* London: Rockliff, 1957.

Cramer, Steven. Rev. of *Fate,* by Ai. *Poetry* 159 (Nov. 1991): 108.

Davidson, James. *The Greeks and Greek Love: A Bold New Exploration of the Ancient World.* New York: Random House, 2009.

Davis, Gladys Rockmore, as told to Jean Anderson. "I Love to Eat—But I Hate to Cook." *Ladies' Home Journal* Dec. 1958: 64.

de Beauvoir, Simone. *The Second Sex.* Trans. Constance Borde and Sheila Malovaney-Chevallier. New York: Vintage, 2011.

De Certeau, Michel. *The Practice of Everyday Life.* Trans. Steven Rendall. Berkeley, CA: University of California Press, 1984.

De Lauretis, Teresa. *Technologies of Gender: Essays on Theory, Film, and Fiction.* Bloomington, IN: Indiana University Press, 1987.

"Do Do-Gooders Do Good?" Editorial. *Ebony* Mar. 1948: 46.

"Do Negroes Hate Themselves?" Editorial. *Ebony* Mar. 1949: 52.

Dooley, Maura, ed. *Making for Planet Alice: New Women Poets.* Newcastle upon Tyne: Bloodaxe, 1997.

Doreski, C. K. *Writing America Black: Race Rhetoric in the Public Sphere.* Cambridge: Cambridge University Press, 1998.

Dowson, Jane. "'Older Sisters Are Very Sobering Things': Contemporary Women Poets and the Female Affiliation Complex." *Feminist Review* 62 (Summer 1999): 6–20.

Dowson, Jane, and Alice Entwistle. *A History of Twentieth-Century British Women's Poetry.* Cambridge: Cambridge University Press, 2005.

Drake, St. Clair, and Horace R. Cayton. *Black Metropolis.* New York: Harcourt, Brace and Co., 1945.

Drucker, Johanna. *SpecLab: Digital Aesthetics and Projects in Speculative Computing.* Chicago: University of Chicago Press, 2009.

Duffy, Carol Ann. Interview by Andrew McAllister. *Bête Noire* 6 (Winter 1988): 69–77.

———. *Selected Poems.* London: Penguin, 1994.

———. *Selling Manhattan.* London: Anvil, 1987.

———. *Standing Female Nude.* London: Anvil, 1985.

DuPlessis, Rachel Blau. *Blue Studios: Poetry and Its Cultural Work.* Tuscaloosa, AL: University of Alabama Press, 2006.

———. *Genders, Races and Religious Cultures in Modern American Poetry, 1908–1934.* Cambridge, Cambridge University Press, 2001.

———. *H.D.: The Career of That Struggle.* Bloomington, IN: Indiana University Press, 1986.

———. "Romantic Thralldom in H.D." *Signets: Reading H.D.* Eds. Susan Stanford Friedman and Rachel Blau DuPlessis. Madison, WI: University of Wisconsin Press, 1990. 406–29.

———. "Social Texts and Poetic Texts: Poetry and Cultural Studies." *The Oxford Handbook of Modern and Contemporary American Poetry,* ed. Cary Nelson. Oxford: Oxford University Press, Forthcoming.

Edmunds, Susan. *Out of Line: History, Psychoanalysis, and Montage in H.D.'s Long Poems.* Stanford, CA: Stanford University Press, 1994.

"Educating Our White Folks." Editorial. *Ebony* Mar. 1952: 98.

The Egyptian. Dir. Michael Curtiz. 1954. Twentieth-Century Fox. Boying [Hong Kong]. 2005. DVD.

Ellison, Ralph. *Invisible Man.* 1952. New York: Vintage, 1989.

Elna. Advertisement. *Ladies' Home Journal* Apr. 1955: 211.

Erkkila, Betsy. *The Wicked Sisters: Women Poets, Literary History, and Discord.* New York: Oxford University Press, 1992.

Erskine, John. *The Private Life of Helen of Troy.* Indianapolis, IN: Bobbs-Merrill, 1925.

"Etiquette of Race Relations." Editorial. *Ebony* Dec. 1949: 78.

Forché, Carolyn. "Sentenced to Despair." Rev. of *Killing Floor,* by Ai. *Washington Post* Mar. 11, 1979: Book World sec.: F2. *LexisNexis.* Web. Dec. 15, 2007.

Ford, Karen Jackson. *Gender and the Poetics of Excess: Moments of Brocade.* Jackson, MS: University Press of Mississippi, 1997.

———. "The Sonnets of Satin-Legs Brooks." *Contemporary Literature* 48.3 (Fall 2007): 345–73.

Fowler, H. W. *A Dictionary of Modern English Usage.* 2nd ed. Rev. and ed. Sir Ernest Gowers. Oxford: Oxford University Press, 1965.

France, Linda, ed. *Sixty Women Poets.* Newcastle upon Tyne: Bloodaxe Books Ltd., 1993.

Fraser, George MacDonald. *The Hollywood History of the World.* New York: Beech Tree Books, 1988.

Freud, Sigmund. "An Example of Psycho-Analytic Work." *An Outline of Psychoanalysis.* Trans. James Strachey. New York: W. W. Norton & Co., 1989. 63–78.

Friedberg, Anne. "Approaching Borderline." *H.D.: Woman and Poet.* Ed. Michael King. Orono, ME: National Poetry Foundation, 1986. 369–90.

Friedan, Betty. *The Feminine Mystique.* 1963. New York: Dell, 1983.

Friedman, Susan Stanford. "Creating a Women's Mythology: H.D.'s *Helen in Egypt.*" *Signets: Reading H.D.* Eds. Susan Stanford Friedman and Rachel Blau DuPlessis. Madison, WI: University of Wisconsin Press, 1990. 373–404.

———. "Hilda Doolittle (H.D.)." *Dictionary of Literary Biography: American Poets, 1880–45.* Vol. 45. Detroit: Gale Research Press, 1983. 115–49.

———. *Mappings: Feminism and the Cultural Geographies of Encounter.* Princeton, NJ: Princeton University Press, 1998.

———. *Psyche Reborn: The Emergence of H.D.* Bloomington, IN: Indiana University Press, 1981.

Frigidaire. Advertisement. *Ladies' Home Journal* Dec. 1956: n.p.

———. Advertisement. *Ladies' Home Journal* Feb. 1957: n.p.

Frost, Elisabeth A. *The Feminist Avant-Garde in American Poetry.* Iowa City, IA: University of Iowa Press, 2003.

Fry, Roger. "An Essay in Aesthetics." *Modern Art and Modernism: A Critical Anthology.* Eds. Francis Frascina and Charles Harrison. New York: The Open University, 1982. 79–87.

Fussell, Betty. *My Kitchen Wars.* New York: North Point Press, 1999.

Gallagher, Jean. "H.D.'s Distractions: Cinematic Stasis and Lesbian Desire." *Modernism/modernity* 9.3 (Sept. 2002): 407–22.

Gemin, Pamela. Introduction. *Sweeping Beauty: Contemporary Women Poets Do Housework.* Iowa City, IA: University of Iowa Press, 2005. xiii–xxviii.

Gibson. Advertisement. *Good Housekeeping* July 1950: 34.

Gilbert, Sandra M., and Susan Gubar, eds. *The Norton Anthology of Literature by Women.* 1985. New York: W. W. Norton & Co., 2007.

―――. *Shakespeare's Sisters: Feminist Essays on Women Poets.* Bloomington, IN: Indiana University Press, 1979.

Gilbert, Sandra M. Interview. *Voices and Visions: Sylvia Plath.* Dir. Lawrence Pitkethly. New York: Center for Visual History. PBS. 1988.

Gill, Jo. "*The Colossus* and *Crossing the Water.*" *The Cambridge Companion to Sylvia Plath.* Ed. Jo Gill. Cambridge: Cambridge University Press, 2006. 90–106.

―――. *Women's Poetry.* Edinburg: Edinburgh University Press, 2007.

Ginsberg, Allen. *Howl and Other Poems.* San Francisco, CA: City Lights Books, 1956.

Gioia, Dana. "Ai." *The Hand of the Poet.* Rodney Phillips et al. New York: Rizzoli, 1997.

"God's Angry Men." Editorial. *Ebony* Dec. 1957: 66.

"God's Dilemma." Editorial. *Ebony* June 1956: 86.

Gordon, Eleanor Risteen. "Daddy, Mummy and Stevie: The Child-Guise in Stevie Smith's Poetry." *Modern Poetry Studies* 11.3 (1983): 232–44.

Graham, Judith. *Pictures on the Page.* Sheffield: National Association for the Teaching of English, 1990.

Green, Veronica. *The Rhythm of Our Days: An Anthology of Women's Poetry.* Cambridge: Cambridge University Press, 1991.

Greer, Germaine, ed. *101 Poems by 101 Women.* London: Faber and Faber, 2001.

Gregory, Eileen. *H.D. and Hellenism: Classic Lines.* Cambridge: Cambridge University Press, 1997.

Gregson, Ian. *Contemporary Poetry and Postmodernism: Dialogue and Estrangement.* New York: St. Martin's, 1996.

Hadas, Rachel. "Ai." *The Oxford Companion to Twentieth-Century Women's Poetry in English.* Ed. Ian Hamilton. Oxford: Oxford University Press, 1994. 7.

Hall, Linda. *An Anthology of Poetry by Women: Tracing the Tradition.* London: Cassell, 1994.

Hall, Mordaunt. "Helen, the First." Review of *The Private Life of Helen of Troy* (First National movie). *New York Times* Dec. 10, 1927: 14. *ProQuest Historical Newspapers.* Web. Apr. 10, 2007.

Hammer, Langdon. "Plath's Lives: Poetry, Professionalism, and the Culture of the School." *Representations* 75 (Summer 2001): 61–88.

Hart, Martin B. *The American WideScreen Museum.* 1995–2010. Web. Feb. 20, 2011. <www.widescreenmuseum.com>.

H.D. "The Cinema and the Classics II: Restraint." Aug. 1927. *Close Up* 1.2. New York: Arno House, 1971. 110–14.

———. *Collected Poems 1912–1944.* New York: New Directions, 1983.

———. *The Gift.* New York: New Directions, 1982.

———. *Helen in Egypt.* New York: New Directions, 1961.

———. Letter to Bryher. 1934. *Analyzing Freud: Letters of H.D., Bryher, and Their Circle.* Ed. Susan Stanford Friedman. New York: New Directions, 2002. 444.

———. *Palimpsest.* 1926. Carbondale, IL: Southern Illinois University Press, 1968.

———. *Trilogy.* New York: New Directions, 1973.

Hedreen, Guy. "The Cult of Achilles in the Euxine." *Hesperia* 60.3 (July–Sept. 1991): 313–30.

Helen of Troy. Dir. Robert Wise. 1956. Warner Brothers. Warner Home Video, Inc., 2004. DVD.

Helena. Dir. Manfred Noa. Bavaria Film. 1924. Müncher Filmmuseum. Video. n.d.

Helle, Anita. "Reading Plath Photographs: In and Out of the Museum." *The Unraveling Archive: Essays on Sylvia Plath.* Ed. Anita Helle. Ann Arbor, MI: University of Michigan Press, 2007. 182–210.

Heller, Zoë. "Ariel's Appetite." Rev. of *The Unabridged Journals of Sylvia Plath. New Republic* Dec. 19, 2000: 30–33.

Hogue, Cynthia. *Scheming Women: Poetry, Privilege, and the Politics of Subjectivity.* Albany, NY: State University of New York Press, 1995.

Homer. *The Iliad.* Trans. Robert Fagles. New York: Penguin, 1990.

Hopewell, Katherine. "'The Leaven, Regarding the Lump': Gender and Elitism in H.D.'s Writing on the Cinema." *Feminist Media Studies* 5.2 (2005): 163–76.

Horak, Jan-Christopher. "Sauerkraut & Sausages with a Little Goulash: Germans in Hollywood, 1927." *Film History* 17.2/3 (2005): 251–60.

Horkheimer, Max, and Theodor W. Adorno. *Dialectic of Enlightenment.* 1944. New York: Continuum, 2001.

"How to Treat a Negro." Editorial. *Ebony* May 1958: 44.

Howe, Florence, and Ellen Bass, eds. *No More Masks! An Anthology of Poems by Women.* Garden City, NY: Anchor, 1973.

Hughes, Frieda. Forward. *Ariel: The Restored Edition.* Sylvia Plath. New York: HarperCollins, 2004.

Hughes, Gertrude Reif. "Making It *Really* New: Hilda Doolittle, Gwendolyn Brooks, and the Feminist Potential of Modern Poetry." *On Gwendolyn Brooks: Reliant Contemplation.* Ed. Stephen Caldwell Wright. Ann Arbor, MI: University of Michigan Press, 1996. 186–212.

Huk, Romana. *Stevie Smith: Between the Lines.* New York: Palgrave Macmillan, 2005.

Hulse, Michael, David Kennedy, and David Morley, eds. *The New Poetry.* Newcastle upon Tyne: Bloodaxe Books, Ltd., 1993.

Huyssen, Andreas. *After the Great Divide: Modernism, Mass Culture, Postmodernism.* Bloomington, IN: Indiana University Press, 1986.

Ingram, Claudia. "Mixed Ancestry, Writers of." *The Oxford Companion to Women's Writing in the United States.* Eds. Cathy N. Davidson and Linda Wagner-Martin. Oxford: Oxford University Press, 1995. 572.

———. "Writing the Crises: the Deployment of Abjection in Ai's Dramatic Monologues." *Literature Interpretation Theory* 8:2 (1997): 173–91.

International Harvester. Advertisement. *Ladies' Home Journal* July 1951: 167.

"Interviewing Helen." Featurette. *Helen of Troy.* Dir. Robert Wise. 1956. Warner Brothers. Warner Home Video, Inc. 2004. DVD.

Intolerance: Love's Struggle Throughout the Ages. Dir. D. W. Griffith. 1916. Triangle Film Corp. Kino Video, 2002. DVD.

Jackaman, Rob. *Broken English/Breaking English: A Study of Contemporary Poetries in English.* Madison, NJ: Fairleigh Dickinson University Press, 2003.

Jackson, Walter A. "White Liberal Intellectuals, Civil Rights and Gradualism, 1954–60." *The Making of Martin Luther King and the Civil Rights Movement.* Eds. Brian Ward and Tony Badger. London: Macmillan, 1996. 96–114.

James, Henry. *The Turn of the Screw.* Illus. Mariette Lydis. New York: The Heritage Press, 1949.

Jameson, Fredric. *The Geopolitical Aesthetic: Cinema and Space in the World System.* Bloomington, IN: Indiana University Press, 1992.

———. *Postmodernism or, The Cultural Logic of Late Capitalism.* Durham, NC: Duke University Press, 1991.

———. *Signatures of the Visible.* New York: Routledge, 1990.

Jenkins, Henry. "Introduction: Childhood Innocence and Other Modern Myths." *The Children's Culture Reader.* Ed. Henry Jenkins. New York: New York University Press, 1998. 1–37.

Juhasz, Suzanne. *Naked and Fiery Forms: Modern American Poetry by Women, a New Tradition.* New York: Octagon Books, 1976.

Junket. Advertisement. *Ladies' Home Journal* Feb. 1958: 72.

Kaplan, Cora, ed. *Salt and Bitter and Good: Three Centuries of English and American Women Poets.* New York: Paddington Press, Ltd., 1975.

Kasischke, Laura. "Dinner." *Sweeping Beauty: Contemporary Women Poets Do Housework.* Ed. Pamela Gemin. Iowa City, IA: University of Iowa Press, 2005. 64–65.

Kennedy, David. *New Relations: The Refashioning of British Poetry, 1980– 1994.* Bridgend, Wales: Seren, 1996.

Kennedy, Sarah. "Maid." *Sweeping Beauty: Contemporary Women Poets Do Housework.* Ed. Pamela Gemin. Iowa City, IA: University of Iowa Press, 2005. 73.

Kent, George E. *A Life of Gwendolyn Brooks.* Lexington, KY: University Press of Kentucky, 1990.

———. "Aesthetic Values in the Poetry of Gwendolyn Brooks." *A Life Distilled: Gwendolyn Brooks, Her Poetry and Fiction.* Eds. Maria K. Mootry and Gary Smith. Urbana, IL: University of Illinois Press, 1989. 30–46.

Kidd, Kenneth. "Prizing Children's Literature: The Case of Newbery Gold." *Children's Literature* 35.1 (2007): 166–90.

Kilcup, Karen K. "Dialogues of the Self: Toward a Theory of (Re)reading Ai." *Journal of Gender Studies* 7.1 (1988): 5–20.

Kinnahan, Linda. *Lyric Interventions: Feminism, Experimental Poetry, and Contemporary Discourse.* Iowa City, IA: University of Iowa Press, 2004.

———. "'Now I am *Alien*': Immigration and the Discourse of Nation in the Poetry of Carol Ann Duffy." *Contemporary Women's Poetry: Reading/Writing/Practice.* Eds. Alison Mark and Deryn Rees-Jones. London: Macmillan, 2000. 208–25.

Klemin, Diana. *The Art of Art for Children's Books: A Contemporary Survey.* New York: Clarkson N. Potter, Inc., 1966.

Kline, Stephen. "The Making of Children's Culture." *The Children's Culture Reader.* Ed. Henry Jenkins. New York: New York University Press, 1998. 95–109.

Kristeva, Julia. *The Portable Kristeva*. Ed. Kelly Oliver. New York: Columbia University Press, 1997.

Lane, Anthony. "Young Blood." Rev. of *Sylvia,* dir. Christine Jeffs. *The New Yorker* Oct. 20, 2003: 206–07.

Lant, Antonia. "The Curse of the Pharaoh, or How Cinema Contracted Egyptomania." *Visions of the East: Orientalism in Film.* Eds. Matthew Bernstein and Gaylyn Studlar. New Brunswick, NJ: Rutgers University Press, 1997. 69–98.

Larsen, Jeanne. "Myth and Glyph in *Helen in Egypt*." *San Jose Studies* 13.3 (Fall 1987): 88–101.

Laux, Dorianne. "Reetika Arranges My Closet." *Sweeping Beauty: Contemporary Women Poets Do Housework.* Ed. Pamela Gemin. Iowa City, IA: University of Iowa Press, 2005. 84–85.

Lefebvre, Henri. *Critique of Everyday Life, vol. 1.* 1947. Trans. John Moore. London, Verso, 1991.

———. *Critique of Everyday Life, vol. 2: Foundations for a Sociology of the Everyday.* 1961. Trans. John Moore. London: Verso, 2002.

Lewis, Michael. "How to Make a Killing from Poetry: A Six Point Plan of Attack." *Poetry* 186.4 (1986): 358. *LexisNexis*. Web. Aug. 28, 2007.

Lindberg, Kathryne V. "Whose Canon? Gwendolyn Brooks, Founder at the Center of the Margins." *Gendered Modernisms: American Women Poets and Their Readers.* Eds. Margaret Dickie and Thomas Travisano. Philadelphia, PA: University of Pennsylvania Press, 1996. 283–311.

Loizeaux, Elizabeth Bergmann. *Twentieth-Century Poetry and the Visual Arts.* Cambridge: Cambridge University Press, 2008.

Lomax, Louis E. "The White Liberal." *The White Problem in America.* Ed. *Ebony* magazine. Chicago: Johnson Publishing, 1966: 39–46.

Lux. Advertisement. *Ladies' Home Journal* Oct. 1953: 6.

Lysol. Advertisement. *Ebony* Dec. 1950: 83.

———. Advertisement. *Ebony* Apr. 1953: 45.

———. Advertisement. *Ladies' Home Journal* Feb. 1954: 120.

———. Advertisement. *Ladies' Home Journal* Oct. 1956: 157.

———. Advertisement. *Ladies' Home Journal.* Feb. 1957: 143.

Mandel, Charlotte. "Garbo/Helen: The Self-Projection of Beauty by H.D." *Women's Studies* 1–2 (1980): 127–35.

———. "The Redirected Image: Cinematic Dynamics in the Style of H.D." *Literature/Film Quarterly* 11.1 (1983): 36–45.

Marchand, Roland. *Advertising the American Dream: Making Way for Modernity, 1930–1940.* Berkeley, CA: University of California Press, 1985.

Markey, Janice. *A Journey into the Red Eye: The Poetry of Sylvia Plath—A Critique.* London: The Women's Press, Ltd., 1993.

Marling, Karal Ann. *As Seen on TV: The Visual Culture of Everyday Life in the 1950s.* Cambridge, MA: Harvard University Press, 1994.

Marriott, Stuart. "Pictures Books and the Moral Imperative." *What's in the Picture? Responding to Illustrations in Picture Books.* Ed. Janet Evans. London: Paul Chapman Publishing, Ltd., 1998. 1–24.

May, Elaine Tyler. *Homeward Bound: American Families in the Cold War Era.* New York: Basic Books, 1988.

McCabe, Susan. *Cinematic Modernism: Modernist Poetry and Film.* Cambridge: Cambridge University Press, 2005.

McEwen, Christian. *Naming the Waves: Contemporary Lesbian Poetry.* Freedom, CA: The Crossing Press, 1989.

McGinley, Phyllis. "Cooking to Me Is Poetry." *Ladies' Home Journal* Jan. 1960: 66–67.

McQuade, Molly. "Poetry." Rev. of *Vice: New and Selected Poems,* by Ai. *Washington Post* Apr. 25, 1999, Book World sec.: X04. *LexisNexis.* Web. Aug. 28, 2007.

Michelis, Angelica, and Antony Rowland. Introduction. *The Poetry of Carol Ann Duffy: "Choosing tough words."* Manchester: Manchester University Press, 2003.

Middlebrook, Diane Wood. "What Was Confessional Poetry?" *Columbia History of American Poetry.* Eds. Jay Parini and Brett C. Millier. New York: Columbia University Press, 1993. 632–49.

Miller, Douglas T., and Marion Nowak. *The Fifties: The Way We Really Were.* Garden City, NY: Doubleday, 1977.

Mitchell, W. J. T. *Picture Theory: Essays on Verbal and Visual Representation.* Chicago: University of Chicago Press, 1994.

Modleski, Tania. *Loving with a Vengeance: Mass-Produced Fantasies for Women,* 2nd ed. New York: Routledge, 2008.

Montefiore, Jan. *Feminism and Poetry: Language, Experience, Identity in Women's Writing.* Rev. ed. London: Pandora, 2004.

Mootry, Maria K. "'Down the Whirlwind of Good Rage': An Introduction to Gwendolyn Brooks." *A Life Distilled: Gwendolyn Brooks, Her Poetry* and Fiction. Eds. Maria K. Mootry and Gary Smith. Urbana, IL: University of Illinois Press, 1989. 1–17.

———. "'Tell It Slant': Disguise and Discovery as Revisionist Poetic Discourse in *The Bean Eaters*." *A Life Distilled: Gwendolyn Brooks, Her Poetry and Fiction*. Eds. Maria K. Mootry and Gary Smith. Urbana, IL: University of Illinois Press, 1989. 177–92.

Moretti, Franco. *Modern Epic: The World-System from Goethe to García Márquez*. London: Verso, 1996.

Morris, Adalaide. *How to Live/What to Do: H.D.'s Cultural Poetics*. Urbana, IL: University of Illinois Press, 2003.

Morrison, Toni. *Playing in the Dark: Whiteness and the Literary Imagination*. Cambridge, MA: Harvard University Press, 1992.

Moses, Kate. Interview. *Sylvia Plath*. Prod. and dir. Ilana Trachtman. Working Dog Productions. *Biography*. A&E, Dec. 27, 2004.

Mullen, Bill V. *Popular Fronts: Chicago and African-American Cultural Politics, 1935–46*. Urbana, IL: University of Illinois Press, 1999.

Murdock, Cloyte. "Land of the Till Murder." *Ebony* April 1956: 91–96.

Murray. Advertisement. *Ladies' Home Journal* Nov. 1951: 89.

The Muse Strikes Back: A Poetic Response by Women to Men. Eds. Katherine McAlpine and Gail White. Brownsville, OR: Story Line Press, 1997.

"Needed: A Negro Legion of Decency." Editorial. *Ebony* Feb. 1947: 36.

Nelson, Deborah. "Plath, History and Politics." *The Cambridge Companion to Sylvia Plath*. Ed. Jo Gill. Cambridge: Cambridge University Press, 2006.

"No Biz for Show Biz." Editorial. *Ebony* Oct. 1947: 42.

"Nobody Loves Them." Editorial. *Ebony* Sept. 1956: 68.

O'Brien, Sean. *The Deregulated Muse*. Newcastle upon Tyne: Bloodaxe Books, Ltd., 1998.

Ohi, Kevin. *Innocence and Rapture: The Erotic Child in Pater, Wilde, James and Nabokov*. New York: Palgrave Macmillan, 2005.

Omi, Michael and Howard Winant. *Racial Formation in the United States: From the 1960s to the 1990s*. New York: Routledge, 1994.

Ortega, Kirsten Bartholomew. "The Black Flâneuse: Gwendolyn Brooks's *In the Mecca*." *Journal of Modern Literature* 30.4 (2007): 139–55.

Ostriker, Alicia Suskin. *Stealing the Language: The Emergence of Women's Poetry in America*. Boston: Beacon Press, 1986.

Patterson, Christina. "Carol Ann Duffy: Street-Wise Heroines at Home." *Independent* [London] Oct. 2, 1999: Features sec.: 9. *LexisNexis*. Web. Sep. 27, 2007.

"Penny for Their Thoughts." Editorial. *Ebony* Nov. 1957: 56.

Penguin Modern Poets, Volume 2: Carol Ann Duffy, Vicki Feaver, Eavan Boland. London: Penguin, 1995.

Perloff, Marjorie. "Icon of the Fifties." *Parnassus* 12–13 (1985): 282–85.

———. *Radical Artifice: Writing Poetry in the Age of Media*. Chicago: University of Chicago Press, 1991.

Pickett, Wilson. "Everybody Needs Somebody to Love." *The Wicked Pickett*. New York: Atlantic Records, 1966. Record.

Piercy, Marge. *Early Ripening: American Women's Poetry Now*. London: Pandora, 1987.

Plath, Sylvia. *Ariel. The Restored Edition*. New York: HarperCollins, 2004.

———. *The Bell Jar*. 1963. New York: Harper and Row, 1971.

———. *Collected Poems*. Ed. Ted Hughes. 1981. New York: HarperPerennial, 1992.

———. *Letters Home: Correspondence, 1950–1963*. Ed. Aurelia Schober Plath. New York: Harper and Row, 1975.

———. *The Unabridged Journals of Sylvia Plath, 1950-1962*. Ed. Karen V. Kukil. New York: Random House, 2000.

Pryor, Thomas M. "Thomas and Jessel Near Picture Deal." *New York Times* Feb. 4, 1952: 13. *ProQuest Historical Newspapers*. Web. Apr. 10, 2007.

Pumphrey, Martin. "Play, Fantasy, and Strange Laughter: Stevie Smith's Uncomfortable Poetry." *Critical Quarterly* 28.3 (1986): 85–96.

Radway, Janice. "The Readers and Their Romances." *Feminisms: An Anthology of Literary Theory and Criticism*. Eds. Robyn R. Warhol and Diane Price Herndl. Rev. ed. New Brunswick, NJ: Rutgers University Press, 1997: 574–608.

Raine, Craig. *Rich*. London: Faber, 1984.

Rankin, Arthur C. *The Poetry of Stevie Smith: "Little Girl Lost."* Gerrards Cross, Buckinghamshire: Colin Smythe, 1985.

Rees-Jones, Deryn. *Carol Ann Duffy*. Writers and Their Work. Plymouth, UK: Northcote House Publishers, Ltd., 2002.

———. *Consorting with Angels: Essays on Modern Women Poets*. Highgreen: Bloodaxe Books, Ltd., 2005.

———. *Modern Women Poets.* Highgreen: Bloodaxe Books, Ltd., 2005.

Rich, Adrienne. *The Fact of a Doorframe: Poems Selected and New 1950–1984.* New York: W. W. Norton & Co., 1984.

River and Carolina Rice. Advertisement. *Ladies' Home Journal* Mar. 1955: 148.

Roberts, Neil. "Duffy, Eliot, and Impersonality." *The Poetry of Carol Ann Duffy: "Choosing tough words."* Eds. Angelica Michelis and Antony Rowland. Manchester: Manchester University Press, 2003. 33–46.

"Rogues, Riches and Race." Editorial. *Ebony* Oct. 1948: 62.

Rose, Jacqueline. *The Haunting of Sylvia Plath.* Cambridge, MA: Harvard University Press, 1991.

Rosenbaum, Susan B. *Professing Sincerity: Modern Lyric Poetry, Commercial Culture, and the Crisis in Reading.* Charlottesville, VA: University of Virginia Press, 2007.

Ross, Kristin. *Fast Cars, Clean Bodies: Decolonization and the Reordering of French Culture.* Cambridge, MA: MIT Press, 1995.

Rowan, Carl. "What Faubus Did for the Negro." *Ebony* Dec. 1957: 123–26, 128.

Rowland, Antony. "Love and Masculinity in the Poetry of Carol Ann Duffy." *English* 50.198 (2001): 199–218.

Rumens, Carol, ed. *Making for the Open: The Chatto Book of Post-Feminist Poetry 1964–1984.* London: Chatto & Windus, 1985.

———. "My Leaky Coracle." Rev. of *Making for Planet Alice*, ed. Maura Dooley. *Poetry Review* 86.4 (Winter 1996/1997): 26–27.

———, ed. *New Women Poets.* Newcastle upon Tyne: Bloodaxe Books, Ltd., 1990.

Russell, Sue. "Act of Reclamation." Review of *Greed,* by Ai. *Kenyon Review* 17.1 (1995): 150–56.

Sajé, Natasha. "Song of the Cook." *Sweeping Beauty: Contemporary Women Poets Do Housework.* Ed. Pamela Gemin. Iowa City, IA: University of Iowa Press, 2005. 114.

Salzman, Eva, and Amy Wack, eds. *Women's Work: Modern Women Poets Writing in English.* Bridgend, Wales: Seren Books. 2008.

Scannell, Vernon. "Voice-Overs." Rev. of *Selling Manhattan,* by Carol Ann Duffy. *Poetry Review* 77.4 (Winter 1987/88): 36–37.

Scott, Diana. *Bread and Roses: An Anthology of Nineteenth- and Twentieth-Century Poetry by Women Writers.* London: Virago, 1982.

Seaman, Donna. Rev. of *Vice: New and Selected Poems*, by Ai. *Booklist* 95.12 (Feb. 15, 1999): 1028. *Gale.* Web. Feb. 21, 2011.

Segal, Alan F. "*The Ten Commandments*." *Past Imperfect: History According to the Movies*. Ed. Mark C. Carnes. New York: Henry Holt & Co., 1995. 36–38.

Segnitz, Barbara, and Carol Rainey. *Psyche: The Feminine Poetic Consciousness, An Anthology of Modern American Women Poets*. New York: The Dial Press, 1973.

Severin, Laura. *Poetry Off the Page: Twentieth-Century British Women Poets in Performance*. Burlington, VT: Ashgate, 2004.

———. *Stevie Smith's Resistant Antics*. Madison, WI: University of Wisconsin Press, 1997.

Sexton, Anne. *The Complete Poems*. Boston: Houghton Mifflin, 1999.

Shearin, Faith. "The Sinking." *Sweeping Beauty: Contemporary Women Poets Do Housework*. Ed. Pamela Gemin. Iowa City, IA: University of Iowa Press, 2005. 127.

Shohat, Ella. "Gender and Culture of Empire: Toward a Feminist Ethnography of the Cinema." *Visions of the East: Orientalism in Film*. Eds. Matthew Bernstein and Gaylyn Studlar. New Brunswick, NJ: Rutgers University Press, 1997. 19–66.

Silverstein, Louis H. "Herself Delineated: Chronological Highlights of H.D." *Signets: Reading H.D.* Eds. Susan Stanford Friedman and Rachel Blau DuPlessis. Madison, WI: University of Wisconsin Press, 1990. 32–45.

Simpson, Joan Murray, ed. *Without Adam: The Femina Anthology of Poetry*. London: Femina Books, Ltd., 1968.

Sinfield, Alan. *Dramatic Monologue*. London: Methuen, 1977.

Sivulka, Juliann. *Soap, Sex, and Cigarettes: A Cultural History of American Advertising*. Belmont, CA: Wadsworth, 1998.

Smith, Stan. "'What like is it?': Duffy's *Différance*." *The Poetry of Carol Ann Duffy: "Choosing tough words."* Eds. Angelica Michelis and Antony Rowland. Manchester: Manchester University Press, 2003. 143–68.

Smith, Stevie. "Angels and Horrors." Rev. of *Poor Monkey: The Child in Literature*, by Peter Coveney. *Time and Tide* Jan. 11, 1958: 49.

———, ed. *The Batsford Book of Children's Verse*. London: B. T. Batsford, Ltd., 1970.

———. "Book Notes." *Modern Woman* Aug. 1947: 40.

———. "Books for Children." *Modern Woman* Jan. 1947: 73.

———. *Cats in Colour*. London: B. T. Batsford, Ltd., 1959.

———. "Children's Christmas Books." *Modern Woman* Jan. 1945: 81.

———. *Collected Poems*. New York: New Directions, 1983.

———. "Dumb Friends in Fiction." *Observer Weekend Review* Dec. 19, 1965: 23.

———. "Goodness Is Good for You." *The Spectator* Nov. 11, 1960: 750.

———. "Poems in Petticoats." Rev. of *Without Adam: The Femina Anthology of Poetry*. Ed. Joan Murray Simpson. *Me Again: Uncollected Writings of Stevie Smith*. Eds. Jack Barbera and William McBrien. New York: Vintage Books, 1983. 180.

———. "Skating to Ely." *The Spectator* Nov. 28, 1958: 775–76.

———. "World of Practical Girls." *John O'London's Weekly* Nov. 25, 1949: 729.

Sobchack, Vivian. "'Surge and Splendor': A Phenomenology of the Hollywood Historical Epic." *Film Genre Reader II*. Ed. Barry Keith Grant. Austin, TX: University of Texas Press, 1995. 280–307.

Solomon, Jon. *The Ancient World in the Cinema*. Rev. ed. New Haven, CT: Yale University Press, 2001.

Spahr, Juliana. Introduction. *American Women Poets in the 21st Century: Where Lyric Meets Language,* eds. Claudia Rankine and Juliana Spahr. Middletown, CT: Wesleyan University Press, 2002. 1–17.

Spillers, Hortense. "Gwendolyn the Terrible: Propositions on Eleven Poems." *A Life Distilled: Gwendolyn Brooks, Her Poetry and Fiction*. Eds. Maria K. Mootry and Gary Smith. Urbana, IL: University of Illinois Press, 1989. 224–35.

Sternlicht, Sanford, ed. *In Search of Stevie Smith*. Syracuse, NY: Syracuse University Press, 1991.

Stetson, Erlene, ed. *Black Sister: Poetry by Black American Women, 1746–1980*. Bloomington, IN: Indiana University Press, 1981.

Stevens, Wallace. *The Collected Poems of Wallace Stevens*. New York: Vintage Books, 1982.

Steward, Julie Sims. "Pandora's Playbox: Stevie Smith's Drawings and the Construction of Gender." *Journal of Modern Literature* 22.1 (1998): 69–91.

Storey, Mark. "Why Stevie Smith Matters." *Critical Quarterly* 21.2 (1979): 41–55.

Sucaryl. Advertisement. *Ladies' Home Journal* May 1959: 42.

Sully, James. *Studies in Childhood.* New edition. New York: D. Appleton and Co., 1910.

Sylvia. Dir. Christine Jeffs. 2003. Focus Features. Universal Studios: 2004. DVD.

Taber, Gladys. "Poet's Kitchen." *Ladies' Home Journal* Feb. 1949: 56+.

"Tabloid Hack Attack on Royals, and Beyond." *New York Times.* Sept. 5, 2010. Web. Sept. 15, 2010.

Tate, Claudia. "Anger So Flat: Gwendolyn Brooks's *Annie Allen.*" *A Life Distilled: Gwendolyn Brooks, Her Poetry and Fiction.* Eds. Maria K. Mootry and Gary Smith. Urbana, IL: University of Illinois Press, 1989. 140–50.

Taylor, Henry. "Gwendolyn Brooks: An Essential Sanity." *On Gwendolyn Brooks: Reliant Contemplation.* Ed. Stephen Caldwell Wright. Ann Arbor, MI: University of Michigan Press, 1996. 254–75.

The Ten Commandments. Dir. Cecil B. DeMille. 1956. Paramount. Paramount: Special Collector's Edition. 2004. DVD.

Terada, Rei. "After the Critique of Lyric." *PMLA* 123.1 (Jan. 2008): 195–200.

Thaddeus, Janice. "Stevie Smith and the Gleeful Macabre." *In Search of Stevie Smith.* Ed. Sanford Sternlicht. Syracuse, NY: Syracuse University Press, 1991. 84–96.

Thomas, Jane. "'The chant of magic words repeatedly': Gender as Linguistic Art in the Poetry of Carol Ann Duffy." *The Poetry of Carol Ann Duffy: "Choosing tough words."* Eds. Angelica Michelis and Antony Rowland. Manchester: Manchester University Press, 2003. 121–42.

Thompson, Era Bell. "Some of My Best Friends Are White." *The White Problem in America.* Ed. *Ebony* magazine. Chicago: Johnson Publishing, 1966. 153–58.

Tibbets, Elizabeth. *Sweeping Beauty: Contemporary Women Poets Do Housework.* Ed. Pamela Gemin. Iowa City, IA: University of Iowa Press, 2005. 140.

"Time to Stop Crying Wolf." *Ebony* June 1952: 116.

Tompkins, Jane. "Me and My Shadow." 1987. *Feminisms: An Anthology of Literary Theory and Criticism.* Eds. Robyn R. Warhol and Diana Price Herndl. Rev. ed. New Brunswick, NJ: Rutgers University Press, 1997. 1103–16.

Trailer. *Helen of Troy.* Dir. Robert Wise. 1956. Warner Brothers. Warner Home Video, Inc. 2004. DVD.

Tuma, Keith, ed. *Anthology of Modern British and Irish Poetry.* Oxford: Oxford University Press, 2001.

Ulmer, Gregory L. *Internet Invention: From Literacy to Electracy.* New York: Longman, 2003.

Untermeyer, Louis, ed. *Modern American Poetry and Modern British Poetry.* New and enlarged ed. New York: Harcourt, Brace & World, Inc., 1958.

Van Dyne, Susan R. *Revising Life: Sylvia Plath's Ariel Poems.* Chapel Hill, NC: University of North Carolina Press, 1993.

Vanci-Perahim, Marina, ed. *Man Ray.* Trans. Willard Wood. New York: Harry N. Abrams, 1998.

Wagner, Linda Welshimer. "*Helen in Egypt*: A Culmination." *Contemporary Literature* 10.4 (Autumn 1969): 523–36.

Wagner-Martin, Linda. "Plath's *Ladies' Home Journal* Syndrome." *Journal of American Culture* 7 (Spring/Summer 1984): 32–38.

Walker, Cheryl. *Masks Outrageous and Austere: Culture, Psyche, and Persona in Modern Women Poets.* Bloomington, IN: Indiana University Press, 1991.

Walker, Nancy A. *Shaping Our Mothers' World: American Women's Magazines.* Jackson, MS: University Press of Mississippi, 2000.

Walsh, Jessica. "Stevie Smith: Girl, Interrupted." *Papers on Language & Literature* 40.1 (Winter 2004): 57–87.

Watts, Emily Stipes. *The Poetry of American Women from 1632 to 1945.* Austin, TX: University of Texas Press, 1977.

Webster, Harvey Curtis. "Pity the Giants." Review of *The Bean Eaters, Annie Allen,* and *A Street in Bronzeville,* by Gwendolyn Brooks. *On Gwendolyn Brooks: Reliant Contemplation.* Ed. Stephen Caldwell Wright. Ann Arbor, MI: University of Michigan Press, 1996. 19–22.

Wheatley, David. "Closely Glossed." Review of *The Girl Who Married the Reindeer,* by Eiléan Ní Chuilleanáin. *Times Literary Supplement* Sep. 6, 2002: 24.

Wheeler, Lesley. *The Poetics of Enclosure: American Women Poets from Dickinson to Dove.* Knoxville, TN: University of Tennessee Press, 2002.

"Will U.S. Cities Become Negro?" Editorial. *Ebony* Aug. 1952: 90.

Williams, William Carlos. *Selected Essays.* New York: New Directions, 1969.

Williamson, Judith. *Consuming Passions: The Dynamics of Popular Culture*. London: M. Boyars, 1986.

Wilner, Eleanor. Foreword. *The Extraordinary Tide: New Poetry by American Women*. Eds. Susan Aizenberg and Erin Belieu. New York: Columbia University Press, 2001. xxiii–xvi.

Wilson, Dorothy Clarke. *The Prince of Egypt*. Philadelphia: The Westminster Press, 1949.

Winkler, Martin M. *Cinema and Classical Texts: Apollo's New Light*. Cambridge: Cambridge University Press, 2009.

———, ed. Introduction. *Troy: From Homer's* Iliad *to Hollywood Epic*. Malden, MA: Blackwell Publishing, 2007. 1–19.

Wojahn, David. Review of *Sin,* by Ai, *New York Times Book Review* June 8, 1986: 38.

Yeats, W. B. *Selected Poems and Two Plays of William Butler Yeats*. Ed. M. L. Rosenthal. New York: Collier Books, 1966.

Yenser, Stephen. "Recent Poetry: Five Poets." *Yale Review* 68.4 (June 1979): 557–77.

Yorke, Liz. *Impertinent Voices: Subversive Strategies in Contemporary Women's Poetry*. London: Routledge, 1991.

Zivley, Sherry Lutz. "Sylvia Plath's Transformations of Modernist Paintings." *College Literature* 29.3 (2002): 35–56.

Index

Page locators in *italics* indicate figures.

Achilles, 28, 30–41, 42–43, 44–45
Adams, Nick, 117
Adams, Ryan, 121
Adcock, Fleur, 13, 14
advertising
    Bon Ami jet-woman, 144–45, *145*
    and domesticity, 139–40, 141–43
    and femineering, 135, 142
    Lysol, 128–30
aesthetics, 15, 53
African Americans
    black press, 87–88
    and liberalism, 86–87
    and Little Rock Nine, 113–16
    stereotypes of, 88, 99–100
    and white liberals, 85–87, 100–103,
        104–7, 112–17
    and zoot suits, 92–94
Agamemnon, 38, 39
Ai
    array of characters, 149–50
    "Evidence," 169–70
    "Hitchhiker," 157, 159–62
    "The Kid," 156, 157, 158–59
    mainstream recognition of, 16
    and media monologues, 168–73
    "Penis Envy," 152, 154–56
    "Recapture," 167
    reviews of *Cruelty*, 166–67
    signature style, 19–20, 173

Aizenberg, Susan, 15
Albers, Randall, 167
Aldington, Richard, 32
Alexander, Elizabeth, 148
Alice stories, 53, 181
Alvarez, Julia, 147–48, 179
ambiguity and women's poetry
    anthologies, 179–81
Amen (Amun) temple, 33, 36, 42–43,
    45, 46, 193*n*21
Anderson, Marian, 108
Angelou, Maya, 186, 187
anthologies
    domestic label, 121–25
    editors and women's poetry label, 11,
        14–16
    mass market popularity, 177–79,
        178
    and mythic figures, 181–82
    poetry of Ai and Carol Ann Duffy,
        167–68
    topical arrangement of, 9
    in the United Kingdom, 12–14
    in the United States, 11–16
appliances as mechanical spouses,
    139–43
Ardizzone, Edward, 18, 64–68, *67*
Asian inscrutability trope, 57, *58*, 59
Auden, W. H., 128, 132–33
Axelrod, Steven Gould, 127

Babb, Valerie, 98
Baker, Houston A., 84
Barbera, Jack, 56, 68
Barresi, Dorothy, 147
Barthes, Roland, 19, 124, 128–30, 143, 182, 184
Bass, Ellen, 12
Batsford Colour Books series, 64
Baudelaire, Charles, 52, 74
Baxter, Anne, 35
Bayley, Sally, 123
de Beauvoir, Simone, 146
Belieu, Erin, 15
Benjamin, Walter, 62
Bennett, Paula Bernat, 8
Bernikow, Louise, 2, 12, 14
Bertram, Vicki, 13
Biden, Joe, 155
Bishop, Elizabeth, 13, 186
Black Arts Movement, 8, 118
Black Boy (Wright), 87
black masculinity, 92–94
Black Metropolis (Drake and Cayton, eds.), 87, 92
Black press, 87–88
Black Sister (Stetson, ed.), 13, 118, 196n3
Blackford, Holly, 52–53
Blake, William, 53, 60, 66, 70, 71, 72, 73, 79, 151
The Bloodaxe Book of Contemporary Women Poets (Couzyn, ed.), 13–14, 122, 123
Blue Book (Post), 107–8
Bluemel, Kristin, 61, 70
Bolden, B. J., 90, 97
Bon Ami jet-woman, 144–45, 145
Bontemps, Arna, 87
The Borrowers (Norton), 54
Bourdieu, Pierre, 185
Bowlby, Rachel, 127
Bradstreet, Anne, 12
Brain, Tracy, 122
Brando, Marlon, 162, 163
Brantlinger, Patrick, 4

Brawley, Tawana, 169
Bread and Roses (Scott, ed.), 14
Brittan, Simon, 169
Brooks, Gwendolyn
    Annie Allen, 98–107
    The Bean Eaters, 107, 114
    "Beverly Hills, Chicago," 98, 102–3
    "A Bronzeville Mother Loiters in Mississippi. Meanwhile, A Mississippi Mother Burns Bacon," 110–12, 117–18
    "The Chicago Defender Sends a Man to Little Rock," 114–16
    cross-racial audience, 84, 88–92, 96–98, 117–19
    as cultural outsider, 84–86
    and Ebony magazine, 83–87
    "I love those little booths at Benvenuti's," 98–102
    "The Last Quatrain of the Ballad of Emmett Till," 112
    "The Lovers of the Poor," 107
    mainstream recognition, 16, 196n18
    Maud Martha, 84
    "Men of careful turns, haters of forks in the road," 103–7
    "The Mother," 117
    relations with white liberals, 85–87, 96–97, 100–103, 104–7, 112–17
    A Street in Bronzeville, 83, 87
    "The Sundays of Satin-Legs Smith," 88–92, 95–97
    use of oxymorons, 90–91, 107
    use of parody and mock grandeur, 89–90
Browning, Robert, 151, 153, 164
Bryant, Carolyn, 110
Bryant, Roy, 110
Budge, E. A. W., 35
Burr, Zofia, 85, 87, 118
Byron, Glennis, 151, 159

Cain, James M., 160–61
Calloway, Cab, 92

Calvert, Karin, 78–79
Carroll, Lewis, 53, 54
Carter, Hodding, 112
Cayton, Horace R., 87, 92, 94, 96
Century of the Child, 17, 54
de Certeau, Michel, 103, 176–77
Chandler, Raymond, 161
Chavez, Cesar, 92
Chicago's South Side (Bronzeville), 83,
    87, 90–92, 96, 99, 101–2, 107
Child Study Movement, 52–53, 75–79
children's culture and childhood
    and modernism, 52–54
    multiple meanings of childhood, 51
    mythology of Western child, 70–72
    and Stevie Smith, 51–54
Children's Ways (Sully), 52
A Child's Christmas in Wales (Thomas),
    65
de Chirico, Giorgio, 127
Chronicles of Narnia (Lewis), 54
cinema
    cineliteracy of H.D., 23
    depictions of Egypt, 33, 45–46,
        48–49
    depictions of Homeric kings, 39
    feminization of epic form, 33–35, 39
CinemaScope
    and Egyptomania, 33, 45–46
    and Helen in Egypt, 37–38, 48–49
    panoramic views and grandiose sets
        of, 22
    and women's poetry studies, 185–86
civil rights movement, 86, 97, 112–17
Cixous, Hélène, 7, 175
Cleopatra (film), 27
Close Up (journal), 25, 32
Clytemnestra, 38
Colbert, Claudette, 35
Cold War geopolitics, 47–48
Collins, Patricia Hill, 85
Conboy, Martin, 170
confession as key signature, 3, 150
Connor, Rachel Ann, 23

consumerism, 176–77
cooking, 133–35
cosmic love, 32, 41, 43
Couzyn, Jeni, 13–14, 123
Coveney, Peter, 54, 70–72, 75, 76, 77,
    78
critique as key signature, 3
cultural studies
    and literary analysis of poetry, 3–5
    mythology of Western child, 71–72
    women as cultural insiders, 1–2,
        4–5, 182–86, 183

Darclea, Edy, 26, 26
Darwin, Charles, 55
Davidson, James, 32
Dean, James, 149, 162
Deen, Paula, 147
Demeter, 43
DeMille, Cecil B., 23, 24, 26, 27, 46
developmental psychology, 54–55, 57,
    59–61
devouring mother figure, 69–70, 69
dialogue balloons, 66–67, 67
Dickens, Charles, 53, 71, 72, 107
direct address modes, 86, 152, 154
domesticity
    and advertising, 139–40, 141–43
    and cooking, 133–35
    domestic label and WP studies,
        121–25
    jet-woman and transcendence,
        143–48, 145
    and Plath's signature style, 10, 130,
        143, 146–48
    and Smith's illustrations of women,
        68, 69
    and supernatural entities, 132–33
    and women's magazines, 131–32
Dooley, Maura, 11, 14, 122–23
Doreski, C. K., 86–87, 107
Dove, Rita, 186, 187
Dowson, Jane, 6, 16
Drake, St. Clair, 87, 92, 94, 96

dramatic monologue
   gendered double standard of, 19–20
   and judgment of women's poetry,
     150–52
   and killer lyrics, 149–50
   reinvention as "media monologues,"
     168–73
   reworking of, 189n2
Drucker, Johanna, 64
Duffy, Carol Ann
   on anthologies, 167
   array of characters, 149–50
   and consumerism, 177
   "Education for Leisure," 156–58, 168
   "Human Interest," 152–54
   mainstream recognition of, 16
   and media monologues, 168–73
   "Poet for Our Times," 169, 170–72
   "Psychopath," 19–20, 159–60,
     162–66, 168, 169
   signature style, 19–20, 152–53, 173
   "Standing Female Nude," 168
   Standing Female Nude, 15
   tabloid journalism and diction style,
     1, 170–73
   "Warming Her Pearls," 168
DuPlessis, Rachel Blau, 3, 9–10, 21, 29,
   185, 187

Early Ripening (Piercy, ed.), 14, 167
East Lynne (Wood), 71
Eaverly, Mary Ann, 35, 46
Ebony (magazine)
   on civil rights movement, 97
   editorials on race relations, 9, 18,
     103, 105, 106, 107–9
   on Emmett Till lynching, 109, 112
   and Gwendolyn Brooks, 83–87
   on Little Rock Nine, 113–14
   and Lysol advertising, 129
   on migration of Southern blacks, 91, 96
   and white liberals, 86–87, 89, 96–97,
     113–14, 116–17
   and "whiteness," 84–85, 86

Edmunds, Susan, 35, 47
Egypt, 33, 45–46
The Egyptian (film), 22, 35, 45–46
Eisenhower, Dwight D., 47, 113
ekphrastic poems, 128, 186
Eleusis, 42, 43
Eliot, T. S., 24, 42, 151, 180
Elle (magazine), 131–32, 133, 180
Ellis, Ruth, 165
Ellison, Ralph, 94
Empson, William, 179
Entwistle, Alice, 6
Erkkila, Betsy, 7, 104
Erskine, John, 26, 191–92n8
Euphorion, 32, 42
"Everybody Needs Somebody to Love,"
   161–62
Everywoman, 181–82
The Extraordinary Tide (Aizenberg and
   Belieu, eds.), 14, 15, 167–68

*The Faber Book of 20th Century
   Women's Poetry* (Adcock), 13
The Fall of Troy (film), 25
family photography and developmental
   psychology, 59–62, *61*
Faubus, Governor Orval, 113
femineering, 142–46, *145*
feminism
   and criticism of form in women's
     poetry, 13
   and criticism of romance plots, 30
   and critiques of "Psychopath," 166
   dissonant response to H.D.'s
     mythmaking, 21–22
   and distancing from WP label,
     15–16
   "feminist ekphrasis" and Surrealism,
     128
   feminist experimental poetry, 9
   French feminism and poetry
     criticism, 6–7
   and interpretive biases in women's
     poetry studies, 150–52

and women's magazines, 131–32
women's writing as act of theft,
    175–77
Feminism and Poetry (Montefiore), 6
feminist literary criticism, 2–5, 80–81
feminization
    depiction of Theseus in *Helen in
        Egypt,* 40–41
    and human interest stories, 152
    popular cinema and epic forms,
        33–35, 39
    in *The Private Life of Helen of Troy*
        (film), 27
femme noir of antiquity, 35
Forbes, Esther, 54
Forché, Carolyn, 149, 167
Ford, Karen Jackson, 8, 94
form
    in "Beverly Hills, Chicago," 101
    and debates on quality of women's
        poetry, 9, 13–14
    denial of ballad form in "A
        Bronzeville Mother," 111
    diction, 90, 99–101, 126, 154
    end rhymes in "The *Chicago
        Defender,*" 115
    in "Evidence," 170–72
    form-problem of *Helen in Egypt,*
        22–24, 30–31, 47
    l'écriture féminine, 6, 134, 172, 175
    Petrarchan sonnet, 153
    rhyme in "Education for Leisure," 157
    staggered quatrain, 112
Fowler, H. W., 171
France, Linda, 14–15, 168
Fraser, George MacDonald, 21
Freud, Sigmund, 55, 56, 57, 60, 71, 72,
    75, 79, 127
Friedan, Betty, 128, 131, 142–43
Friedman, Susan Stanford, 4, 21, 22,
    27, 39
Froebel, Friedrich, 54
Frost, Elisabeth, 9
Frost, Robert, 106

Fry, Roger, 53
Fussell, Betty, 135

Gallagher, Jean, 23
Garbo, Greta, 23, 184
Gemin, Pamela, 19, 147
gender
    and "The Applicant," 140–43
    and approaches to women's poetry
        studies, 4–5
    and criticisms of Brooks' poetry, 85,
        118–19
    crossing gender identity, 150–52
    gender relations in *Helen in Egypt,*
        30–31
    and gendered double standard of
        dramatic monologue, 19–20
    linguistic studies of gender
        differences, 6
    and "lyric intervention," 150–51
    and "The Photograph," 61, *61*
    and women's identities under
        patriarchy, 5
gender roles
    "Childe Rolandine," 52
    "The Colossus," 128–30
    in *Helen in Egypt,* 32
    in "Men of careful turns," 98
    and portrayal of heroines, 25
    "practical girls" and child
        protagonists, 63
ghost story trope, 75–78
Gilbert, Sandra, 5, 129
Gill, Jo, 5, 126
Ginsberg, Allen, 176
Gioia, Dana, 154
Giovanni, Nikki, 12, 13
Gordon, Eleanor Risteen, 52
Graham, Judith, 65
Great American Negroes (Richardson,
    ed.), 87
Great Migration, 91
the Greeks and views of Helen, 27–28,
    44

Greene, Graham, 65
Greer, Germaine, 11, 15, 117
Gregory, Eileen, 28
Gregson, Ian, 149, 166, 171
Griffith, D. W., 24, 25, 26
Gubar, Susan, 5

Hall, G. Stanley, 52
Hall, Linda, 9
Hammer, Langdon, 135
Hardy, Thomas, 126
Harlem Renaissance, 88
H.D.
    cineliteracy of, 23
    and cinematic allure of Helen, 10
    on cinematic excesses, 25–26
    as cultural insider, 33–35
    exclusion of in anthologies, 2, 12, 22
    The Gift, 33
    on Griffith's *Intolerance,* 25
    "Helen," 27–28
    "Hermes of the Ways," 175
    image of wide scope, 46
    Imagist aesthetic of "Helen," 27–28
    "Leda," 28–30
    mainstream recognition of, 16
    on Noa's *Helena,* 26
    Trilogy, 26, 175
    and women's writing as act of theft,
        175
    See also *Helen in Egypt*
"headline language," 171
Hedreen, Guy, 32
Helen in Egypt
    CinemaScope context of, 22–24,
        37–38, 41–42, 48–49
    and Cold War geopolitics, 47–48
    critique of martial masculinity,
        38–39, 192n9
    depiction of Achilles in, 28, 30–41,
        42–43, 44–45
    depiction of Helen in, 30–38
    "Eidolon," 31, 39, 41–45
    as epic-romance love story, 30–31

feminization of epic form, 33–35
form-problem of, 23, 30–31
and hyperformalism, 24
inflection of historical epic film, 21,
    32–33
"Leuké," 31, 32, 40–41
"Pallinode," 31, 33–34, 37–39
scarf motif and Orientalism, 37–38,
    40, 44, 193n15
use of headnotes in, 31
Helen of Troy (film), 17, 23, 34, *34,* 39,
    48, 193n17
Helena (film), 26, *26,* 27, 32–33, 38
Helle, Anita, 121
Hellenism, 21–22
Heller, Zoë, 123
Hemans, Felicia, 122
heroines, 25, 30–33, 35, 36–37, 191n7
Hill, Anita, 155
historical epic film, 21, 22, 24, 25, 26
Hobbes, Thomas, 73
Hogue, Cynthia, 7
Homer, 35
Hopewell, Katherine, 23
Horne, Lena, 84
Howe, Florence, 12, 13, 22, 117, 118,
    122
Hughes, Gertrude Reif, 111
Hughes, Langston, 83
Hughes, Ted, 125
Huk, Romana, 8, 52, 56
Hyde Park, 100–103
hyperformalism, 22, 24, 163

identity politics, 9
the Iliad, 30, 35, 38, 48
The Image of Childhood (Coveney), 71
image-text relations
    Ardizzone illustrations, 64–68, *67*
    in Smith's illustrations, 63–64
    and WP studies, 182–87, *183*
Imagist poetry, 21, 27–28, 32
imperialist inflections of developmental
    psychology, 54–55, 57, 59–61

Ingram, Claudia, 159
innovation, 1–2, 8–9, 25
Intimate Journals (Baudelaire), 52
Intolerance (film), 24, 25, 26
Invisible Man (Ellison), 94
Iphigenia, 32, 38
Irigaray, Luce, 6
irony, 153, 155, 159
Isis, 35

Jackaman, Rob, 163–64, 169, 171
Jackson, Walter A., 92
James, Henry, 53, 75, 76, 77, 79
Jameson, Fredric, 23, 172
Jeffs, Christine, 121
Jenkins, Henry, 81
Johnson, Georgia Douglas, 13
Johnson, John H., 84, 116
journalistic tropes, 152–53
Joyce, James, 53, 71, 72
Juhasz, Suzanne, 5, 84

Kaeser, H. J., 64
Kaplan, Cora, 3, 13
Karnak, 46–47
Kasischke, Laura, 147
Kate Greenaway Medal, 65
Keith, Harold, 54
Kennedy, David, 152, 160, 171, 172
Kent, George E., 85, 88, 94, 103, 107,
    114
Key, Ellen, 54
key signatures, 1–5, 16–20
Kidd, Kenneth, 59
killer lyrics
    and anthologies, 167–68
    counterintuitive innovations, 19–20,
        150, 167
    and dramatic monologue, 151–52
King, Rodney, 154
King Lear, 156
Kinnahan, Linda, 9, 150, 153
Kipling, Rudyard, 60
Kitt, Eartha, 35

Klee, Paul, 53, 127–28, 130
Klemin, Diana, 64
Korda, Alexander, 27
Koresh, David, 168
Kristeva, Julia, 2–3, 7, 80–81
Kumin, Maxine, 124
künstlerromans, 53

Lacan, Jacques, 6
Ladies' Home Journal, 19, 123, 124,
    129, 131–32, 133–34, 139,
    144–45
"Lady Poets," 12, 22
Lamarr, Hedy, 22
The Land of the Pharaohs (film), 45
Lander, Christian, 117
Landis, Paul, 141
Lane, Anthony, 121
Lant, Antonia, 33
The Last Days of Pompeii (film), 25
Latina (magazine), 179
de Lauretis, Teresa, 136
Lawrence, D. H., 71, 72
Lawrence, Elizabeth, 85
layout and book illustrations, 64, 66,
    68–70, *69*
l'écriture féminine, 6, 134, 172, 175
Lefebvre, Henri, 19, 115, 124, 130–32,
    133–36, 143, 180, 184
Lewis, C. S., 54
Lewis, Michael, 169
liberalism, 85–87, 96–97, 100–103,
    104–7, 112–17
Lifting Belly High conference, 10,
    190n10
Lindberg, Kathryne, 87, 100
literary tradition, 8–9, 21
Little Rock Nine, 113–16
Little Tim and the Brave Sea Captain
    (Ardizzone), 65–66, *67*
Loizeaux, Elizabeth Bergmann, 128
Lomax, Louis E., 104
Loves of Three Queens (film), 22, 39
Lowell, Amy, 12

Loy, Mina, 186
lyric
    debate over, 8–9
    and interdisciplinary studies, 187–88
    killer lyrics, 149–50
    linguistically experimental poetry,
        190n9
    "lyric intervention," 150–51

Magritte, René, 139
Making for Planet Alice (Dooley, ed.),
    11, 178, *178*, 180–81
Making for the Open (Rumens, ed.), 11,
    13, 15
Making Friends With Black People
    (Adams), 117
Malcolm X, 92
Mandel, Charlotte, 23, 33
Marchand, Roland, 140, 184
Markey, Janice, 141
Marling, Karal Ann, 133
marriage, 140–42
Marriott, Stuart, 66
Mary Poppins in the Park, 54
masculinity and killer lyrics, 150, 159–63
"mass culture," 179, 199n5
May, Elaine Tyler, 94, 143
McAllister, Andrew, 163, 166
McBrien, William, 56
McCullers, Carson, 72, 76
McEwen, Christian, 80
McGinley, Phyllis, 99, 133
McRobbie, Angela, 184
media
    censorship and portrayals of African
        Americans, 88
    intersections with poetry, 18–19
    and killer lyrics, 152
    mass market popularity of
        anthologies, 177–79, *178*
    media monologues, 19–20, 168–73
    tabloid media, 9
The Member of the Wedding
    (McCullers), 72, 76

Menelaus, 33, 36, 38, 39
Middle East, 47–48
Middlebrook, Diane, 145
Milam, J. W., 110
Millay, Edna St. Vincent, 2, 12, 124,
    131–32, 179, 187
Milton, John, 31
Mimff-Robinson (Kaeser), 64, 65
mise-en-page, 64–70, *67, 69*
mistaken identity trope, 34, 44
Mitchell, W. J. T., 186
Modern English Usage (Fowler), 171
Modern Women Poets (Rees-Jones, ed.),
    6, 15, 158, 168
Modleski, Tania, 36, 184
Monroe, Marilyn, 142, 149, 181
Montefiore, Jan, 6, 22, 29
Monumentalfilm, 25
Moore, Marianne, 8, 12, 13, 124
Mootry, Maria, 87, 111, 118
Moretti, Franco, 42–43, 47, 48
Morris, Adelaide, 10, 23–24
Morrison, Toni, 97
Moses, Kate, 121
Mullen, Bill V., 84, 89, 91
Murdock, Cloyte, 109–10, 112
mythology
    Hollywood's Americanization of, 9
    mythic figures in women's poetry
        anthologies, 181–82
    mythmaking in H.D.'s poetry,
        21–22

NAACP (National Association for the
    Advancement of Colored People),
    84, 112–13
Naming the Waves (McEwen, ed.), 80
"NEETs," 157
Negro Digest (magazine), 83, 84
Nelson, Deborah, 140
New Women Poets (Rumens, ed.), 11
No More Masks! (Howe and Bass, eds.),
    12, 22, 117, 118, 122, 187–88
Noa, Manfred, 26, 27

Norton, Mary, 54
The Norton Anthology of Literature by Women (Gilbert and Gubar, eds.), 55, 168

Odysseus, 38
offset printing and book illustrations, 64
Ohi, Kevin, 76
Omi, Michael, 98, 117
101 Poems by 101 Women (Greer, ed.), 11, 117
"optical unconsciousness," *61*, 62
Ostriker, Alicia Suskin, 6, 9, 21, 29, 175
Othello, 155

Paradise Lost (Milton), 31
Paris (character), 30–36, 39, 40, 43, 44
Parks, Robert E., 98
patriarchy, 7
Patterson, Christina, 168
Perloff, Marjorie, 132, 172
Persia, 42, 43
Petry, Ann, 87
Picasso, Pablo, 53
Pickett, Wilson, 161–62
Piercy, Marge, 14, 167
Plath, Sylvia
    "An Appearance," 138–39
    "The Applicant," 122, 140–42
    "Ariel," 143, 145
    Ariel, 19, 121–22, 130, 132–35, 138–40, 143–48, *145*
    "The Bee Meeting," 134
    The Bell Jar, 133
    "A Birthday Present," 132
    "Black Rook in Rainy Weather," 126
    classical allusions of, 129
    "The Colossus," 128–30
    The Colossus, 128–30
    "The Courage of Shutting-Up," 139
    as cultural icon, 187
    "Cut," 134–35, 147

"The Disquieting Muses," 127
domesticity and signature style, 10, 18–19, 125–31, 143, 146–48
extraordinary depictions of everyday objects, 130–35
"Fever 103°," 134, 143, 145–46
"The Ghost's Leavetaking," 127–28
and horizontal cultural studies, 183–84
"I Am Vertical," 183–84
jet-woman and transcendence, 143–48, *145*
"Kindness," 132
"Lady Lazarus," 143, 151
"Lesbos," 126, 127, 139, 147
mainstream recognition of, 13, 16
"Morning Song," 139, 145
"Mrs. Cherry's Kitchen," 137
"Poems, Potatoes," 126–27
"Second Winter," 133
technology and romance, 135–43
"Two Views of a Cadaver Room," 138
Unabridged Journals, 121, 123
"Wintering," 134
"Words heard, by accident, over the phone," 136–37
Polyxena, 40
POOL film collective, 191n4
Poor Monkey (Coveney), 54, 75, 76
popular culture
    critiques of, 2
    meanings of, 179, 199n5
    and "proper" domain of women's poetry, 8
    and signature style in women's poetry, 1–2
    and women's poetry studies, 4–5, 185–86
Portland Vase, 32
Portrait of the Artist as a Young Man (Joyce), 53
Post, Emily, 107
post-feminist women's poetry, 11

The Postman Always Rings Twice (Cain), 161

poststructuralism, 10

Potter, Beatrix, 54

Pound, Ezra, 24, 25, 32, 42

presidential election of 1956, 112–13

The Prince of Egypt (Wilson), 24

printing techniques and book illustrations, 64

The Private Life of Helen of Troy (Erskine), 26, 191n8

The Private Life of Helen of Troy (film), 26–27

Proteus, 42, 193n21

Psyche (Segnitz and Rainey, eds.), 12, 13, 22, 80, 118–19, 122, 181

psychoanalysis and poetry criticism, 10

psycho-biographical framework for poetry studies, 5, 7–8, 23–24

Pumphrey, Martin, 52, 60

"quality" vs. form debate in women's poetry, 12, 13–14

race relations
  "Beverly Hills, Chicago," 98, 102–3
  black cultural politics and liberalism, 86–87
  "The *Chicago Defender* Sends a Man to Little Rock," 114–16
  and criticisms of Brooks' poetry, 85–86
  crossing race identity, 150–52
  Ebony magazine editorials on race relations, 103, 105, 106, 107–9, 116–17
  "I love those little booths at Benvenuti's," 98–102
  "The Lovers of the Poor," 107
  "Men of careful turns, haters of forks in the road," 103–7
  Parks's race relations cycle, 98
  school desegregation, 113–16
  and stereotypes of African Americans, 99–100

and "The Sundays of Satin-Legs Smith," 96–97

Radway, Janice, 25, 30

Raine, Craig, 121–22

Rainey, Carol, 12, 118, 151

Ramsey, JonBenet, 150

Ray, Rachael, 147

Rees-Jones, Deryn, 6, 15, 165, 168, 169

Reeves, Rosser, 140

refraction of society in literature, 185–86

revisionist mythmaking, 6, 23–25, 27–29, 38–39, 48–49

rhyme and rhythm
  assonance, 48, 106–7, 148
  in "Beverly Hills, Chicago," 101, 102
  in "Education for Leisure," 157
  end rhymes, 115
  in "The Ghost's Leavetaking," 127
  irregular meter, 60
  off and slant rhyme, 60
  transverse slant rhyme, 126

Rich, Adrienne, 12, 124, 146–47, 186

Richardson, Ben, 87

Rifles for Watie (Keith), 54

Roberts, Neil, 166

Rodari, Gianni, 62

romance, popular
  and depiction of Achilles in *Helen in Egypt*, 35–36
  feminist criticism of, 30
  of "Leda," 28–30

romantic relations and technology, 135–43

Romanticism
  and "Bog-Face," 69–70
  and children's poetry anthologies, 66
  and constructions of the child, 18
  cultural mythology of Western child, 71–72
  and dramatic monologue, 151
  and "Infant," 73–74
  and innocent/knowing child, 73–75
  and "The Turn of the Screw," 75–79

Roosevelt, Eleanor, 86, 112–13
Rose, Jacqueline, 123, 124
Rosenbaum, Susan, 134
Rousseau, Jean-Jacques, 71, 73, 74, 81
Rowan, Carl, 113–14
Rowland, Antony, 162
Rukeyser, Muriel, 11, 13, 14
Rumens, Carol, 11, 13, 15, 177–79, 180
Russell, Sue, 154, 169

Sajé, Natasha, 148
Salt and Bitter and Good (Kaplan, ed.),
    12–13, 122
Salzman, Eva, 11, 15, 117
Sarton, May, 124
Scannell, Vernon, 164
Schlesinger, Arthur, Jr., 112
Scott, Diana, 14
The Second Sex (de Beauvoir), 146
Segnitz, Barbara, 12, 118, 151
semiotic discourse theory, 2–3, 80–81
Sendak, Maurice, 64
Severin, Laura, 52
Sexton, Anne, 13, 129, 146–47
Shakespeare, 155, 156
Shearin, Faith, 147
Shelley, Percy Bysshe, 66
shopping and stealing metaphor, 176
signature style, 1–2, 8–9, 16–20
Silverstein, Shel, 68
Simpson, Joan Murray, 11, 12, 14, 80
Sinatra, Frank, 86
Sinfield, Alan, 151, 164
Sitwell, Edith, 3, 81, 187
Sivulka, Juliann, 139
Sixty Women Poets (France, ed.), 15,
    158, 168
Smith, Stan, 156
Smith, Stevie
    and Ardizzone's illustrations, 64–68,
        67
    The Batsford Book of Children's Verse
        (Smith, ed.), 54
    "Bog Face," 68–70, 69

Cats in Color, 54, 64
Child Study theory, 57, *58*, 59–62,
    61
criticisms of, 51–52
as cultural insider, 54, 57, 79
as cultural outsider, 51–52
"Darling Daughters," 54
image-text relations, 63–64, 186
"Infant," 73–74
"Lady 'Rogue' Singleton," 63
"The Last Turn of the Screw," 75–79
"Little Boy Lost," 54
mainstream recognition, 16, 194n1
"My Hat," 63
"Not Waving But Drowning," 52, 70
"Nourish Me on an Egg," 74–75, *75*
"The Orphan Reformed," 54
"Papa Love Baby," 54–57, *58*
on perceptions of children, 72
"The Photograph," 54–55, 59–62,
    61
reinvention of childhood, 73–75
reversal of parent/child relations,
    55–56
review of Coveney's *Poor Monkey*,
    70–72
reviews of children's literature,
    53–54, 62–68
on romanticism, 72–73
"The Sad Mother," 70
signature style, 17–18, 51–54,
    62–63, 68–70, *69*
use of feminine end-rhyme, 56
and woman-poet-as-child, 79–81
Sobchack, Vivian, 22, 24
social philology, 9–10
Solomon, Jon, 39
South Side of Chicago (Bronzeville),
    83, 87, 90–92, 96, 99, 101–2, 107
Southerners, 91, 93, 114–16
Spillers, Hortense, 87, 103, 104
stealing metaphor of women's writing,
    175–77
Stein, Gertrude, 3, 8, 12, 81, 128, 187

stereotypes
 of African Americans, 88, 99–100
 in "Education for Leisure," 156–57
 and poetry anthologies, 179–80
 stereotypical subjects and women's
  poetry, 4
 of women's poetry, 187
Stetson, Erlene, 13, 118, 196n3
Stevens, Wallace, 184
Stevenson, Adlai, 112–13
Stevenson, Robert Louis, 52
Steward, Julie Sims, 52
Stewart, Martha, 121, 147
The Street (Petry), 87
Studies in Childhood (Sully), 52
Stuff White People Like (Lander), 117
subversion
 H.D.'s Helen poems, 21
 Ostriker and, 6
 and Smith-as-child, 52
 and women's poetry, 2–3, 14
Suez Crisis, 47
Sully, James, 52, 59
Surrealism, 126, 127–28, 130, 139
Sweeping Beauty (Gemin, ed.), 19, 122,
  130, 147–48, 182
Sylvia (film), 121
synthesthesia, 101

Taber, Gladys, 131–32
tableau vivant, 28
Tan (magazine), 84
Tate, Claudia, 87, 104
Taylor, Henry, 103–4
technology and domesticity, 135–43
Telephone Tales (Rodari), 62
temples, Egyptian, 33, 36, 42–43,
  45–46
The Ten Commandments (1923 film),
  46
The Ten Commandments (1956 film),
  17, 23, 24, 35, 46
Tender Buttons (Stein), 128
Terada, Rei, 187

Thaddeus, Janice, 52
Thatcher, Margaret, 156, 157
Theseus, 31, 32, 40–41
They Seek a City (Bontemps), 87
Thomas, Clarence, 154, 155–56
Thomas, Dylan, 65
Thomas, Jane, 165
Thompson, Era Bell, 84, 100, 108–9,
  114
Tibbets, Elizabeth, 147
Tierney, Gene, 35
Till, Emmett, 109–12
Tim All Alone (Ardizzone), 65, 67–68,
  67
To the Lighthouse (Woolf), 53
transcendence and everyday life,
  130–35
transgression, 2–3, 8
Travers, P. L., 54
Trilogy, 21, 26, 175
Trojan War, 29
Troy, 44–45
Truman, Harry, 97
Tupperware, 125
The Turn of the Screw (James), 75–76,
  78
Tyson, Mike, 154

Ulmer, Gregory, 46
Untermeyer, Louis, 124

The Valley of the Kings (film), 45
Van Dyne, Susan, 143
Vanci-Perahim, Marina, 126
Vanity Fair (magazine), 179
Vice (Ai), 16, 168
Vogue (magazine), 179
voice and cross-gender dramatic
  monologue, 150–52

Wack, Amy, 15, 117
Wagner, Linda, 40
Wagner-Martin, Linda, 123
Walker, Cheryl, 7–8

Walker, Nancy, 124
Washington, Desiree, 154
We Have Tomorrow (Bontemps), 87
Webster, Harvey Curtis, 117
Welles, Orson, 35
Western civilization and developmental
    psychology, 54–55, 57, 59–61
What Maisie Knew (James), 53
Wheatley, David, 11
Wheeler, Lesley, 8, 87
whiteness
    "Beverly Hills," 98, 102–3
    and Brooks' portrayal of Till
        lynching trial, 110–12
    "The *Chicago Defender* Sends a Man
        to Little Rock," 114–16, 118–19
    criticisms of Gwendolyn Brooks, 84
    and *Ebony* magazine, 84–85
    "I love those little booths at
        Benvenuti's," 98–102
    "Men of careful turns," 104–7
    "The Sundays of Satin-Legs Smith,"
        88–92
    white beauty standards, 83
Whitman, Walt, 176
Wilkins, Roy, 113
Williams, William Carlos, 183
Williamson, Judith, 61
Wilner, Eleanor, 14
Wilson, Alex, 116
Wilson, Dorothy Clarke, 24
Winant, Howard, 98, 117
Winkler, Martin, 39
Wise, Robert, 34
Without Adam (Simpson, ed.), 11, 80,
    181
Wojahn, David, 161
woman-poet-as-child, 79–81
women's magazines, 131–32, 180, 184

Women's Work (Salzman and Wack,
    eds.), 11, 117
Wood, Mrs. Henry, 71
Woolf, Virginia, 53, 71, 72
Wordsworth, William, 70, 72, 73, 150
The World Split Open (Bernikow, ed.),
    2, 11, 12
WP (women's poetry)
    and ambiguity, 179–81
    and anthologies, 117–19, 177–79, *178*
    assumptions about, 4–5, 187
    and domesticity, 121–25
    image-text relations, 182–87, *183*
    interpretive biases, 150–52, 166,
        172–73
    jet-woman and transcendence at
        home, 143–48, *145*
    and motherhood, 117–18, 122
    and mythic figures, 181–82
    popular culture and location of
        signature style, 1–2
    and publishing industry, 10–16
    refraction of society in, 185–86
    in the United States and the United
        Kingdom, 5–6, 11–16
    women poets as cultural insiders,
        1–2, 4–5, 182–87, *183*
    "women's themes" in poetry books, 9
    "women's voice," 7
    and WP label, 11, 14–16
Wright, Richard, 83, 87, 88

Yeats, W. B., 28
Yorke, Liz, 7
Yorkshire Ripper, 150, 166

Zodiac Wheel, 41, 45
"Zoot Suit Riots," 92
zoot suits, 87–97

CPSIA information can be obtained at www.ICGtesting.com
Printed in the USA
BVOW021509110512

289849BV00006B/2/P